Using Co
in Business

Joel Shore

with Bryan Pfaffenberger

que CORPORATION
LEADING COMPUTER KNOWLEDGE

Using Computers in Business

Library of Congress Catalog No.: 89-62444

ISBN 0-88022-470-3

92 91 90 89 8 7 6 5 4 3 2 1

Interpretation of the printing code: the rightmost double-digit number is the year of the book's printing; the rightmost single-digit number, the number of the book's printing. For example, a printing code of 89-1 shows that the first printing of the book occurred in 1989.

DEDICATION

To my parents, Milton and Lucille; my beloved wife, Mary;
and, of course, my son Patrick, the best darn soccer player
in the entire Neary Elementary School fourth grade.

—JSS

Publishing Director

Lloyd J. Short

Production Editor

Gregory Robertson

Editors

Kelly D. Dobbs
Jeannine Freudenberger
Jay McNaught
Richard Turner

Technical Editor

Bryan Pfaffenberger

Editorial Assistants

Renée Ackermann
Stacie Lamborne

Index

Sherry Massey

Book Design and Production

Dan Armstrong
Jodi Jensen
Lori A. Lyons
Jennifer Matthews
Cindy L. Phipps
Joe Ramon
Dennis Sheehan
Louise Shinault

Composed in Garamond and Excellent No. 47
by Que Corporation

About the Author

Joel Shore

Joel Shore is senior editor of the networking section for *Computer Reseller News*, a weekly industry trade publication. He is also president of Documentation Systems, a Southborough, Massachusetts management consulting firm that provides personal computing solutions to small businesses. Mr. Shore teaches personal computing and small-business courses at Massachusetts Bay Community College in Wellesley, Massachusetts; he is a contributing columnist to *WordPerfect Magazine* and speaks frequently at several of the Boston Computer Society's special interest groups. He is a coauthor of Que Corporation's *Using WordPerfect 5* and *WordPerfect Tips, Tricks, and Traps*, 2nd Edition, and was the technical editor for Que's *WordPerfect QuickStart*, *dBASE IV QuickStart*, and *dBASE IV Que Cards*.

Contents at a Glance

Table of Contents

Acknowledgments

My wife, Mary, has no doubt felt at times abandoned for the sake of my computer. Yet without her unflagging support and understanding, this book could never have come to be. I am forever grateful for her patience and the many nights she spent curled up with a Dick Francis mystery novel instead of her husband.

Thanks, also, to my son, Patrick, who put aside his vast library of recreational software long enough to let me borrow *my* computer. He is truly a joy to behold.

Que's Karen Bluestein took my original outline and honed it into a well-organized, focused work. It was Karen who supported my efforts through those stressful periods when I disconnected my answering machine in an effort to hide from her deadlines.

Que's Lloyd Short always managed to find me when those deadlines were being stretched. Thanks to him for his creative detective work.

And special thanks to Jeff Acerson, vice president for corporate communications at WordPerfect Corporation, in Orem, Utah. It was he who in November of 1987 suggested that I contact Que to discuss my desire to "do a little writing on the side." His good name, when spoken, caused doors in the publishing world to open as if by magic. Little did I know then that my moonlighting would soon become a career.

Trademark Acknowledgments

Que Corporation has made every effort to supply trademark information about company names, products, and services mentioned in this book. Trademarks indicated below were derived from various sources. Que Corporation cannot attest to the accuracy of this information.

1-2-3, Lotus, VisiCalc, and Symphony are registered trademarks and Allways is a trademark of Lotus Development Corporation.

3Com is a registered trademark and EtherNet is a trademark of 3Com Corporation.

Apple, Macintosh, AppleTalk, MacProject, and LaserWriter are registered trademarks and Finder and MultiFinder are trademarks of Apple Computer, Inc.

ARCnet is a registered trademark of Datapoint Corporation.

Ashton-Tate, Framework, and dBASE are registered trademarks and dBASE IV is a trademark of Ashton-Tate Corporation.

AT&T is a registered trademark and UNIX is a trademark of AT&T.

Centronics is a registered trademark of Centronics Data Computer Corporation.

COMPAQ Deskpro 286 and Deskpro 386 are registered trademarks of COMPAQ Computer Corporation.

CompuServe is a registered trademark of CompuServe, Inc. and H&R Block, Inc.

Dow Jones News/Retrieval is a registered service mark of Dow Jones & Company, Inc.

EPSON is a registered trademark of Epson America, Inc.

FoxBase+ is a trademark of Fox Software, Inc.

Hercules Graphics Card is a trademark of Hercules Computer Technology.

LaserJet is a trademark of Hewlett-Packard Co.

IBM is a registered trademark and DisplayWrite, OS/2, and PS/2 are trademarks of International Business Machines Corporation.

Leading Edge is a registered trademark of Leading Edge Products, Inc.

MCI Mail is a registered service mark of MCI Communications Corporation.

MS-DOS, XENIX, and Microsoft are registered trademarks of Microsoft Corporation.

Novell and NetWare are registered trademarks of Novell, Inc.

PageMaker is a registered trademark of Aldus Corporation.

PostScript is a registered trademark and Adobe Illustrator is a trademark of Adobe Systems, Inc.

Quicken is a registered trademark of Intuit Software.

The Source is a service mark of Source Telecomputing Corporation.

Super Project is a registered trademark of Computer Associates.

TOPS is a registered trademark of Centram Systems West, Inc.

WANG is a registered trademark of Wang Laboratories, Inc.

WordPerfect is a registered trademark of WordPerfect Corporation.

Introduction

Difficult as it may be to believe, personal computers have been in existence for only a short while. Apple Computer brought out the first commercially successful machine in the late 1970s and took the hobbyist and education markets by storm. But the very idea of using a *personal* computer in a business environment did not yet merit serious consideration, due to several factors. Those early machines lacked the computational horsepower needed by business, and directors of large corporate mainframe computer installations were afraid that decentralization would dilute their authority and cloud their jurisdiction. In addition, few software programs were available for business use. After all, playing Pac Man would hardly be condoned by the boss.

It wasn't until IBM's introduction of the original Personal Computer that the use of individual desktop computers was legitimized.

Since that fateful day in 1981 (when Apple, then the market leader, took out full-page newspaper ads welcoming IBM), technology breakthroughs have come with breathtaking frequency. Those 1981 computers, long since relegated to the scrap heap by many industry pundits, have been surpassed by several generations of desktop computers. Today's personal computers deliver more processing power than their room-size mainframe computer ancestors of just ten years ago.

Many early business users of personal computing technology leap-frogged their competition to gain competitive advantages that, in some cases, were measured in years. In other cases, those who got behind because they could not provide customer service levels on a par with their newly automated competitors fell by the wayside, eventually closing their doors.

As we enter the 1990s, the opportunities for small businesses that have not yet automated are virtually limitless. Near-miraculous gains in employee productivity, accuracy, and morale are now within the grasp of those who are willing to devote time—the most precious of all assets—to the proper planning, analysis, acquisition, and installation of computers in order to assist in the operation of a business enterprise.

Today's businesses, with ever-increasing demands placed on them by their clientele, competition, and vendors, in many cases have reached the point where the mere addition of more employees is no longer enough. These businesses have arrived at a crossroads, and the automation of business operations by way of personal computers has become not a luxury, but a necessity.

Who Should Use This Book?

If you own or operate a small business and have considered adding a computer to your operation, this book is for you. If your experience with computers is modest or nil, you should feel comfortable reading this book: you will find no technobabble here.

Whether your business is that of accountant, lawyer, general contractor, caterer, landscaper, or door-to-door car waxer, you can achieve extraordinary gains in productivity by automating the creating of customer bills, tallying their payment, managing your inventory, or scheduling your day's work.

This book has been designed with the owner, supervisor, or manager of a business in mind, not the *type* of business you run. The concepts and techniques contained here are probably very much like those you now use every day.

How Is This Book Organized?

Each chapter in *Using Computers in Business* focuses on a particular aspect of computerizing a small business. Much of the book is based on the case study of a bed and bath accessory retail store that sells from inventory on the sales floor and accepts custom orders. The bed and bath case study is a compilation of true experiences from many business, that have been woven together as a typical small-business example. Mark and Marian, the proprietors of this small business, are fictional characters based on real people.

The appendixes serve as an adjunct to the rest of the book, providing information that you can use in your computerization project.

How To Use This Book

Because this book follows a case study of business computerization from beginning to end, you should join in at the beginning and come along for the entire adventure. Although certain sections of the book can be read out of order, the intent is for you to follow the case study computerization project from conceptualization through analysis, acquisition, installation, testing, and implementation.

What's in This Book?

Chapter 1, "Is it Time To Computerize?," defines some of the terms used throughout the book. This chapter provides you with some clues that may indicate that the time for computerization has arrived. You think about what you want to accomplish by computerizing, and you learn about the tangible and intangible results of computerization. This chapter discusses good and bad reasons for buying a computer system, alternatives to computers are explored, and the entire computerization process is introduced. You learn about the steps involved in the computerization process, and you also are introduced to human factors that come into play when you undertake a computerization project. This chapter tells you about the two costs of computerizing: financial and nonfinancial—and, finally, shows you how to establish meaningful criteria to quantify and measure your success.

Chapter 2, "Taking the First Steps toward Computerization," introduces the case study of a bed and bath accessories shop owned by Marian and her husband Mark. This case study is referred to throughout the book. In this chapter, you see why information drives a business and why inaccurate or untimely information can lead a business down the path to potential ruin. A *needs analysis,* the first step in computerizing, is examined in detail. This chapter tells you what to observe and what information needs to be collected to lay a proper foundation for your project. Finally, you learn to develop a plan and establish a budget for the project.

Chapter 3, "Identifying Your Software Needs," shows you how to get the most out of the money you spend on software. First, you learn to put together a shopping list of requirements your software must meet. Next, the chapter shows you how to decide what software you need and where and how to buy it. A discussion of public domain software, shareware, and custom software ends the chapter.

Chapter 4, "Finding Business Solutions in Application Software," gives an overview of the major types of software available. This chapter discusses word processors; spreadsheets; databases; and telecommunications, integrated, accounting, desktop publishing, project management, statistical analysis, and time-billing software packages.

Chapter 5, "Making Hardware Purchasing Decisions," examines virtually every type of hardware you may need for your project. This chapter explains the differences between single-user and multiuser systems. Next, you get the information you need to decide on a hardware platform (IBM-compatible or Apple Macintosh) and operating system. A discussion of hardware terminology follows. You are introduced to the microprocessor chip (the computer's brain), two types of memory (read-only and random-access), and ports, through which your computer connects to other devices. You learn about storage options, from floppy and hard disk drives to tape drives and the new optical drives. Display monitors are discussed, as are output devices, including printers, plotters, facsimile (FAX) machines, and modems for transmitting data over telephone lines. Input devices, including mice and scanners, are examined, as are the building blocks of local area networks, including servers, workstations, cabling, adapter cards, and network operating systems. A discussion of accessories (surge protectors, cables, and switch boxes and buffers) is included as well. The chapter continues by telling you how to prepare yourself for a trip to your local computer store. Sample computer system configurations give you an idea of how to meet needs for different software applications. The chapter concludes with a section that looks at the physical surroundings with which your employees and the computer system must coexist. You learn about the furniture you need, including proper work surfaces and chairs; electrical power requirements; protection in the event of a power outage; heating, ventilating, and air conditioning (HVAC) requirements; lighting; static electricity control; sound control; and the choice between computers that sit *on* or computers that sit *beside* your desk.

Chapter 6, "Getting Help from a Consultant," introduces the different players who may play major roles in your project. Because you cannot be an expert in every endeavor, you hire specialists. (Do you hire an accountant to do your books?) Computerization may require you to hire a consultant to manage and guide you through your project. This chapter shows you where to find a consultant, what to expect, and how to manage him or her. You also meet other players: custom software program developers and technical writers.

Chapter 7, "Deciding Where To Buy Your Computer Equipment," is a veritable what's what of where you can buy your computing solutions. You are introduced to the different *channels* through which computers are sold, including retail stores, independent retailers, value-added resellers (VARs), mail-order houses, mass merchandisers, warehouse stores, and office supply superstores. This chapter helps you decide whether buying used computing equipment makes sense for you. If it does, you see where to buy used equipment, from catalogs and brokers to the auction notices in your Sunday paper. You learn what the price of equipment *really* includes and why simply comparing prices may be akin to comparing apples and oranges. Finding vendors is explored, from the yellow pages and computer magazines, to trade groups, competitors, and consultants. When you finish this chapter, you will understand why it is important to evaluate your vendor—someone with whom you will deal before, during, and after the sale. Finally, you examine refund and exchange policies, hardware and software warranties, and the types of recourse available to you if you are not getting the service you expect.

Chapter 8, "Implementing Your New System," guides you through the preparations you need to make before pieces of hardware begin to arrive. You learn about developing a floor plan that takes into account work flow, electrical and cabling needs, telephones, and lighting considerations. Equipment security—the protection of your hardware—and data security—the protection of information vital to your business—are examined. When the big day—and your hardware—arrives, you need to install your system. Setting up your hardware, installing software, and testing your equipment are explored. Next, you learn about which software application to implement first. This chapter also shows why a plan with a low risk and high payoff is ideal but not always practical. Finally, four common applications—accounts receivable, time billing, word processing, and database management—are scrutinized as possible choices for initial implementation.

Chapter 9, "Testing Your System," examines the critically important process of system testing to make sure that your computer system performs the tasks you require in the way you expect and with accurate results. You follow the development of a test plan and the creation of test data, a test script, and manual calculation of results to compare to your computer-generated output. You step through the process of performing the test, reconciling test results, and getting together with your project team daily to examine the results and compare notes. You also learn about running "parallel" systems—running both your old manual and new computer-based systems side-by-side during the transition period. Finally, when everyone is satisfied with the results, you "cut the cord" and leave your old manual system behind forever.

Chapter 10, "Training," examines the requirements for ensuring that all users understand how to interact with your new system. Who should provide training, how much it should cost, whether it should be done in a classroom setting or at your premises are the questions discussed. The need to learn one program at a time, allocation of sufficient training time, and cross-training are also examined.

Chapter 11, "Living with Your System," introduces you to the daily routine that eventually will become second nature. This routine includes daily system start-up, housekeeping and administration, addition of new users, deletion of users, file backup, and daily shutdown. You also see why it is important to store copies of data off-site and how you can control the cost of supplies. This chapter covers *standards,* as well, including documentation of procedures and operational policies that are necessary to ensure smooth operation, and early detection of potential difficulties.

Chapter 12, "Expecting the Unexpected," examines delays that can occur during the planning, analysis, development, and implementation phases of your project and tells how you can build in slack time or adjust your project schedule as necessary. You also learn about incorrect data results and hardware failure and ways to respond to these occurrences. Finally, you see that what you have sought to replace—a manual, noncomputer system—is a necessity as an emergency backup in case a malfunction forces you to shut down your computers.

Appendix A, "Computer Publications," provides a list of publications that cover the computing industry. Some of the publications (*PC Magazine* and *PC World*, for example) are available on magazine stands and provide general interest coverage. Others (*PC Week* and *InfoWorld*, for example) are weekly newspapers intended for those who work with or acquire personal computers in volume. Other publications (*Computer Reseller News, Macintosh News,* and *Reseller Management*) are intended for those in the trade of selling computer equipment. These periodicals are listed so that you know what your computerization advisors are reading.

Appendix B, "A Contract for Developing Custom Software," is a sample contract, which you can use as a model when contracting for custom programming services. Such a contract may be negotiated by you or by a consultant that you have retained for your project. In either case, you should be sure that an attorney representing you is involved in the process. The contract in the appendix is a sample only. Laws vary from state to state and province to province, so your contract may be quite different.

Appendix C, "Cost/Benefit Analysis," is a step-by-step walk-through of the cost/benefit analysis procedure. As a part of the computerization process, you perform a cost/benefit analysis to determine whether the funds you plan to invest in computerization will be recovered in a reasonable length of time, or you will be better off investing that same money in a certificate of deposit at your local bank.

Appendix D, "An Overview of DOS," discusses the most commonly used operating system software. Knowing something about DOS enhances your ability to use your computer. This appendix explains the fundamentals of DOS and its structure, purpose, and functions.

Appendix E, "An Overview of 1-2-3," covers the most popular spreadsheet program. This appendix explains what a spreadsheet is and then talks about the features of 1-2-3 that make it so popular.

Appendix F, "An Overview of WordPerfect," is about one of the most commonly used high-end word processors. The basics of WordPerfect are explained, giving you a solid foundation on which to build as you explore the program's more advanced features.

Appendix G, "An Overview of dBASE," discusses a powerful and popular database that is commonly used in business. This appendix explains in more detail what a database management system is and how it is used. dBASE capabilities in particular are covered here.

What's Not in This Book?

A book that describes the detailed installation of specific software packages for individual types of businesses would require a book tens of thousand of pages long. Due to space considerations, dealing with specific brand-name software packages is not included. For assistance with an individual package, seek help from its manufacturer, the dealer from whom you purchased it, or computer user groups in your area.

This book is based on the premise that today's personal computers provide sufficient computing power, storage, and flexibility to run almost any business. For that reason, the use of minicomputers, such as those from Digital Equipment Corporation, Data General Corporation, IBM, NCR, Unisys, and other manufacturers, is not covered.

CHAPTER 1

Is It Time To Computerize?

People who run a business, whether it is large or small, want that business to grow and prosper, an aspiration that is part of the American dream. Often those aspirations are realized; yet many smaller businesses never grow as their owners had hoped, due to the hundreds of reasons that cause businesses to stagnate or falter. One of the most common reasons is the failure to manage properly the information that forms the basis of the business's day-to-day operations. Making decisions with information that is not complete, accurate, and timely can be downright risky.

This chapter is an introduction to the process of computerizing your business operations. You learn that computerizing is much more than just a trip to the local computer store; it's a multistep process requiring a significant amount of analysis and planning. You also find out about good and not-so-good reasons for buying a computer, and learn how to establish criteria for measuring the success of your computerization project.

What Does Computerizing Mean?

Somewhere every day a small business owner walks into a computer store and becomes smitten with the fastest, sleekest-looking, most colorful desktop computer that money can buy. "That's for me!" says our executive, and the computer salesperson, not wanting to be denied a handsome commission, cries "It's you!" The salesman directs one of the store's support staff to carry the newly purchased collection of boxes from the store and load them into the car. It may well be the last time this new computer owner sees either of them. After a short drive back to the office, the intrepid businessman lugs the boxes inside and begins to unpack.

Now the trouble begins. "How do I hook up all of this equipment? What are these things called disks? The computer must be hardware, but what is software? Did I buy any software? How do I turn it on? And what am I going to do with it?"

That kind of situation occurs all the time. The president of one of the country's largest automotive engine rebuilders (more than 100 employees) decided in 1983 that it was time to "computerize the business." He went to a computer store, bought several desktop computers with the intention of interconnecting them and using shared software programs to, as he said, "run the business." As of March 1989, the equipment, now hopelessly obsolete, still sits in the original sealed boxes. And the investment of close to $30,000? It's a total loss. Surely this is not computerizing.

So what is computerizing?

Computerizing is a carefully planned process that results in an easy-to-use, properly sized system that automates selected business operations and so improves the profitability of a business. Computerizing is not, never has been, and never will be a shopping spree at your local computer store.

Words To Live By

Before embarking on your journey, you should become familiar with some new terminology. For now, you can keep it simple. A detailed glossary is included as an appendix to the text. The following terms are basic to a discussion of computerizing your business:

Computer: an electronic device that stores and processes data

Computerizing: a carefully planned process that results in an easy-to-use, properly sized system that automates selected business operations and improves the profitability of a business

Data: the raw numbers and text (such as sales figures and customer addresses) generated by and used in your business. You can obtain computer programs that, among other things, transform these numbers into information—data that has been selected, sorted, and presented so that it is meaningful to you.

Hardware: the physical devices that constitute a computer system, including but not limited to the computer itself, a display monitor, keyboard, storage devices, and printer. A computer cannot do anything without software.

Information: data processed and arranged into any format that is meaningful to you

Software: instructions (usually called programs), stored on magnetic disk or tape, that tell the computer hardware what to do. Accounting systems and word processors are two different types of software.

How To Determine Whether the Time Has Come

Did you wake up this morning at 3:00 a.m. and say to yourself "It's time to computerize"? Probably not or, if you did, you were probably in the middle of a nightmare. Deciding that it's time to begin using computers in your business often is more akin to a dam bursting: the decision is a result of many small incidents building up over a period of time into an intolerable problem, rather than a sudden decision out of the blue. An important factor in reaching this realization is recognizing those situations where computerization can help.

Look at your business not in the way that you normally do, but rather as an outsider might see it. The best way to do this is to pretend you are considering buying this business. As a potential buyer, you want to examine every aspect of the business with a critical eye. The object of this exercise is to cut the emotional ties that bind you to your business so that you can make purely objective observations.

Walk into your business some morning and look around as if you had never been there before. What business are you in? For present purposes, selling shoes, groceries, or mufflers are the same; your business is selling inventory. Are you an accountant, attorney, or architect? If so, then your product is your time. Butchers, bakers, and candlestick makers are all in the business of manufacturing and selling. The type of business you operate determines the type of information that is generated. That information needs to be managed effectively to operate a successful business. Is it?

What you find should come as quite a shock to you. Even though your business is profitable, you should find many opportunities for greater profitability. Incidentally, if you are unable to find any missed opportunities, do either of the following: repeat the exercise more carefully, or send your resume to the Fortune 500 companies—they need people like you.

Lost Business

In a retail business, every person who walks into your store represents a sale. If you have what the person is looking for, that person may become a customer and buy the item. If you don't have the item in the desired size and color, you have lost a sale. If this happens more than once to the same customer, it's less likely that he or she will return. You have lost current and future business.

Unrealized Business

Suppose that the person in the preceding paragraph tells his or her friends that you are always out of stock on certain items. These friends represent business that can never be realized because they probably will not bother to come into your store.

Paperwork Levels

Imagine that you are an independent jobber selling custom-printed computer forms. You visit a customer and write up an order. Next, you contract the design of the form to a freelance graphic artist. After customer approval, you hire a printer to produce a proof. Once the customer approves the proof, you give the go-ahead to the printer, who prints and ships the job.

Keeping track of each job requires a great deal of paperwork. Order forms, contracts, and artwork must be kept in order. Approvals and dates must be carefully recorded. You receive bills from the subcontractors, that you must pay. You send a bill to the customer and eventually receive payment. If the customer is an educational institution, you may need to waive sales taxes.

This business is awash in paperwork. Data is everywhere, but not information. Do you need a list of customers who are late paying their bills? Good luck!

Duplication of Effort

A small accounting firm that maintains the books for 200 local independent physicians sends a monthly bill to each client for professional services rendered. Each month, an administrative assistant spends an entire weekend of overtime preparing the bills, which do not generally vary because each client's monthly flat rate usually remains the same. A secretary spends two full days typing envelopes.

Keeping Track of Accounts Receivable

The office manager of the small accounting firm mentioned in the preceding paragraph records each payment in a loose-leaf notebook set up with each client on a separate page. Not only is this manual process error-prone, but imagine if the owner of the business asks for a list of all clients who are behind in payments by 30, 60, 90, or more days. It recently took the office manager three days to compile the report by hand.

Keeping Track of Accounts Payable

The printing jobber owes money to his subcontractors. But the only way he can tell a bill was accidentally overlooked is because, like clockwork, one month later he gets another bill from the same subcontractor. The second bill is stamped *OVERDUE* in red ink, and he is informed that his current order will not be shipped until payment is received in full. But he needs that shipment to fill a dozen custom orders, all of which now will be at least a week late. How many of those customers will return?

Recognizing these black holes of lost profitability can sometimes be painful, especially if the business is one that you created and have nurtured over the years. Keep in mind that every situation you discover represents an opportunity.

> Always keep a written list of your opportunities. Use this list to set priorities and assess risks.

What Do You Want To Accomplish?

A computer system represents an investment of several thousand, or perhaps tens of thousands of, dollars. If you plan to invest in a computer system, you should have a clear idea of what you intend to do with that system. Although clearing a stack of paperwork off the counter may be commendable, it is not an accomplishment that justifies the money you invested in the system. Strive for results that make your money well-spent.

The results you achieve can be classified as either tangible or intangible. Tangible results, those that can be quantified and measured in dollars and cents, have a direct bearing on the bottom line. Intangible results are those that cannot be easily quantified. If you are considering bank financing for your computer system, you should not include intangibles in any proposal you prepare for the bank. Bankers, as a rule, tend to be conservative and discount any claims that are based on "gut feelings" or cannot otherwise be substantiated. If you must mention intangible results when making a proposal to your bank, be sure to do so in an appendix.

Tangible Results of Computerization

Will the solution you implement save money? Can you show exactly how much will be saved? If you answered yes to both questions, then you are dealing with a tangible result. Some examples of tangible results are described in the following paragraphs.

Cost Reduction

When you cut current spending, you are reducing costs. Suppose that you now spend $30 per page to have your price list professionally typeset, but you determine that you can eliminate this spending by installing a desktop publishing system. If your price list is 10 pages long and requires monthly updating, you reduce costs by $3,600 per year by using an in-house desktop publishing system.

Cost Avoidance

Future spending that becomes unnecessary represents cost avoidance. Suppose that your business is expanding so rapidly that your current staff cannot handle the time-consuming task of affixing price labels to each item in your retail store. You contemplate hiring an additional employee to do this job. This employee will cost $22,000 per year, including benefits.

A new $12,000 point-of-sale computer, however, makes it unnecessary to affix price labels to each item because the computer can read bar codes. You avoid spending $10,000 the first year you use the computer.

As you think about avoiding or reducing costs, however, bear in mind that you may be creating new, unanticipated costs—costs that are directly attributable to the new computer system. The desktop publishing system that saves so much money in professional typesetting fees, for instance, requires expensive toner cartridges at regular intervals. And suppose that the point-of-sale computer system you acquire is so difficult to program that you and your employees finally conclude that you cannot perform this task yourselves. You must hire a database consultant three times per year at $2,500 per session to perform system updating; the costs you thought you were avoiding reappear in another context.

> When you reduce or avoid one cost, you may create another.

If this point seems discouraging, take heart: you really *can* avoid or reduce costs by computerizing your business. To do so successfully, however, you must try to anticipate not only how much the computer system will save, but also how much it will cost in recurrent or system maintenance expenditures. You will find tips and advice on anticipating these expenditures in the section titled "Cost Factors of Computerization." In the meantime, remember that foreseeing such expenditures can greatly enhance your credibility when you bring a proposal to a bank.

Intangible Results of Computerization

Many of the results that initially appear to be tangible should be considered intangible because they cannot be quantified

...y substantial degree of exactness. This section deals with ...e intangible results.

Reduction in Staff

You may be surprised to see this heading under "Intangible Results of Computerization," because many people believe that a primary reason for installing computer systems is to do away with salaried employees. Business experience, however, indicates that it is only rarely the case that a new computer system can render a human employee redundant. People are flexible, adaptable, and capable of learning new solutions to new problems. Computers, in contrast, can perform a few tasks very efficiently and very rapidly, but the range of their prowess is limited, and it is difficult and costly to adapt them when circumstances change. For this reason alone, you should not assume uncritically that a computer can replace a human employee. The former mayor of San Francisco, Diane Feinstein, recently complained that despite spending more than $60 million on computer systems, the city was unable to dispense with a single salaried employee! In case after case, attempts to do away with employees by installing computers have backfired on managers—often in ways that would be laughable if the costs were not so high, as in the case of the firm that suddenly found itself with an *increased* payroll after installing an expensive computer system that was supposed to reduce payroll expenses—which it didn't. The company was forced to hire a full-time computer technician just to keep all the supposedly "job killing" computers running.

To be sure, there are situations in which you can legitimately claim that a computer system will reduce staff—especially if one or more of your employees performs a single task (but no other tasks), and this task can be accomplished by a computer. Suppose that you employ a part-time employee on Saturdays to type form letters to customers on your mailing list. Because this task can be performed by a computer word processing system, you can legitimately claim that installing the system will permit you to reduce your payroll expenditures. But such situations are considerably rarer than many business managers, computer sales personnel, and inexperienced computer specialists imagine. And remember, too, the problem of unanticipated expenses. After you install the new system that does away with a marginal and low-salaried employee, *someone* must learn how to create and maintain a form-letter application with WordPerfect—and if you have to engage an outside consultant or expert to create the application, the result may actually be *increased* salary expenditures.

> Salary reduction is only rarely a tangible result of computerization.

Increased Sales

You might at first consider increased sales to be a tangible result. The difficulty with this reasoning becomes clear when you attempt to quantify these sales. By how much will sales increase? You can never be sure. What if you decide that your system will ensure that you have the proper inventory from which to sell four additional pairs of shoes a day? This, too, is problematic. What constitutes proper inventory? How does that inventory translate into four additional sales per day rather than three or five? Although it's likely that your computer system will provide the information you need to make decisions that ultimately may increase business, your accountant probably will remain skeptical.

Improved Inventory Posture

If your business carries an inventory of any kind, you may install a computer and software that provides information to help you manage your inventory better. By adjusting the inventory mix, you may be able to do the same amount of business from less inventory or possibly more business from the same amount of inventory. With fine-tuning, you may even achieve the best of both worlds and do more business less inventory. Because you have no way of knowing how much more business or how much less inventory, however, you should consider improved inventory posture to be an intangible result.

Higher Stock Turn Ratios

A stock turn ratio is the rate at which you sell your inventory. Goods that sit on the shelf for long periods of time cost you money, but merchandise that sells quickly is turned into cash that you can use to purchase more stock. Again, because the change in stock turn ratios cannot be quantified, you should consider it an intangible result.

Shortened Reaction Times

The time it takes for you to figure out what is selling well and how fast it is selling is reaction time. A long reaction time means later ordering of replenishment merchandise, which results in later delivery. If you run out before your new order arrives, you lose business. Shortening the reaction time may translate into additional business, but because you cannot tell how much additional business would be generated, shortened reaction time, too, is an intangible benefit.

Increased Efficiency

A true classic. Ask almost anyone why they computerized and you're likely to hear "so we could be more efficient." Did you ever stop to think that increased efficiency may mean ordering the wrong merchandise faster? Business experience proves conclusively that no computer can guarantee increased efficiency. If the system is not carefully planned, tested, and implemented, it is more likely to introduce inefficiencies, which your customers are sure to notice.

A poorly designed point-of-sale computer system at a computer retail store provides a telling case in point. This system is set up so that the sales clerk must ask every customer for his or her name, address, telephone number, and future purchasing interests before it is possible to compute the sales tax and total. Obtaining this information for major purchases makes good sense, but it only serves to irritate customers who drop in just to buy a magazine or some other smaller purchase. After undergoing five minutes of interrogation just to pay cash for a box of disks, some customers will decide to shop elsewhere.

> Installing a computer system does not guarantee increased efficiency.

Increased Personal Time

When you own your own business, you easily can spend 80 or more hours a week at work. You might want to work less so that you can spend more time with your family. Your desire is certainly understandable and much preferable to being a slave to the business. Just remember that increased personal time is not a true reduction in staff (because you're not about to take a cut in pay) but rather an intangible result.

Improved Quality of Work Life

Automating mundane tasks so that they no longer need to be performed by employees usually results in happier employees. Happier employees perform better, care more about their work, and stay with the company. Happier employees contribute to the bottom line because they produce more. An improved quality of work life is a wonderful concept and it truly works, but it cannot be quantified. Keep this one in the intangible results column.

Cost Factors of Computerization

The costs of computerizing your business fall into two broad categories: financial and nonfinancial. Both have a bearing on the bottom line and should be considered carefully before making any purchase.

Financial Costs of Computerization

You cannot buy a computer without spending money. But the following financial cost factors, not always obvious, need to be recognized:

- *Hardware*. This factor is the cost for the computer, printer, monitor, and other associated devices.
- *Software*. You need software to make your computer function. Software can be purchased off-the-shelf, as in the case of word processing or accounting packages, or it can be custom-designed if required. Custom software, because it generally has no mass-market appeal, can be extremely expensive.
- *Environment*. Depending on the physical layout and cleanliness of your place of business and the quantity and type of computer equipment, you may need to modify the physical surroundings in which your computer system will be installed. Computers cannot tolerate dusty or dirty environments, may have special electrical or temperature requirements, and the display monitors should be shielded from the glare of fluorescent lights.
- *Outside Expenses*. Jimmy Durante once said, "Everybody wants to get into the act." He may well have been talking about consultants. Your accountant and attorney certainly should be involved in financial

and contractual matters. In addition, you may feel more comfortable hiring an impartial consultant to perform your needs analysis, make recommendations, and deal with computer salespeople. Finally, if you need custom-designed software, it will be necessary to contract with an independent programmer or a software company.

- *Training*. Your employees need to learn how to use and care for the computer system. Depending on the complexity of the installation, training can be provided by tutorial exercises included with the hardware and software, by computer sales professionals, by your outside consultant, by the custom software developer, or by companies that specialize in computer training.

  In addition to paying the trainers, an expense is associated with the time you must allocate to your employees for training. And remember that training never ends. You always need to train new employees and to retrain old-timers to keep them sharp.

- *Consumables*. Computer systems are like sharks; their appetites are endless. Disks, paper, ribbons, and toner cartridges are significant ongoing expenses.

- *Repair Costs*. Like all electromechanical devices, computer systems do break down from time to time. How you plan for and handle "down time" is a function of the size and complexity of your system.

  A single central computer to which many individual display monitors are connected is usually covered by an on-site service contract because a central computer failure puts everyone out of commission. Be sure that the contract specifies both average response time and maximum response time. Individual personal computers and associated devices can be covered with on-site or drop-off (depot) contracts or with no contract at all. If you can function without the broken machine for a week, you probably are better off with no contract. If you cannot live without that particular device, consider a service contract that provides for an equivalent loaner machine while yours is in the shop.

- *Insurance.* Whether you own your computing equipment outright or have arranged for outside financing, you should look into insurance. Although insurance carriers differ somewhat, usually you can cover hardware, software, data loss, and sometimes even loss of revenue, although that can be difficult to prove. Talk to your business insurer.

Nonfinancial Costs of Computerization

The nonfinancial costs of computerization are no less important than the financial costs. The following factors deserve close scrutiny:

- *Time.* Is there ever enough time? You need time to analyze your business, time to decide what to computerize, time to search for software and hardware solutions, time to install, time to test, time to train, time to explain, and more.

- *Disruption of Business Operations.* Without a doubt your new system will disrupt business even before it is installed. You will be away from the business while you shop for solutions, you may need to rearrange furniture or displays to accommodate the new equipment, and workers may need to install cables or new electrical service.

  Once the computer system is running, there is a period of adjustment as your employees, customers, and vendors learn to work with the system. People, being single-minded, can process only one thought at a time. While concentrating on the system—even if only for a moment—it will be impossible to concentrate on the business.

- *Frustration*. For any computer user, novice or expert, frustration is forever just one erroneous keystroke away. Frustrated employees are neither happy nor productive, both of which take a toll on the business. Patience is indeed a virtue, and your employees will constantly look to you as a role model. If you hate your system, so will they.

Good Reasons for Purchasing a Computer

If you intend to finance your system with outside funds, such as a bank loan, it becomes imperative that your reasons be financially justified in terms of tangible results, as explained in the preceding section. Yet there are other good reasons to computerize besides the ones you can quantify.

One such reason is to keep up with or get ahead of the competition. The explosion in video rental stores, is a case in point. The early entries in this growing market kept track of their rentals by using index card systems derived from manual lending library procedures. Although such a system may have been slow, unwieldy, and prone to error, customers came, saw, and rented nonetheless. But the market changed nearly overnight. Computer systems were developed specifically for retail video rental stores and soon any store without such a system was operating at a distinct competitive disadvantage. It became clear that a system was required just to keep pace with the competition. Today, a look through the appropriate trade journals lists no fewer than 32 companies manufacturing software for this market.

Another unquantifiable reason to computerize is to gain a strategic *advantage* over your competition (instead of just keeping up with it). A major midwestern supplier of machine parts, for instance, provided its customers with personal computers, software, and telecommunications equipment that enabled these customers to order parts quickly, easily, and cheaply from the customers' own offices. Because it was so much easier to order parts from this supplier, customers started using this ordering system for all or most of their parts needs instead of going to the supplier's competition, which was effectively locked out of the new ordering system. The supplier increased its market share dramatically, and higher profits followed.

> You can use computer technology to keep up with the competition. Even better, you can use it to *change the rules* so that you gain a strategic advantage over your competition.

Not-So-Good Reasons for Purchasing a Computer

Every intelligent discussion has two viewpoints. In addition to good reasons, then, there are also some not-so-good reasons for buying a computer.

At the top of the list of not-so-good reasons is what Douglas Carlston, the president of Broderbund Software, calls "computer fever." Fascinated with technology as a child, Carlston later took a law degree and opened a legal firm in Maine. Soon after meeting a colleague who had installed a sophisticated microcomputer system, Carlston concluded that he had to computerize his law office and purchased several microcomputers. But "computer fever" soon overtook his interest in law, and instead of concentrating on the legal software he envisioned writing, he created a game called *Galactic Empire*. Happily for Carlston, the game turned out to be the key to a new, multimillion-dollar business, but it spelled the end of his legal career. Carlston now recognizes that his interest in computerizing his law firm was only a rationalization for his real interest, namely, playing with computers.

Carlston's story has a happy ending, but few cases of computer fever produce such good results. In the late 1970s, a small law firm in the San Francisco Bay area hoped to gain a strategic advantage over its competition by computerizing virtually every facet of its operations. But the real reason was the computer fever of one of the firm's founders, who wanted to create all the necessary programs himself. The result was computer-assisted disaster of the worst kind: the bug-ridden programs made it impossible for the firm to determine who owed it money. Unable to collect on client fees, the firm was forced to cease all operations.

> If you show any signs of computer fever, do not computerize your business unless you are absolutely sure that you are doing so for sound business reasons. Play with computers at home, not at work.

A computer system, no matter how well designed and implemented, cannot save a business that should not have existed in the first place. Several years ago a national seafood restaurant chain opened several outlets in New England. Despite computerized cash registers for inventory control and sales tracking and computer-controlled cooking equipment to ensure consistency of product, the company closed every one of these outlets less than a year after they had opened. The problem, of course, was the wrong product in the wrong geographic area. When you can walk into virtually any local restaurant or market and purchase seafood caught fresh that very morning, a chain of restaurants selling deep-fried, previously frozen, processed, batter-dipped seafood is, well, like a fish out of water.

Other Things To Try First

You may be surprised to read the following in a book on computerization:

> Computers are not always the best choice. Investigate the alternatives first.

Buying a computer is just one of many alternatives that you can choose to achieve an intended result. In large corporations the concepts of price/performance ratio and payback are scrutinized carefully for any proposed solution. Price/performance ratio means simply getting the "biggest bang for the buck." It's good advice and applies to businesses both large and small. Payback is an indication of how long it will take for the money you spend on the computer to be returned. You will examine a cost/benefit analysis later in this book.

Consider Less Expensive Noncomputer Solutions First

Because of the expense required, you should list all possible solutions and consider these alternatives before deciding on a computer. You can buy a $59 software program that makes your $6,000 computer function like a $10 pocket calculator, but would that make sense? A better alternative would have been simply to buy a $10 pocket calculator and save the other $6,049. Think about the price/performance ratio and payback!

Suppose that an attorney is considering a system to replace a manual typewriter to help prepare various legal documents. She can buy an electric typewriter, an electronic typewriter, a document preparation system, or a personal computer with a word processing program. Each alternative comes with its own set of advantages and disadvantages. The electric typewriter is inexpensive but does not have a memory to simplify the preparation of nearly identical documents. The electronic typewriter may add simple spell checking and a bit to the price but little else. A document preparation system (a specialized computer that lives up to its name and no more) will certainly solve the immediate problems but will not allow client invoices to be prepared. A personal computer when equipped with the appropriate software can undertake a range of tasks far too long to list here. After studying the alternatives, the attorney chooses the personal computer because it represents a solution that can produce the required results at the required time and also perform other tasks (like billing clients).

Outside Service Bureaus

Another important alternative is going outside for solutions. If, for example, you are having difficulty keeping up with the stringent governmental requirements for payroll tax reporting, you may find that an outside payroll service offers the best solution. If you are not interested in maintaining your company's financial records, consider hiring a client accounting service that will do it for you. Not only will you be relieved of a task you dislike, but you also will have more time to concentrate on your business. The attorney in the preceding example considered using an outside secretarial service, but eventually discarded that alternative because none of the staff was familiar with legal terminology and there was a two-day minimum turnaround time on the preparation of documents.

Understanding the Computerization Process

Buying and installing computer hardware and software is just one part of the overall computerization process—and it is neither the beginning nor the end of the process. Before investing in a system, you should formulate very specific ideas regarding what it is you actually want the computer system to do. And because it is nearly impossible to do this without a clear understanding of your current business procedures, a detailed examination of your business should be undertaken first. These topics are explored in detail throughout this book.

Analysis of the Current System

"To know where you are going, you have to know where you have been" goes an old saying. Take this advice to heart when thinking about a computer system. Because you are looking to automate, consolidate, or otherwise improve current operating practices, it is vital for you to have the clearest, most in-depth understanding of these practices possible.

Use the analysis process to examine your business, its component procedures, and their interrelations. Analyze your business to understand how information flows between people, which paper forms are used and for what purpose, and to discover opportunities for improving accuracy.

You find a comprehensive guide to needs analysis in Chapter 2, "Taking the First Steps toward Computerization."

Matching a Solution to Your Needs

Once you have completed your analysis, you can start thinking about solutions. Learn what a solution is—and is not.

> A solution is a process that you use to solve a problem. A computer is not a solution; it is a method of applying a solution.

Although this book explores the computer as the method for applying your solution, you should always consider noncomputer, less expensive solutions first. If you determine that rearranging your employees' desks improves the flow of information to an acceptable degree, then a computer may not be necessary.

Once you have concluded that a computer system is a requirement, you then begin the search for the software that best suits your business and its needs. This search can be time-consuming—for example, more than 200 word processing programs exist for the IBM PC family of computers alone.

Always consider software before shopping for hardware. It makes no sense to buy a computer only to discover later that the perfect software solution for your business runs only on a different type of machine.

You find an overview of the tool-selection process in Chapter 3, "Identifying Your Software Needs"; Chapter 4, "Finding Business Solutions in Application Software"; and Chapter 5, "Making Hardware Purchasing Decisions." Chapter 7, "Deciding Where To Buy Your Equipment," explores your options in choosing a vendor or vendors for the software and hardware you have selected, and Chapter 6, "Getting Help from a Consultant," explains how to obtain the assistance of a professional consultant as you navigate the tricky waters of a system purchase.

Testing Your System

With your system delivered and installed, testing—a vital activity—is next. Carry both healthy optimism and vigorous skepticism into the testing process: optimism because you certainly want your project to succeed, and skepticism because you should not make business decisions based on information generated by your computer system until you have thoroughly tested and certified the accuracy of that information.

Implementing Your System

Once your system has been successfully installed and tested, it's time to implement it—that is, to work the computer system into the day-to-day fabric of your business's activities. The key here is to take it one step at a time. You should begin with a single application and perform tests on noncritical or simulated transactions until you and your employees are confident of the results. In this stage, you face a major and often trying task: training your employees to use the system. Chapter 8, "Implementing Your New System," explains the implementation process in detail.

Using Your Computer System

Once the system becomes part of your daily business operations, you must see to it that the system is properly maintained and that operation standards are routinely met. The best computer system in the world, after all, will produce undesirable results if it is not taken care of and used properly. You will need to consider, too, the unhappy prospects of theft, vandalism, and sabotage, as well as the problem of deciding when the growth of your business calls for expansion or replacement of your system.

The Human Side of Computerization

As the computerization process has been described here, it sounds like a cut-and-dried, rational process. But people are involved, and an intelligent plan for computerizing your business begins with a recognition of this fact. Your employees and your customers will all be affected as you computerize your business, in ways that range from positive to negative. As the owner of the business, it is up to you to anticipate the effects of computerization on people and take action so that the positive effects outweigh the negative ones.

Computer Phobia

As you test and implement your new system, you will probably become caught up in the excitement and novelty of experiencing a powerful new technology—especially if you have just a touch of computer fever. If so, you may be all the more surprised that your employees do not share your enthusiasm for the new system. Some employees, to be sure, may welcome it with open arms. Others will cooperate dutifully, even if they are not so enthusiastic. But some may display signs of what researchers call "computer phobia," a deep-seated fear of computers that may lead them to avoid the computer—or at the worst, to try to sabotage the system by cutting wires, dumping beverages into computer enclosures, or running magnets across disks. When a new computer system was implemented for a police station, for instance, the system implementor was surprised to find out one day that an officer had apparently put two bullets through a video display device.

Feelings of fear and resentment about computers stem from a variety of irrational beliefs. Some employees may believe that the arrival of a new computer system is just the first step in a process that will culminate in the loss of their jobs. Others may fear they cannot operate the computer because of deficiencies in their mathematical or technical backgrounds, and that the computer will make them look stupid. Still others may feel that the computer is going to force them to do business in a dehumanized way, isolated from others, as they are reduced to mere button-pushers who are no longer performing an interesting or valuable service.

The best way to deal with fearful employees is to address these fears openly at the outset. Make it clear that the purpose of the system is to help all employees serve customers more effectively. Make it clear, too, that the computer applications you will ask them to use do not require advanced mathematical or technical abilities, and that all employees will be given the opportunity to learn to use the programs at their own pace and from their own level, without negative performance appraisals if they take somewhat longer than others to learn. Finally, make it clear that the purpose of the system is not to create a dehumanized environment or reduce employees to mere button-pushers. On the contrary, the system's purpose is to help all employees improve the level and quality of the service or product that is delivered to the firm's customers. And invite your employees' feedback if they have reason to feel that the computer is not living up to its promise.

Some employees may feel threatened by computerization because they fear that the computer, with its interactive textual display and command menus, will reveal their low level of literacy, which they had been able to disguise previously. Unlike the irrational fears of computer phobia, these concerns are well grounded. As Shoshona Zuboff has argued in *The Age of the Smart Machine* (New York: Basic Books, 1988), the essence of computerization is the translation of a firm's *oral* culture into explicit, *textualized* representations in computer displays—representations that some employees will not be able to read. In large firms, implementing a computer system frequently leads to the discovery that some employees, who appear to be literate in other contexts, are not able to comprehend computer-displayed menus. After a computerization effort revealed such problems, a company in Massachusetts conducted literacy tests and found that *one out of every five* of its employees was functionally illiterate. The introduction of the computer into the work environment does not *create* this problem; it just *exposes* it and in so doing forces businesses to face up to the phenomenal problems of public illiteracy in this country. One recent study found that although 95 percent of U.S. adults aged 21 to 35 can read simple passages, only a very small percentage could understand complex material. One out of three adult Americans is either functionally illiterate or only marginally competent in basic reading and writing skills.

Except in extreme cases of computer phobia or illiteracy, you should avoid forcing a resistant employee into a marginal job or out of the firm. Doing so will send the wrong message about your intentions to other employees, who might be sitting on the fence, wondering whether the system really is a threat to their jobs. A little patience on your part, and perhaps some outside training or counseling for the employee, are humane solutions to the problem of a computer-phobic employee—and what is more, these solutions make it clear that you are sincere in your claim that the system is no threat to your valued employees. Remember: in the hands of hostile, alienated employees, even the most brilliant technical systems will perform far below their potential.

Even if all your employees are enthusiastic about the system, they may take much longer to learn how to use it effectively than you had anticipated. Despite all the advertising hype about "user friendliness," the fact remains that today's computers and applications can be challenging to learn. Fortune 500 companies are spending millions of dollars on in-house and external training programs, which have emerged as one of the most dangerous hidden costs of computerizing business practices. If you are computer literate yourself, you may have forgotten how long it took *you* to learn MS-DOS, dBASE, and 1-2-3, and how much frustration you had to endure. Put yourself in your employees' shoes, and remember your own days as a computer novice!

Will the Computer Change Your Business?

Research on the impact of computers on organizations has demonstrated one fact beyond a doubt: it is virtually impossible to predict with any certainty how a computer system will affect an organization. Computers do not "automatically" lead to job loss or "dehumanization" any more than they "automatically" lead to increased efficiency or productivity. It all depends on how the system is designed, conceived, implemented, and used.

Ideally, the system helps you and your employees provide a better service or a better product to your customers. This entire book is designed to help you achieve this goal, but one point can be made straightaway. The way you have organized your business represents the accumulated experience of many years of human effort. You should never willingly surrender this accumulated experience by adopting a computer system whose limitations force you to change the way you do business. If you honestly feel that a system which is being recommended to you would force you to alter existing and *successful* methods of selling, servicing, communicating, or interacting, look for a different system.

> Do not change your business to conform to a computer system; change the computer system to conform to your business.

The only exception to this rule is that computerizing your business may provide you with new opportunities to gain a strategic advantage over your competition. As you become more aware of what your computer system might do for you, think of ways you can use it to change the rules of the game to favor you. Most video rental stores, for example, employ software that records each customer's rentals by title. With a little extra programming effort, this software could be altered so that it automatically analyzes each customer's rental patterns (such as preference for children's, action, or comedy films). This information could be used to generate customized mailings that contain information about forthcoming films in a given category and an offer to reserve the new films for the customer's use on a given day—for a small reservation fee, of course.

How Your Customers Will See Your Computer System

An example cited earlier described customers' frustrations with a point-of-sale system that required them to provide their name, address, telephone number, and future buying plans just to buy a $4 magazine with cash. As this example suggests, customers may perceive the new system positively—or negatively. In general, the system should never appear to force the customer into an inconvenience that is mandated by the system and that employees are helpless to avoid. On the contrary, the customer's interaction with the system (or view of it as employees interact with it) should drive home the central reason it was implemented in the first place: to provide the customer with better service and a better product. If your customers are telling you that the system gets in the way of service and quality, it's time to take a very critical look at what you have done.

Even where good intentions are made clear at the outset, however, it may take time to gain customer acceptance. When supermarkets first installed electronic point-of-sale terminals with bar code readers, for instance, many customers were uncomfortable with the technology and suspected that the system failed to ring up their sales accurately. After scrutinizing their receipts a few times, however, most customers conclude that the system really is accurate, even more so than older methods, and they may also conclude that it saves them waiting time at the checkout line.

Measuring Your Success

With the substantial investment of both time and money required to conceive of and install a computer system, it's natural to want to know whether the effort was a success. To determine the success of your effort, you should establish a list of criteria for success.

The length of the list is not important. The criteria you develop, however, should be quantifiable standards (in terms of amounts and timetable) that do not change as your automation project progresses.

Suppose that you take many custom orders from your customers and that many orders are eventually canceled because they were filled incorrectly, only partially, or kept the customer waiting too long. To say that you want to cut down on the number of canceled orders does not constitute a valid criterion for success because you can cut down by one and claim victory even though the cost of the system was not recouped by the one order.

Although it is clear that you want to cut down on the number of canceled orders, it's unlikely that you will eliminate them. Pick a reasonable number that presents both a challenge and a good chance for success. Striving for unattainable goals only hurts your employees' morale. Establish a timetable, because you cannot wait forever.

After reconsideration you may develop a criterion along the lines of "after 6 months with the new system, we want to cut the number of canceled custom orders by 35 percent." What is the difference? You have established an event (reduction of canceled orders), a quantifiable and reasonable amount (35 percent), and a timetable (6 months).

> Establish criteria for success that include quantifiable milestones over specific periods of time.

Justifying the Expense with a Cost/Benefit Analysis

Once you have decided exactly what you want your computer to do and have established the criteria for measurement, you should undertake a cost/benefit analysis to determine whether the expense of the system is justified. Your cost/benefit analysis will produce two pieces of information: payback (the number of months or years it will take to recoup your investment) and internal rate of return (a measure of the profit that your computer investment can be reasonably expected to return).

Assessing Risk

Any project, no matter how carefully planned, always has a certain degree of risk associated with it. Imagine that you want to build a wood deck for your home. The idea is good, your plans are accurate, and you have purchased all the right materials. Where's the risk? You may measure the lumber incorrectly and cut the support beams too short. Or you may build your deck closer to the property line than local zoning laws allow.

Computer projects are no different. You may tackle too large a project, and you may purchase an inappropriate or inadequate solution.

Consider risk and payoff. Think of payoff as the overall combination of benefits, payback, price/performance ratio, internal rate of return, and positive effects on your business. It is natural, of course, to strive for the maximum payoff—but at what risk?

The chart shown in figure 1.1 plots risk against payoff.

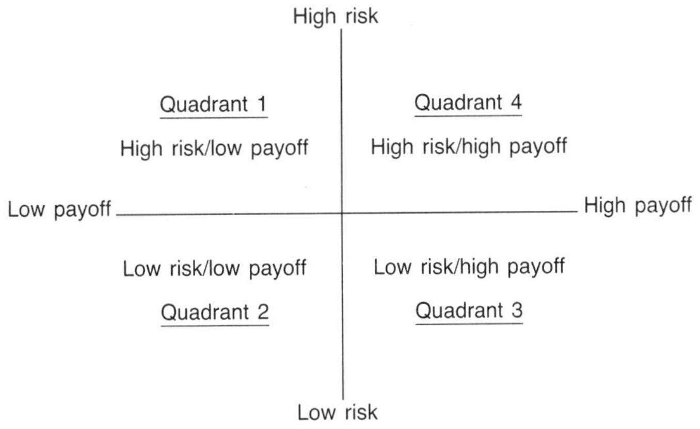

Fig. 1.1. *Risk versus payoff.*

Quadrant 1 illustrates a high risk/low payoff scenario—a choice that no competent business executive would ever consider.

Quadrant 2, low risk/low payoff, is akin to the saying "nothing ventured, nothing gained."

Quadrant 3, low risk/high payoff, is the goal for which your project should strive. Think of it another way: a $1 raffle ticket promising a $1,000 prize is surely low risk/high payoff, but a different formula, say, a $750 ticket with a $1,000 prize, would fall into quadrant 1, high risk/low payoff.

Finally, quadrant 4, high risk/high payoff, is where you are likely to find today's wildly successful entrepreneurs, those willing to bet it all for huge returns.

For a sample cost/benefit analysis, see Appendix C.

Chapter Summary

In this chapter, you thought about your business, how it operates, and whether there are opportunities for improving its profitability. You learned a little about computers, good and not-so-good reasons for acquiring one, and why you should examine noncomputer alternatives. You discovered that purchasing the computer is just one part of an overall process that begins with analysis and ends with never-ending training. You learned about the costs of computerization, the importantance of establishing measurement criteria, and the necessity for undertaking a cost/benefit analysis.

In the next chapter, you learn more about the analysis process, establishing a budget, and environmental requirements for your new system.

CHAPTER 2

Taking the First Steps toward Computerization

Years ago IBM used the word *THINK* as its motto. Just *THINK*. No more, no less. Walk into a large corporate data processing center, and there it was—*THINK*. You could always see it—*THINK*. One glance was enough to make you do just that: think.

That old IBM motto certainly comes into play when you consider a computer system for your small business. For your purposes, consider updating the motto to *Think before You Buy*.

Before you rush out to purchase computer equipment, you need to undertake a needs analysis of your business. This analysis process is an exercise that helps you document your business and determine what you want to automate and to what degree. Not until your needs are known should you consider specific software and hardware solutions.

This chapter examines the needs analysis process and explains how to establish a budget for your automation project.

A Realistic Story

To understand the process of carrying out a needs analysis and the need for a book like this, you can benefit from the realistic story of Mark and Marian, the owners of a bedroom and bath accessories store. Their story was selected to demonstrate what can happen to a successful small business when information management goes awry. Although the story is about a retail establishment, the scenario could be easily applied to just about any type of business, even yours.

Fortunately, this story has a happy ending. The owners distanced themselves from their emotional involvement with their business and took the time to perform an objective analysis. They sought outside expertise when unsure of their next step. This conservative approach was eventually rewarded by a successful automation project that, when supplemented by advertising, brought in and kept customers both new and old. The names of the proprietors have been changed.

Mark and Marian, husband and wife, run a successful bedroom and bathroom accessories shop located in a suburban shopping mall. They have been in business for six years. The store is in a prime location and is almost always filled with customers. Some are eyeing a solid oak towel rack while others look through the huge selection of designer shower curtains. In another part of the store, customers are placing orders for custom-made bed comforters and pillows or checking on orders placed earlier.

But something is not quite right. The towel racks are frequently out of stock. The more popular shower curtains are always "due in any day," while the least popular models are in plentiful supply. Even worse is the Custom Orders department. Customers are complaining. It seems that some orders placed weeks ago were never called in to the factory. Other orders were filled only partially. Some customers were never notified that their orders had arrived weeks ago.

No doubt about it, Mark and Marian are standing in quicksand. They are gradually drowning in their own success. To help them, an adviser needs to know two things: what is happening and what should be done about it. Now, examine their situation more closely.

What business are Mark and Marian in? Retail sales is correct, but take it a step further and divide the business into two separate operating units: sales of on-hand inventory and custom orders. Keep in mind that *what* they sell is irrelevant. Next, analyze what is happening in each of the two operating units or departments.

First, Mark and Marian are losing business in towel racks and shower curtains because they have lost track of which items are the most and the least popular. They need to track each item's sales and its on-hand availability so that they can make decisions about reordering.

Now what about the Custom Orders department? Each order is written on a 4-by-6-inch index card. Each card is then filed under the customer's last name in one of three cardboard boxes: orders not called in, pending orders, and orders received. Some cards were accidentally filed in the pending box even though those orders had not been called in. Cards for large orders contain writing on the back that might have been overlooked. Most cards contain orders for items from different manufacturers. Because Mark calls half the manufacturers on Monday and Marian calls the rest on Tuesday, Mark leaves those cards on the counter Monday night because none of the three boxes is appropriate. And because there is no easy way to gather all the ordered items for each manufacturer, it's easy to miss one or more.

Mark and Marian have all the data they need to run the Custom Orders department, but they have lost control of the organization and management of that data. Without control, it becomes just a matter of time before the bottom falls out.

Depending on your point of view, Mark and Marian have either a crisis that threatens to put them out of business or an opportunity to make their business thrive once again. This book, of course, assumes that you subscribe to the latter point of view. Although your business is probably far healthier than Mark and Marian's, many of the solutions they discovered and implemented can be applied no matter what type of business you operate.

Informational Needs

Every business has informational needs. In fact, information is the basis upon which every business must operate. A retail business must keep track of what is sold and what remains in inventory. A lawn service must keep track of each customer's lawn size and date of last service to calculate how much fertilizer to buy and when to apply it. A law firm must keep detailed records of each attorney's time so that clients are billed accurately. A magazine must know when your subscription expires so that you won't receive issues for which you haven't paid.

After one particularly painful Saturday in which numerous custom orders were canceled, Mark and Marian decided that something finally had to be done. The time for action had come.

How To Perform a Needs Analysis

Several steps need to be taken before you can shop for your system as an educated consumer and one already familiar with the concept of computerization. You probably studied the local business environment before you started or purchased your business, just as you probably asked about the quality of the local school system before purchasing your home. You need to go through a similar process before you buy a computer system.

What Is a Needs Analysis?

Simply put, a needs analysis is a process you perform that results in the following items:

- ❑ A statement that identifies problems within your business
- ❑ Information about your business that must be taken into account when searching for solutions
- ❑ A statement of exactly what you want to accomplish and the degree to which you want to accomplish it

Developing a Problem Statement

No one likes to admit that a problem exists in a business, but you are probably shopping for a computer system as a solution to a business problem. The first step in arriving at the solution is the development of a written problem statement, a very broad general acknowledgment that a situation requiring further study exists.

The owners of the bed and bath store thought long and hard about their problem statement. At first, they had difficulty finding a common thread. After all, what did out-of-stock shower curtains have to do with improper filling of custom orders? These were separate departments, run by different people, in different parts of the store.

Eventually Mark and Marian saw the light: they realized they were facing the *same kind of difficulty in both departments*. Their business was awash in information, but they were not using it effectively, so they developed the following problem statement:

> We need a better way to take advantage of the information used in our business.

This is a momentous occasion! Examine the problem statement carefully. It is a simple declaration—no more, no less. A problem statement is significant not only for what it includes but also for what it excludes. This problem statement is neither positive nor negative in tone and does not reach a conclusion or suggest a course of action.

When you develop your problem statement, be sure that it

- ❑ *Recognizes opportunity.* Even the healthiest business has untapped potential. Mark and Marian recognized that although their business was sick, it was not terminally ill. Put another way, the outlook is positive, and Mark and Marian assume that it can be made healthy again.

- ❑ *Refrains from making recommendations.* Saying "we need to computerize the business" is inappropriate and may lead to a solution for a problem that never existed. Mark and Marian could have invested thousands of dollars in a computer system only to find later that a fourth cardboard box for the custom orders would have sufficed.

- ❑ *Refrains from being overly specific or overly broad.* Developing a problem statement that is too specific is akin to treating a symptom instead of the disease. Imagine that the problem statement in the example had been purely a reaction to the canceled custom orders. This narrow focus would have treated the resulting symptom, the canceled orders, while overlooking the larger picture—the inability to manage information, not just for custom orders, but for the entire store.

  Conversely, a problem statement that is too broad does not establish enough of a basis for further examination. To say "our profits are too low" isn't particularly useful. Did you ever hear of a company that didn't want to make more money?

- *Lays the foundation for detailed analysis.* Specifying a course of action ("we need a computer and a word processing program") as a problem statement may lead you to implement a solution that does not achieve the intended result. An automation project requires careful thought and a detailed, multifaceted analysis of the business.

- *Lays the foundation for measuring the project's success.* Is it enough to know that you bought and installed a computer? It shouldn't be. In the end, after all the equipment is installed and operating, you should be able to measure, in quantifiable terms, whether the project was a success and the degree of success.

Getting Information from Your Employees

Developing a good problem statement is not easy. Seek help. Talk to the experts—your employees. As the owner or operator of a business, you may be too involved to see what is happening around you or too removed from the daily operation to understand its nuances.

What do your employees find wasteful or error-prone? Do they find it impossible to keep hot-selling items in stock? Does your legal secretary complain about the way time billing is handled? Are your accountants wasting time preparing client tax returns by hand?

> It is your employees, not you, who will live with the computer system. Keep them involved.

You may find that employees are reluctant to open up to the boss. They may feel that these problems are a negative reflection on your abilities. To overcome this natural apprehension, you can hold a series of meetings away from the business, perhaps as a conference with dinner. You also can retain the services of an outside consultant, an option to be examined later.

Collecting Samples of Your Internal Business Forms

Depending on the nature of your business, you may have few or many internal business forms. If you are typing purchase orders for inventory, you need samples to make sure that your new system can handle every piece of information. Are you making shoes? If so, any purchase order management system you install needs to handle construction, materials for each component, multiple size runs, and more.

Other forms you should collect are checks (mark them *VOID*), sales slips, invoices, inventory forms, special instruction forms, packing slips, statements, and those hand-drawn forms that seem to come from nowhere.

Collecting Samples of Forms Received from Outside

In addition to your internal forms, it makes sense to complete the set with forms you receive from others. Although these forms may not have a great impact on your system, they can serve as models for any internal forms you redesign.

Developing a Needs Questionnaire

To help get information from customers or vendors, you can try a simple questionnaire. Ask questions that can be answered with a yes or no or that look for a rating from excellent to poor. Vendors usually are glad to take a few minutes (but no more) to answer a questionnaire because it may mean more business for them. Customers on the other hand may need a little incentive. In a retail store you can offer a 5 percent discount; if you are an accountant, you may offer a particular service for free.

Mark and Marian developed the questionnaire shown in figure 2.1 to find out what customers thought about the special orders area.

M&M Bed and Bath Accessories
Customer Questionnaire

Please help us serve you better by taking a minute to answer these questions. As our way of saying thank you, we will deduct $5 from your order of $100 or more.

Are you satisfied with the service you have received in the Custom Orders Department? ☐ yes ☐ no

If you answered "yes," please stop here. A sales associate will collect this sheet. Thank you for your help in improving our business.

Please answer the following questions:

Was your last order filled accurately? ☐ yes ☐ no

Were any items missing? ☐ yes ☐ no

Did you get the right items but in the wrong color or size? ☐ yes ☐ no

Did you receive items that you did not order? ☐ yes ☐ no

How many items were in your last order? ________

How long did it take for your order to arrive? ________

Was that too long? ☐ yes ☐ no

Were you satisfied with the quality of the merchandise you received? ☐ yes ☐ no

Fig. 2.1. *Using a questionnaire to learn customer opinion.*

Design your questionnaire so that it can be filled out quickly by the respondent and analyzed easily by you. This questionnaire is not intended to be used as a scientifically based statistical sampling, but rather as a quick method of measuring customer sentiment. Note too that the last question has nothing to do with the project at hand, but it provides feedback that Mark and Marian decided will be helpful at another time.

Determining How Computers Can Help

You have placed your business under a microscope. Employees have voiced their concerns and suggestions, a mountain of forms has been collected, and you have interviewed just about everyone: customers, vendors, and your accountant. You should have a clear idea about the direction your project should take.

Mark and Marian teamed up with their employees and vendors and learned that as many as 25 percent of all custom orders were incorrect in some way. Together, they decided that it was necessary to cut this error rate in custom orders to 15 percent in the first year and to 5 percent after 18 months. Because you cannot eliminate errors completely, you should never set goals that strive to eliminate all errors. Next, Mark and Marian agreed that the 10-day response time for reordering merchandise should be cut to 5 days. Finally, the team (excluding the outside vendors) discovered that sales had dropped 3 percent in the last year. Determined to reverse that trend, they specified an increase of 1 percent, a net change of 4 percent. These goals are realistic but challenging.

To document their findings, Mark and Marian developed a simple chart listing the problem, error rate, objective, and desired error rate (see fig. 2.2). Note that the chart does not include all findings.

A statement has been developed, and quantifiable goals have been set. Note that Mark and Marian have not yet thought about how to reach their goal. That will not happen until they begin shopping for a system.

Establishing a Budget

Clearly, substantial costs are associated with any computerization project, and it makes sense to keep those

Problem			Objective		
Item	Amount	Cause	Item	Amount	Action
Custom order errors	25%	Manual procedures are error-prone	Process custom orders with fewer errors	15%	Redesign procedures
Reorder cycle is too long	10 days	Manual evaluation of sales figures takes too long	Reduce reorder cycle	5 days	Produce time-sensitive consolidated sales information
Sales are decreasing	-3%	Incorrect mix of inventory	Increase sales	+1%	Modify inventory mix

Fig. 2.2. *Making a list of problems and goals.*

costs as low as possible to achieve the maximum benefit. You also need to determine how much you can afford to spend. If you are simply installing two or three personal computers and printers for word processing, the cost may be about $10,000, and you can keep track of that level of expense. But for larger projects, your accountant should remain closely involved in the process of setting a workable budget.

What Is the Minimum Configuration You Need?

In developing your requirements you probably decided on a certain number of computers to be installed at specific locations. Perhaps you plan to install a computer for each of the ten secretaries your business employs. Consider whether it is necessary to install all ten at one time. You may install only five and discover the same amount of work is being accomplished. Not only have you saved on equipment costs, you have doubled productivity. You are presented with an opportunity to reallocate your manpower.

In a retail operation like Mark and Marian's bathroom accessories store, it's important to decide what can wait. For them, the largest drain on the business was the special orders department, so they decided that it must be computerized as soon as possible. On the other hand, they wanted very much to computerize the sales and inventory portion of the business. They understood that training sales personnel to detect manually inventory surpluses or shortages earlier would help. Mark and Marian decided that they could implement the solution for this part of the business at a later time.

A phased implementation benefits you in two ways. First, you are spreading out your capital investment over a longer period of time. That time means that instead of paying a large sum of money on day one, you can use cost savings generated by the system to purchase additional equipment. In other words, after the initial start-up costs, the system funds itself. Second, you can concentrate your efforts in one area. Like the handyman who never seems to finish a project because he has five going on at the same time, your computer project should be complete in one area before moving on to the next. Mark and Marian understood this and agreed to concentrate their efforts in the special orders area.

Setting Priorities with a Five-Year Plan

A five-year plan? When you don't even know what to have for lunch tomorrow? Perhaps the phrase "five-year plan" sounds too regimented. Think of it more as a five-year vision. For your particular business, maybe it's best to develop a three-year plan. Of course, like anything else in life, this vision is subject to revision or modification.

The five-year plan is an exercise in developing priorities. After you identify the aspects of your business needing automation, you and your team first determine the order in which you want to address each subproject and then the timetable for implementation.

The owners of the bed and bath store developed a project list that contained more than just the special orders and inventory projects. They assigned each subproject a priority: high, medium, or low. High-priority items are those that are critical to the survival of the business, medium-priority items are others that produce quantifiable benefits, and low-priority items are those that are "nice to have." The finished list is shown in figure 2.3.

List of Projects and Priorities

Description	Low	Medium	High
Custom orders department			X
Inventory control			X
Accounts receivable			X
Customer mailing list	X		
Sales analysis		X	
Electronic paperless purchase orders	X		
Sales associates productivity reporting		X	
Customer follow-up letters	X		
Accounts payable		X	

Fig. 2.3. *Setting priorities.*

Allocating the Budget

Determining how the money will be spent is an important step in your project. Allocate too little to one area, and you eventually will need to make someone else's slice of the pie smaller. If that cannot be done, you may find yourself searching for a bigger pie (putting in more money). The best way to avoid these potential problems is to hold money in reserve.

Allocations change. If you plan to spend $500 for a prepackaged order-entry software system and discover that none meets your needs, you have two alternatives. You can buy the package that comes closest to fulfilling your requirements and modify your business procedures to fit, or you can hire someone to develop custom software for your business. Don't be surprised if the custom software costs $10,000 or more. Without mass-market appeal, the programmer must recover all development costs from you.

Dividing the monetary pie is different for every project. What works in an attorney's office surely is not appropriate for a manufacturing operation. The allocations presented here are those developed for the bed and bath store example. You should use them as a starting guideline, but you should make any changes appropriate for your business.

- *Hardware—35%.* Hardware is the major portion of any budget. This category includes all computing equipment, furniture, and electrical work.

  If you plan to connect several computers together in a network, you should allocate funds for cabling and for the server, a special computer that stores everyone's files. For networking, 35 percent may be low.

- *Software—15%.* All the programs you buy—word processing, order entry, accounting, and utilities to help manage your computers—are software. This 15 percent allocation assumes that you are buying off-the-shelf software. For custom program development, this figure could be 50 percent or more.

- *Outside Services—15%.* Outside services are fees paid to people who do not work for you (except for training). Included in this group are accountants, attorneys, and consultants.

- *Training—15%.* The best computer system in the world is worthless to your company if no one understands how to operate it. Training is a crucial expense that should not be overlooked or eliminated.

- *Printing—10%.* Printing includes continuous forms that you feed into your printer. Many office supply mail-order houses carry forms for most of the popular accounting packages. When you order these forms, they are imprinted with your company's name, address, and logo for a personalized look.

  If necessary, you can contract with a forms design company for any custom work. If custom forms are required, you may need to revise this allocation.

- *Reserve—10%.* The reserve allocation of 10 percent is your emergency fund. Never make plans to spend this money. Treat this fund like the dime or quarter that you keep hidden in your wallet or handbag (or shoe) for that emergency phone call.

Mark and Marian decided not to borrow money to fund their project. Instead, they agreed to use as much as $40,000 from their savings. Dividing this amount among the budget categories yielded the results shown in table 2.1.

Table 2.1
Budget by Category

Category	*Percent*	*Amount in dollars (maximum)*
Hardware	35	14,000
Software	15	6,000
Outside services	15	6,000
Training	15	6,000
Printing	10	4,000
Reserve	10	4,000

Depending on the scope of your project, you may create other budget categories, such as advertising or new telephone lines for transmission of data to other computers.

Make frequent checks of your actual expenses against your budget so that you can discover and correct overruns before they jeopardize the project or even your business. Recently, a large northeast multimillion dollar furniture store chain closed 70 stores and eventually filed for bankruptcy. The president of the company blamed cost overruns in a new corporate computer system for the company's woes. The lesson to be learned is simple: no company, big or small, can afford to ignore the budget.

Chapter Summary

Much of this chapter recounts real-life situations. You learned how to perform a needs analysis to determine where your business can benefit from better information management. Next, you reviewed a sample five-year plan that lays out all the subprojects and priorities. Finally, you learned about budget allocations and the importance of constantly reviewing your expenditures. The remainder of this book assumes that, after careful consideration, you have decided that a computer represents the best opportunity for your business. With that decision in mind, follow Mark and Marian as they continue the decision-making process.

CHAPTER 3

Identifying Your Software Needs

Now that you have completed your needs analysis and budget, it's time to select the software and hardware you need. Start with the software. You will know why after reading the following tale.

Imagine that you own a company which designs packaging for new products. It is Sunday morning, and you are scanning the business section of your local newspaper, and you come across a large advertisement placed by a computer store in the area. The store is running a limited-time sale on IBM personal computers. Aware that you are about to computerize the graphic design portion of your business, you drive to the store and start talking with a sales representative.

The sales representative assures you that drawing programs are available for IBM PCs, so you decide to purchase a computer and printer for each of the four graphic artists on your staff. You also buy drawing software for each PC.

Corporate computing center directors live by an age-old saying: nobody ever got fired for buying IBM. That may be true when it comes to large mainframe computers, but you are about to find out that although you may not be fired, you made a serious mistake in buying IBM equipment in this instance.

As it turns out, the Apple Macintosh II would have offered you much more for your graphic arts environment. Why? Because you can purchase software for the Macintosh II that is designed to do sophisticated drawing, support the Pantone Color Matching system, and generate color separations on industrial phototypesetting equipment. No software package for the IBM PC provides the degree of minute control that people in this industry demand.

The moral of the story is clear.

> Find the proper software solution before considering hardware.

Finding the proper software is perhaps the most critical element in developing an overall business solution. The manufacturer of the hardware should become nearly irrelevant in your decision-making process.

Developing a Shopping List of Requirements

Imagine a trip to your local supermarket. To shop efficiently, before you go to the store you need to look through your refrigerator, cabinets, and drawers to identify what you need to buy. Write these items down on a sheet of paper, and you have a shopping list. Organizing the list into logical groups makes your shopping even more efficient, listing the meat items in one group and all the dairy items in another group.

Buying software is no different. With hundreds of accounting packages from which to choose, a requirements list is crucial. You can develop this list yourself or enlist the aid of your consultant and, especially, your accountant.

Figure 3.1 shows the requirements list developed by Mark and Marian for the accounts receivable function of their custom order processing system.

Does the accounts receivable system maintain the following customer data?

- Customer name
- Customer number
- Customer address
- Customer city
- Customer state/province
- Customer ZIP
- Customer contact name
- Customer telephone number
- Customer "bill-to" address
- Customer "ship-to" address
- Comment area for notes
- Terms
- Ship via
- Salesperson code
- Last sale date
- Last sale detail information
- Tax exempt number
- Year-to-date sales
- Year-to-date finance charges
- Calculations of finance charges
- Credit limit
- Credit available
- Highest balance due in last 12 months
- Discount percentage
- Override discount
- Date account opened and by whom
- Apply cash to specific orders

Can the accounts receivable system do all the following tasks?

- Write-off of small differences (user definable) between amounts due and received
- Allocate write-offs to general ledger account
- Run-to-run controls for balancing
- Transaction logging for audit trail
- Reinstate invoices if a customer check bounces
- Generate standard reports
- Daily invoices sorted by Customer, Vendor, Invoice number, Batch
- Daily receipts sorted by Customer, Invoice number, Batch
- Trial balance reports with aging: Current, 30, 60, 90+ days
- Mailing labels
- Rolodex cards
- Dunning letters   Customer statements
- Report generator for customized reports

Does the multiuser (local area network) version have these capabilities?

- Password entry to system
- Multiple levels of security (clerks should not be allowed to enter payments received)

***Fig. 3.1.** Requirements for Mark and Marian's accounts payable module.*

With this requirements list in hand, you are ready to go shopping.

Mark and Marian's list of requirements specifies in detail the minimum requirements their software must meet. When they go shopping, they will do their best to select programs that meet these requirements. The reason? If Mark and Marian are going to solve the problems in their business, the software they choose *must* be capable of handling the specific information they employ every day.

> Once you have formulated your list of requirements, don't settle for software that fails to perform functions that your analysis identifies as crucial to improved profitability.

If you choose a program that fails to handle information crucial to your business, you may conclude that you would have been better off sticking with your present methods!

Admittedly, situations may occur in which you decide to compromise. For example, Mark and Marian found an order-entry package that met most of their needs, but after reading through the documentation and chatting with the firm's technical support people, they discovered that the program could not print a list of all items ordered for each vendor. With this package they would have to print a weekly report of all customer orders placed and pick out by hand the items for each vendor.

When you run into a limitation of this sort, and you will, you must decide whether you can live with it. A limitation you can live with is one that will not seriously degrade the system's potential to increase your firm's profitability. If you honestly feel that the limitation *would* harm your firm's profitability, keep looking.

Remember an important caveat, however. Although it is sound business practice to identify your needs and seek software solutions, you should remain open to a different way of thinking. As you become more aware of the wealth of application software available, you will surely identify programs that might make it possible for you to do business in a new way. To acquaint you with the range of software possibilities currently available, the following chapter contains an extensive survey of software types in today's application software market.

Selecting Software

Shopping for software can be a difficult and time-consuming task. You should plan to spend a sufficient amount of time for proper selection. General purpose software—word processing, for example—is straightforward. Of the several hundred word processing programs currently available, the top five hold about 80 percent of the market. Any one of them is a good choice for memo or correspondence writing. But if you have special requirements, such as foreign language support, the choices require more research.

Software Categories

Software is grouped according to the function it performs.

- *Application Software.* Application software, by far the largest category, includes all the programs that enable the computer to perform business-related tasks. Accounting, inventory control, word processing, spreadsheet, and desktop publishing are but a few of the hundreds of types of application programs available.

- *Systems Software.* Systems software, commonly called the operating system, are specialized programs that enable the computer to perform its basic functions. Without systems software, your computer may not know how to display characters on the screen, send information to the printer, or understand characters that you type on the keyboard. IBM-compatible computers use the Disk Operating System (DOS) or the newer Operating System/2 (OS/2) software to perform these functions. Apple computers use a totally different operating system that is incompatible with IBM equipment and software. Operating systems also vary in ease of use, so you might bear in mind that "user-friendly" operating systems may make it easier for employees to cope with the new computer system. If you connect your computers together in a local area network, you need network operating system software.

- *Utility Software.* Think of utility software as a set of tools that you use to manage your use of the computer. You can purchase utility programs to recover deleted files, reorganize the information on your hard disk, or speed up the movement of the cursor on your screen. Other utility programs provide an instant pop-up calculator, phone directory, and notepad. Many utility programs are designed for terminate-and-stay-resident (TSR) operation. That is, once loaded into the computer's random-access memory (RAM), they are always available and can pop up over any other application software you are running.

Deciding Which Software You Need

Every computer needs operating system software. Although you may pay for the operating system as a separate item, it certainly is not optional. Without operating system software your computer will not even be able to start your accounting software.

Utility software, although optional, is usually inexpensive and can save much time and frustration. A utility program that recovers deleted files can save hours or days of work that would otherwise be spent re-creating the lost data. Other utility software helps you copy data from your hard disk to disks or tape (called *backing up*) or compress data files so that they occupy less disk space.

Application software is the real reason you are purchasing computers, because you want software to help you run your business more efficiently and effectively. The application software you choose depends on the business you operate. An attorney wants application software to prepare legal documents, perform time-tracking and billing, and schedule clients and other appointments. A dairy farmer needs dairy farm and cattle management software. When you read "Find the proper software solution before considering hardware," application software is the software that is meant. The system software is determined by the hardware environment you choose.

Because no business is single-faceted, you need different kinds of application software for different tasks. An office supply retail store may need point-of-sale, sales analysis, inventory control, purchase order management, invoicing, accounts payable, accounts receivable, general ledger, and payroll software, in addition to word processing for correspondence and desktop publishing for designing advertisements.

Finding Software

Software for specialized types of business, called vertical market software because it does not appeal to a broad horizontal range of users, also requires a great deal of research. Not only is much research required, but you should be prepared to play detective to ferret out all the products that serve your industry. It is possible that the perfect software solution for your business may be hiding in the proverbial haystack.

How To Talk to a Computer Salesperson about Software

Buying software, like buying a car, can be a daunting experience. Your inexperience will be obvious immediately, and the salesperson may try to take advantage of it. In addition, retail stores carry only the top-selling software programs. Ask for a program that is not popular, and you will find that program difficult or impossible to find. You could have your consultant obtain the software for you, but what do you do if you choose to deal with the salesperson yourself?

> Retail stores carry only top-selling programs. The ideal program for your business may be available only from a little-known specialty supplier.

First, never buy software during your visit to the store. You are there only to gather experience and to collect as much product literature as possible. Avoid being steered to a product that's unfamiliar to you.

Second, bring at least two copies of your software requirements. Give a copy to the salesperson and explain that you are looking for a package that meets these requirements. When the salesperson asks you "IBM or Macintosh?", say that you will consider a package that runs on either platform. Because you have no hardware at all, this response gives you the best chance you will have to find the perfect match for your business.

If the sales representative is too quick in proposing a particular package, ask why that package is being recommended. Which of your requirements does it meet? What other programs of the same type does the store carry? What other programs of the same type can be specially ordered?

Bear in mind as you shop that each store carries a limited stock, and salespeople naturally have an interest in steering you toward the items they are currently selling. In addition, you should realize that some companies offer salespeople a variety of kickbacks and perquisites; if you receive a particularly strong pitch in favor of SuperDuperCalc, it may be that you're the last remaining sale needed to send the salesperson to Club Med. Don't get snookered!

Computer salespeople have reasons for recommending specific programs or computers, and these reasons may have little to do with meeting your needs.

Ask for detailed literature for the programs recommended to you. If literature is not available, ask for the full address and telephone number of the software manufacturer and call the manufacturer from your office. Don't depend on the salesperson to do this for you. Ask for all available literature and a location near you where the product can be viewed.

In addition to promotional literature, many software programs offer free, or nearly free, demonstration disks. Collect all you can find and experiment with them on a friend's computer. Also, most full-service computer stores have sample copies of actual software products (not demos) installed on their floor model machines. Ask for a comprehensive run-through and be sure to examine the documentation. You learn three things: how to work with the computer, how to interact with the software (Are you comfortable with its "look and feel?"), and the extent of the salesperson's expertise.

Finally, thank the salesperson for his or her assistance and explain that you have additional research to undertake before making a final decision.

Repeat the process at other computer stores. Each may suggest a different software solution, and you may find a salesperson willing to spend time to answer your questions. Plan on paying more at a store offering better service and skilled help.

How To Comparison Shop

Price is not the key when shopping for software. You can view this fact in two ways. First, there are dozens of $99 packages that outperform their more expensive counterparts. Second, you may find the same package sold at wildly varying prices from different sources. So how do you shop for software?

Whether a package costs $25, $99, or $495 should take a back seat to finding the package that is the best fit for your business. That's the reason you established a list of requirements. If the $495 package contains five times as many features as the $99 package, that is one thing. But if the only package that meets your requirements is the $99 package, then give serious thought to going with the less expensive solution.

As to different pricing for the same product, it comes down to the issue of support and expertise. If you buy a software package through a mail-order company, you should expect little or nothing in terms of post-sale technical support. If you buy that same package from a storefront retailer who charges the full list price, you should expect—and demand—advice before the sale and a certain amount of support after the sale. If the retailer offers neither, then take your business elsewhere. After all, the price/performance theory applies here too. Get the most for your money!

Buying Software for Growth

One of the reasons you may be investing in a computer system is to help your business grow. If so, make sure that the application software you buy provides room for that growth.

Consider the experience of the young couple who started a mail-order business. They created a series of rubber stamps with a caricature of a young boy or girl. The stamp was personalized with the name of the boy or girl. To keep track of their customers, the husband and wife purchased an inexpensive order processing, fulfillment, and invoicing system with a capacity of 999 customers. After all, they thought, this venture was merely a hobby that would never attract more than a few hundred customers at best.

It took two months to sell their first hundred rubber stamps. But business exploded after they placed a small advertisement in one of the "women's" magazines found at supermarket check-out lanes. Orders poured in by the thousands. They had to purchase new software and reenter manually all previously accumulated data because the data files of the two software systems were not compatible.

Today, this couple devotes full time to their flourishing mail-order business, which now carries hundreds of items and boasts tens of thousands of customers. The second software system they purchased can easily handle a business of this size and supports a local area network so that several computer operators can enter orders simultaneously.

> Purchase software that provides room for growth in your business.

Public Domain and Shareware Software

When you purchase a software package designed for retail sale, you do not actually own the software. You are only granted a license to use the software; the manufacturer retains title to and ownership of the program. The manufacturer is also protected by copyright laws that prohibit you from making unauthorized copies, even if the software is not copy protected. The Software Publishers Association, an industry trade group based in Washington, D.C., puts it very succinctly: "The unauthorized copying of software is a crime."

Two other licensing arrangements do exist: public domain and shareware.

Public domain software (sometimes called freeware) is free, although you may be required to pay a small disk duplication and handling charge. Sometimes the author asks for a donation, and, although you are not obligated to do so, your donation enables the author to develop new programs. The author, by placing the program in the public domain, relinquishes all rights to the program. You can freely make copies of public domain software. You can obtain public domain software through catalogs and from many computer bulletin boards by downloading via modem.

Shareware is not free; if you use the software, you are expected to register your copy and pay a registration fee to the author. These fees are how the author makes his or her living. You are free to make copies of the software for distribution to others with the expectation that these other users will register their copies. Additional copies you make for computers you own should also be registered.

Public domain and shareware programs abound, and many of them are reliable enough for business use. For example, ProComm, a data communications program for IBM-compatible computers, has been available for years and is almost standard equipment for anyone who owns a modem. (PROCOM PLUS, the newest version of ProComm, is licensed software.)

Do You Really Need Custom Software?

Suppose that you find a $500 software package that meets 95 percent of your needs. If this is the only package under consideration after your research, then it's time to think about custom programming. Imagine that a custom-designed package that provides all the features you demand costs $10,000. Shocked? Don't be. Custom software is that expensive. It cannot be sold to hundreds of thousands of users to keep down the price per copy. It's a one-of-a-kind product built for you and only you. Now it's time for the big question. Are you willing to pay an extra $9,500 to get the missing 5 percent in features? That, unfortunately, is a question this book cannot answer. The decision rests squarely on your shoulders. The best your consultant can do is to identify all the alternatives and make a recommendation. You must make the final decision.

By the way, Mark and Marian opted for the custom solution even though it cost thousands of dollars more. First, by printing the orders in vendor order they saved about 8 hours of manual labor per week. Figuring their fully loaded salaries at $90 per hour, that alone results in a savings of $720 per week, or $37,440 per year. You can see how the custom program, which cost $10,000, will pay for itself three times over in the first year alone.

There is another benefit, too. If five customers order the same item, Mark and Marian's report of orders by vendor will aggregate those five orders into a single line item. Rather than placing five separate orders each for a single unit they can now place just one order for five units and qualify for volume discounts. It's clear from these examples that the best choice for Mark and Marian is an investment in custom software.

Sources of Custom Software

If you are considering custom software, you need to find a programmer. Because programmers are like consultants, many of the same rules apply.

> Make sure that your programmer understands your business.

The programmer should provide references and sample copies of software that you can run on a computer for evaluation purposes. Talk to former and current clients as well as to your competitors. Read trade magazines and attend industry trade shows.

Custom Software Issues

As you have already learned, custom software usually is very expensive. In addition, you must consider the issues of cost overruns, support, and documentation.

Cost Overruns

Imagine that you select a programmer to develop custom software to automate the management of your business. After a lengthy analysis, the programmer presents you with a written document called a *functional specification*, or a *system specification*. The specification contains detailed descriptions of what tasks the system should perform and how those tasks are to be performed. Also, the specification includes layouts of all the screens the system displays and all printed reports. You review the specification, the programmer makes modifications as required, and you sign off on the document, indicating your approval. You and the programmer have agreed on a price of $10,000 and delivery on August 1.

Around July 15 the programmer comes to you and says, "The project is taking longer than I thought. It won't be finished until August 31 and it will cost another $5,000."

What do you do? Because the programmer provided the initial delivery date, you may think it is proper for him or her to absorb the entire overrun cost. The programmer, naturally, would never agree to such a contractual provision. It is reasonable, therefore, to reach some middle ground.

The best way to handle this too-common occurrence is to include provisions in your legal contract with the programmer. It is customary to pay up to an additional 25 percent over the original agreed-to price for any cost overruns. For that $10,000 contract, you should agree to pay up to an additional $2,500. Beyond that, the programmer should pick up the tab. After all, the programmer is a professional and should be able to provide estimates that are "in the ballpark."

Support

Did you ever hear the expression "a six-month contract with a programmer is a contract for life"? This sounds much worse than it really is, but it does make a crucial point. No one will ever know your custom programs as well as their creator. And when modification or enhancements are required, whom do you call first? Why, the original programmer, of course.

In addition, it's likely that the programmer (or someone closely associated with the programmer) will provide training and telephone support to you and your employees. None of these services is free. This is crunch time—when the reasons for your research in finding a programmer become clear.

Custom Software Documentation

Another critical element of custom software development is documentation. You need instructional documentation for the employees who will use the system. This documentation should answer all the questions that arise during normal operation, including daily start-up and shutdown, controls (so that you know that Monday's ending figures are the same as Tuesday's starting figures), system operation, and file backup and restoration.

In addition, you should be provided with complete technical documentation that describes the inner workings of the software. Charts showing the structure of all data files should be included. Also, look for instructions for installing the program, adding or deleting users, and handling any system errors (like damage to a data file) that might occur.

If your system contains levels of security (to keep clerks from printing checks, for example), make sure that restricted documentation is provided in a separate booklet so that you can store it in a safe place without impeding access to other needed documentation.

You and your staff should read all the documentation that your programmer provides. Make sure that any missing items are added, check for accuracy and completeness, and approve it only when you are satisfied that the documentation provides everything that is needed to operate your system without further assistance from the programmer.

Source Code

Not too long ago, a cartoon appeared that depicted a grieving young wife and her small daughter standing in a rainstorm clutching an umbrella. Dressed in black, both were staring down at a freshly filled grave. A gentleman standing close by says, "I'm sorry to trouble you at a time like this, but did he ever mention anything about source code?"

A bit maudlin perhaps, but it certainly drives home the point. Source code, also called program listings, is what the programmer types when writing computer programs. These listings, while they may look unintelligible to nonprogrammers, are instructions to perform all the tasks that make up your custom software system. Your programmer will always maintain your program's source code listings in both printed form for archival purposes and on disk so that the program can be modified as necessary. Without access to disk-based source codes, your programs cannot be modified.

> You must have access to the program listings (source code) for any custom system, no matter how small.

Though the tragedy depicted in the cartoon may be an overstatement, you may find that your programmer has moved away, taken a full-time programming job, or retired from the business. To protect yourself and your sizable investment, you must include in your contract provisions to get copies of all the actual program listings either as hard-copy printouts, on disks, or, ideally, both.

Many programmers balk at the idea of giving away what amounts to their work. If this is the case, negotiate to have the program listings placed in escrow with an attorney. If the programmer does not agree to this solution, find a different programmer.

Chapter Summary

In this chapter, you learned that to make an intelligent hardware choice, you start by ignoring hardware! Instead, formulate a list of requirements that your computer system must meet to address your business needs, and then identify the *application software* that meets these needs. In your search for application software, avoid compromising on your list of minimum requirements. At the same time, however, remain open to software that has business implications you may not have grasped previously.

You also learned to keep in mind the rule *caveat emptor* (let the buyer beware) as you talk to computer salespeople about software. Computer stores carry only best-selling programs. You must undertake research to find sources of vertical-market software that may be ideal for your purposes. Don't overlook public domain and shareware programs. If you cannot find a prepackaged application program that meets your needs, you may be forced to hire a programmer to create custom software. But be forewarned that programmers sometimes fail to understand a firm's business, exceed their budgets, and miss deadlines. You can reduce software development costs by hiring a programmer to customize a programmable application package, such as dBASE IV or 1-2-3, rather than permitting the programmer to write the program from scratch.

CHAPTER 4

Finding Business Solutions in Application Software

Now that you have identified your software needs, it's time to start shopping for software. Your search should not concentrate single-mindedly on meeting the needs you have identified. As you grow more familiar with computers and learn what they can do for your business, you almost certainly will see new ways you can apply computers to solve your business's problems. This chapter surveys the following types of application software packages that are available in today's personal computer marketplace:

- ❏ Word processors
- ❏ Spreadsheets
- ❏ Databases
- ❏ Telecommunications

- ❏ Integrated packages
- ❏ Accounting
- ❏ Desktop publishing
- ❏ Project management
- ❏ Statistical analysis
- ❏ Time billing

Word Processing Programs

By far the most widely used software in personal computing, word processing programs greatly reduce the tedium involved in writing, editing, and printing all forms of written work, ranging from simple letters to book-length technical manuscripts. And you can choose from dozens of programs, ranging from simple, "easy to use" programs to high-end, full-featured powerhouses, such as WordPerfect or Microsoft Word.

For small-business applications, choose a high-end program. These full-featured programs are virtual cornucopias of business solutions. High-end programs are harder to learn than their entry-level counterparts, but the time you spend learning them is amply compensated. High-end features such as outlining, glossaries, mail merging, and macros may be unfamiliar to you, but as you will learn in this section, they are useful business tools.

> For small-business application, choose a full-featured word processing program. Such programs are loaded with tools you can use to solve business problems.

Outlining

Also available as stand-alone programs, outlining features in word processing programs help you plan and organize your work. In outlining mode, you type headings and subheadings, and special commands give you the tools you need to reorganize and restructure the outline quickly. Outlining software is useful for organizing your thoughts for presentations or proposals.

When outlining features are fully integrated with word processing functions, as they are in both the Macintosh and IBM versions of Microsoft Word, these features gain additional value. With Word, you can look at your document in two ways—as an outline (you see only the headings and subheadings) or as an ordinary document. What's more, in the outline mode you can restructure large text domains simply by rearranging the headings or subheadings.

If your business routinely prepares lengthy and complex technical proposals, reports, or documentation, you are well advised to consider a word processing program that includes a well-integrated outlining feature.

Glossaries

In the word processing world, glossaries are not lists of words with their definition. Rather, they are passages of standardized text (called boilerplate) that are stored on disk. The glossary feature gives you a way of adding these passages to a document simply by pressing a key or choosing the passage's name from a menu.

Glossaries have many uses in business writing—especially in business correspondence. Every time you send out a first-class letter in response to an inquiry letter, you establish a contract that is legally enforceable in a court of law. For this reason, it is absolutely vital from a legal standpoint that you word your responses carefully. Terms of sale, warranties, return policies, and other responses should be scrutinized by a lawyer and the wording fixed, if necessary. By storing such passages in glossaries, you guarantee that you—and your employees—will never send out a letter with a carelessly worded passage.

Yet another very good reason for developing a series of glossaries for business correspondence exists. Business communication experts agree that a business letter sends an important message about your business. In every business letter, you should emphasize the positive and focus on the customer's needs. By developing standardized response passages about such matters as late deliveries or packaging errors, you ensure that you always present your company in its best light. At the same time, however, each letter should be personalized and show interest in the customer. You can use glossaries and the word processing program's text-entry features to achieve both goals.

To illustrate how glossaries can be used in a way that ensures standardized wording but shows a personalized touch, a store that sells second-hand computers by mail order has developed a series of glossaries for answering routine inquiry letters. One glossary, called WARRANTY, explains the firm's generous 6-month warranty and tells how a customer can obtain repairs. A second, called SHIPPING, explains the customer's options for arranging shipping. A third, called RETURNS, explains the firm's 30-day return policy. To answer a letter that asks for information on shipping and return policies, the business's owner types the correspondent's name and address, opens with a personal salutation, and adds the SHIPPING and RETURNS glossaries. Finally, she adds a personalized closing, prints the letter, and signs it.

Tables and Lists

Not all word processing programs provide special features for creating tables and lists. High-end packages like WordPerfect and Microsoft Word, however, may include special features that enable you to create a list in two-column format and sort it alphabetically. These features may prove valuable to you if you frequently create and print lists that you distribute to your customers. A video store, for example, keeps a list of all currently stocked video titles in a WordPerfect document, which can be easily edited and sorted as tapes are added to or removed from the list.

A surprising number of businesses give people computer-generated lists printed sloppily on a dot-matrix printer. Remember the last one you received from a video rental shop? Although a dot-matrix printout suggests that the information is up-to-date, you should remember that every time you provide information to your customers you have an opportunity to send a message about your business. For this reason alone, the lists you give them should be attractively designed and printed on a laser printer.

Business Forms

Every business uses forms—invoices, order forms, employee application forms, and more. Although some businesses are more form-happy than others, almost every business finds it necessary to have custom-designed forms typeset and printed. This expense can be avoided if you have a word processing program, like Microsoft Word, which includes form design features, such as the capability to enclose text in boxes. Once you have printed the form, you can have it duplicated cheaply by using an offset printing process. By designing and typesetting the form yourself, you can save hundreds of dollars in form-design, typesetting, and paste-up costs.

The form-design features included in word processing programs are usually quite basic, however, so if you need forms that your customers will use, you are well advised to purchase a stand-alone business form program, such as Smartform Designer (Claris Software), available for Macintosh computers. These programs provide additional tools that, in combination with a laser printer, enable you to design and print many forms, which you can have duplicated by a commercial print shop.

Before dropping everything to design forms for your business, remember that you can save on filing expenses if you enter data (such as customer orders) into forms displayed on computer screens. Moreover, the information you enter on computer-displayed forms can be directly and automatically transferred to a computer version of a general accounting ledger.

Newsletters

If you create newsletters to stay in touch with your customers, you pay big bucks for professional layout and typesetting fees. You can avoid these costs by preparing the newsletter yourself. To do so, you have two options. You can purchase a word processing program with multiple-column and page layout capabilities, such as Microsoft Word or WordPerfect, or you can purchase a program specifically designed for sophisticated page layout applications, such as PageMaker. Which approach is best? Today's high-end word processing programs have narrowed the gulf that once lay between word processing packages and page layout programs, but they haven't closed it. A good page layout program (combined with a laser printer) enables you to produce a very handsome newsletter; a high-end word processing program limits you to producing a merely adequate one.

If you plan to produce newsletters frequently, and especially if you plan to use a page layout program, such as PageMaker, you are well advised to equip your system with a high-resolution, full-page monitor. Such monitors display a visual representation of a full 8 1/2-by-11-inch page, enabling you to visualize the printed page on-screen before printing it. In addition, you should choose a laser printer that recognizes the PostScript printer language. So-called PostScript printers are considerably more expensive than laser printers that do not respond to PostScript, but they produce superior results. With PostScript, graphic images are considerably sharper, and you can include many special effects, including shading and rotated images.

Many people in the desktop publishing industry say that the Macintosh environment is the only serious choice for anyone contemplating the production of a business newsletter. Remember, however, that PageMaker, full-page displays, and PostScript-compatible laser printers are available for IBM Personal Computers and compatibles, as well. You should take other software choices into consideration before letting this one determine your choice of a hardware platform.

Mail Merging and Personalized Form Letters

A communications tool routinely used by large firms is the personalized form letter. Like all form letters, the personalized form letter contains text that is sent to many people. Unlike a true form letter, however, the personalized form letter is addressed to a specific person and looks as if it were sent only to that person—if, that is, the job is done correctly. You have probably received many personalized form letters in which your name is printed slightly off register or in a slightly different color of ink, exposing the ploy.

High-end word processing programs, such as WordPerfect and Microsoft Word, offer mail merging features that are capable of producing high-quality personalized form letters. To create a form-letter application, you create a mailing list and store it in a format the program can read. (You can use a file management or database management program for this purpose.) Then you create the text of the letter. To this letter you add special commands that tell the program how to retrieve the personalized data you want each letter to contain, such as name, address, city, state, ZIP code, and salutation. Finally, the program automatically prints numerous copies of the same letter, each one customized with an individual's name and address. The term *mail merging* sums up what this feature does: the program takes names and addresses from a mailing list and merges them with the text of a form letter.

A more advanced form-letter application takes advantage of conditional mail merging, in which a special passage of text is printed only if information stored with the person's name meets conditions you specify. Suppose that you create a mailing list containing information about whether the person's account is overdue. In the file that contains the text of the letter, you include commands that tell the program to include a request for payment if the account is overdue.

Laser printers are all the rage these days, but anyone planning mail merging applications should include a daisywheel letter-quality printer in his or her purchase plans. The reason? These printers produce letters that look as if they were personally and very professionally typed using a fine office typewriter. The result is a letter that conveys a personal touch as well as immediacy.

Macros

A *macro* is a set of program commands stored in a file the program can read. The commands are intended to be executed sequentially. To execute the commands, you press a key that you have assigned for that purpose. In other words, a macro gives you a way of carrying out several program commands by pressing just one key.

You can use macros to accomplish many tasks, such as giving several formatting commands at once (centering and boldfacing a heading, for example). The best word processing programs, such as Microsoft Word, however, come with macro programming languages that enable you to create custom word processing applications. With Microsoft Word, for instance, you can create a custom user interface that automatically presents the user with a menu of document templates. (A *template* is a skeletal version of a document to which you add specific text.) Among such templates, you might want to include standard versions of business letters, such as requests for payment or responses to employment applications, which need only the addition of the correspondent's name and address to be completed.

Hardware for Word Processing

If you or your employees need to use word processing software for more than a few minutes each day, you are well advised to equip your system with a high-resolution monitor. Resolution refers to the number of dots a monitor can display on-screen. The more dots displayed, the clearer the image—and the less strain on the eyes. Monochrome monitors are generally preferable to color monitors, even if the color monitor has a reasonably high level of resolution. Increasing numbers of word processing systems are equipped with *paper white* monitors, which (like the standard Macintosh display) displays black text on a paper-white background. If you intend to compose newsletters, brochures, or other desktop-published documents, choose a full-page display.

Spreadsheet Programs

Spreadsheet programs got their start in the mid-1970s at Harvard Business School, where Dan Bricklin, an MBA student, found himself wearing out a calculator. His homework assignments forced him to create complex numerical models of business performance—and then, once he had calculated the bottom line, he had to do the calculations all over again after varying one or more of the initial assumptions, such as the rate of interest. Dan envisioned an electronic spreadsheet, an electronic version of an accountant's pad, that would recalculate the bottom line automatically after making changes anywhere on the spreadsheet. The result was VisiCalc, the first electronic spreadsheet program.

VisiCalc was a huge success, but it was soon displaced by 1-2-3, a program for IBM personal computers that seamlessly integrates data management and business graphics functions into the spreadsheet program. In the Macintosh world, the dominant spreadsheet package is Microsoft Excel, which (like

1-2-3) combines a spreadsheet with analytical graphics capabilities.

What Are Spreadsheet Programs For?

On-screen, an electronic spreadsheet resembles an accountant's pad, with its matrix of rows and columns. (You can widen or narrow the columns as you please.) Each intersection of a row and column is a cell, and it is uniquely identified by its row and column number (such as A9 or C34). You can make three kinds of entries in an electronic spreadsheet: text (called labels or headings), numbers, and formulas. The formulas tell the spreadsheet what computations to perform on the numbers you enter. For instance, to add the values in cells A9 and A10, you place the formula *A9 + A10* in cell A11. You can also use built-in functions that sum up ranges of cells, such as an entire column of numbers.

> Don't try to create a general ledger or other accounting applications with an electronic spreadsheet program.

Because electronic spreadsheet programs provide an electronic version of an accountant's pad, many people wrongly assume that spreadsheets are best applied to accounting applications, such as creating a general ledger or storing information about accounts receivable. Although it is possible to create accounting applications with electronic spreadsheets, it is not desirable to do so, because the very nature of electronic spreadsheet programs—the fact that you can so easily *change* the numbers to see how the change affects the bottom line—makes it virtually impossible to maintain a secure audit trail. If you're thinking about doing your own accounting with a personal computer, don't do it with an electronic spreadsheet. (For more information on accounting software, see "Accounting Packages," elsewhere in this chapter.)

What are spreadsheet programs for? They're superb tools for *sensitivity testing*, a form of analysis that begins with the question, "What if?" For example, suppose that you are thinking about purchasing the building in which your retail store is situated. The building has two additional stores, which you could rent. Will the rents pay the mortgage each month if you are able to obtain a loan at 9.75 percent interest? At 10.5 percent? What if you are able to charge $15 per square foot in rent instead of the current $12.50 rate? What if the rate falls to $9.75—will you be able to absorb the loss until rental rates rise again? All these questions are excellent candidates for spreadsheet applications.

When you create a spreadsheet application for sensitivity testing, you use headings, numbers, and formulas to construct a *model* of your business, or some aspect of it. A model is a representation of reality that you can manipulate to see what happens. After you have constructed a model, you can ask many "what-if" questions, such as, How many more employees will I need if sales increase 15 percent? How many more parts must I order from my suppliers if the expected 20 percent increase in orders occurs in the next quarter? and What rent increases can I tolerate before thinking seriously of moving my business? Spreadsheet software provides precisely the tools the owners of small businesses need to think through vexing "what if" questions such as these. That's why spreadsheet programs are among the best-selling of all personal computer application programs.

Spreadsheet Templates

If you're developing a model with general application, such as a loan amortization schedule, there's no need to reinvent the wheel. From user's groups and sources of public domain software you can obtain disks with ready-to-use models for a variety of financial and business spreadsheets.

Analytical Graphics and Presentation Graphics

Today's popular electronic spreadsheet programs are seamlessly integrated with business graphics modules, which generate bar, pie, column, and line charts from the data you enter in spreadsheets. These graphics are called *analytical graphics* because they create a visual representation of the analysis you created numerically. You can use analytical graphics to create a picture of your business at any given point in time. For instance, you can create a pie graph that displays the sales in each department per quarter. Because analytical graphics display numerical data in a form that is much easier to grasp and interpret, using graphics is one of the best ways to see emerging patterns and trends.

The analytical graphics produced by an electronic spreadsheet program usually are distinguished from *presentation graphics*, which are designed for public presentation. Spreadsheet-generated charts and graphs are very useful for analyzing your business, but they have a utilitarian look that makes them unsuitable for public distribution. If you are planning to use charts and graphs in a company publication or in an oral presentation, you need to enhance the graphics by using a presentation graphics package. Increasingly, electronic spreadsheet programs are sold with presentation graphics packages included. Lotus, for instance, is including its Allways presentation graphics package in its popular 1-2-3 program.

To display analytical and presentation graphics on the screen of an IBM-format personal computer, you must purchase a system that has graphics capabilities. For monochrome systems, purchase a video display card that is compatible with the Hercules Graphics Card. For color systems, choose a VGA (video graphics array) display adapter. All Macintosh systems display graphics. For more information on IBM-format video displays and display adapters, see Chapter 5.

Three-Dimensional Spreadsheets

The latest innovation in electronic spreadsheet software is the *three-dimensional* spreadsheet program, which displays not only the usual two dimensions of rows and columns but also a third, depth. With these programs, you can work with two, three, or more spreadsheets in a stack, with the additional spreadsheets positioned "behind" the one that's visible on-screen. What's more, a cell in one spreadsheet can include a formula that automatically posts the value found in another spreadsheet's cell. Using three-dimensional spreadsheet software, then, you can create a model that includes separate spreadsheets for each of ten separate areas of your business, and an eleventh, "master" spreadsheet that contains the bottom lines of each of the ten other spreadsheets. Spreadsheet programs that lack three-dimensional features also provide ways to include data from other spreadsheets, but they are less convenient.

Do you need a three-dimensional spreadsheet? The principles of good spreadsheet design call not for gigantic, complex spreadsheets, but rather very simple ones, which are easy to understand—and less susceptible to mistakes. For this reason, it makes good sense to break a problem down into a series of simple spreadsheets rather than one large, confusing one. On these grounds alone, three-dimensional spreadsheets are highly recommended. If your business is easily segmented into separate operations, such as a business with two separate departments, the three-dimensional structure facilitates the construction of a model that recognizes these segments and enables you to manipulate them independently.

Hardware for Spreadsheet Programs

If you're planning to purchase a three-dimensional spreadsheet program, you must purchase a personal computer that is powerful enough to handle it. In the world of IBM-compatible computers, the 8088, 8086, and the slower 80286 microprocessors are out; you need a computer based on the 80386 or 80486 microprocessors. For more information on microprocessors, see Chapter 5.

Electronic Spreadsheet Perils

A data processing manager in a major firm a few years ago embarked on a unique project: checking the spreadsheets currently used by the firm's major managers to see whether they contained any errors. He found, to his amazement, that not one of these spreadsheets was free of mistakes. Some of the mistakes were small and inconsequential, but others affected the bottom line by as much as an order of magnitude!

Why were so many errors made? The simple truth is that electronic spreadsheets are prone to error. For one thing, the formulas you type in a cell, don't appear in the cell; they disappear, and the program returns the value the formula calculates. With all the formulas hidden away, it's easy to forget about them. What if one of the formulas is wrong? You could use the spreadsheet for years without realizing your error. People do it every day!

Another reason spreadsheets are prone to error is a command that instructs the spreadsheet program to stop recalculating after each data entry. When a spreadsheet becomes large, it can take several seconds to recalculate, so many people turn off automatic recalculation to speed data entry. If they forget to turn recalculation back on after entering the data, however, or if they forget to give the manual recalculation command, the bottom line of the spreadsheet may display an incorrect value.

> Don't ever assume that a spreadsheet is producing a correct answer until you have thoroughly checked all the formulas and made sure that you have recalculated the spreadsheet after the last data entry.

Database Management Programs

A database management program provides tools for creating, sorting, retrieving, and printing data you store on forms. These forms, called *data records*, contain one or more *data fields*, each of which contains some unique numerical, alphabetical, logical, or alphanumeric information. A file containing data records is called a *database*.

A database is analogous to a library's card catalog. Each form (that is, each data record) contains information in distinct data fields (author, title, date of publication, call number, and so on). But card catalogs are notoriously difficult to maintain and use; it's enough of a job to keep a card catalog sorted by author. What would it take to resort 25,000 cards by date of publication? Forget it. The advantage of a computerized data management system is that huge numbers of data records can be re-sorted and shuffled virtually any way you want, and the whole process takes just seconds. For that reason, libraries all over the country are giving up card catalogs and adopting database management software!

A database management program can do much more than sort the data records. You also can use database programs to formulate *queries*, which are computer-readable questions about the information in a database. If you use a database management program to track your inventory, for instance, you can ask the computer, in effect, "For which items is the stock down to 2 or fewer?" After you enter the query, the program selects the data records that meet the criteria you specify, and displays a shortened version of the database, called a *view*. This view lists only the records that conform to the criteria you stated. You can print the view if you want.

Some database management programs enable you to perform numerical queries on data fields that contain numerical data, and this feature can be very valuable. For an inventory database, for instance, you can ask, "What is the current total value of my inventory?"

All database management programs contain *report* functions, which enable you to print the information in the database. These programs vary widely in the capabilities of their report functions, however. With some shareware database programs, you can print each record only in a columnar format. For this reason, that type of program is not very useful for business purposes. You should be able to print the information in your database in a variety of formats, and you should be able to choose just which information you print.

Flat File versus Relational Database Management Programs

Database management programs are of two varieties, called *flat file* and *relational*. For business purposes, you should choose a relational package. The reasons, however, require a little technical explanation.

A flat file program enables you to work with only one database at a time. For many applications, that is not really a severe limitation. Whenever you create a database in which the same information appears more than once, using a flat file program is asking for trouble, for the following reasons.

Suppose that you create an inventory database, and you want to indicate the name and address of the supplier on the data record for each item you carry. Now suppose that you use the same supplier for ten different items. When you create the database, you must type the supplier's name and address ten times. Even that is not a severe problem, especially if you hire a clerical worker to type all the data. Using this procedure, however, multiplies by ten the chance that you or your data entry clerk will make a typing error, and these errors can damage the program's capability to retrieve information. Suppose that nine records contain "Amalgamated Supply, Inc." in the Supplier field, but the tenth field contains "Amalgemated Supply, Inc." A tiny typing mistake, perhaps, but it's enough to cause problems. The next time you query the database by asking, in effect, "Show me all the items I obtain from Amalgamated Supply, Inc.," the program will fail to retrieve the tenth record. Or suppose that you use the program to generate mailing address labels, but one of the records contains the wrong address! Nine of the orders find their way properly to Amalgamated Supply, but one order will be returned to you after a long delay, and you end up with another late order to explain to your customers.

Another problem with flat-file programs surfaces when data changes. Suppose that you get a letter from Amalgamated Supply, Inc., advising you of an address change. With a flat file program, you must access all ten records and manually edit each of them. If your database is very large, updating records can soon become quite a drain on your staff's time.

Relational database management programs solve these problems of data redundancy and updating. Relational databases enable you to work with two or more databases at the same time. You relate the databases to one another (hence "relational") by means of a common field. Suppose that one database contains nothing but a list of suppliers, together with their phone numbers and addresses. Each database also contains a field for the supplier's code name, such as ASI (short for Amalgamated Supply, Inc.). The second database lists the items you carry in your inventory. This database also contains a field for the supplier's code name.

Because both databases have a common data field (supplier code name), you can relate the data in one database to the data contained in the second. To query the database, you ask (in effect), "Use both databases. Now show me all the items I order from ASI, and print ASI's full address." There's no chance that the address will be improperly printed, because you typed it in just one place.

Relational databases do not entirely eliminate the problem of data redundancy, as this example suggests, because you still must type *ASI* in each inventory data record for each item you order from Amalgamated Supply, Inc. Still, it does reduce the possibility that you will make errors—it's much easier to type and check the spelling of ASI than it is to type *Amalgamated Supply, Inc.* Furthermore, some programs permit you to define *masks*, which check your input to make sure that it conforms to a list of permissible entries. If you type *ASU* instead of *ASI*, the program displays an error message. The best programs, at this point, enable the user access to a screen showing the legal entries.

Relational programs greatly facilitate the updating of entries. When Amalgamated Supply, Inc., announces its new address, you change only one record.

> For business applications, choose a relational database management program.

Database Management versus Accounting Program Modules

Like spreadsheet programs, database management programs are general-purpose programs that give you the tools you need to create a huge variety of applications. Some programs offer more flexibility than others, but the good ones enable you to design the data-entry form as you please. At the extreme, you could spend weeks designing a whole series of forms for invoices, custom orders, and the like. Before embarking on a huge enterprise of this sort, however, you should consider whether you want to computerize your business's accounts. If you do, you should purchase point-of-sale, inventory control, and other accounting program modules that are compatible with the accounting software you choose. These programs automatically post all transactions to the general ledger, saving you a great deal of time and trouble. For more information on accounting programs and the modules available with them, see "Accounting Packages," elsewhere in this chapter.

What are database management programs for, then? If you do not plan to computerize your firm's books, and if existing vertical-market programs are not flexible enough to meet your needs, you may find it useful to create databases for inventory control, customer mailing lists, and similar applications. Even if you do plan to computerize your books, you may still find applications for databases that contain nonaccounting information, such as a list of current video tapes stocked by a rental store.

Database Programming Languages

The best database management programs come equipped with a special-purpose programming language. Using this language, you or a consultant can create applications that are customized to your business's needs. A custom application of this type might display a start-up menu of choices and guide the user through each action with instruction screens available on request. For instance, a video rental store can create a menu showing the following options on start-up:

```
Add a new tape to the list

Delete a tape that is no longer carried

Print the list of currently stocked video tapes
```

Database Templates

Just as you can purchase templates or ready-made applications for spreadsheet programs, so too can you purchase templates for database management applications.

Hardware for Database Management

Database management programs run on virtually any personal computer, but if you plan to make heavy use of one, consider equipping your system with a high-resolution color monitor. The better programs enable you to "paint" your data records so that headings and data-entry areas are clearly distinguished by color. The color differences help the eye navigate the screen and ease the task of data entry.

Telecommunications Programs

Equipped with a modem and a telecommunications program, your computer can send and receive information via the telephone system. The modem takes care of the job of modifying your computer's signal so that it can be transmitted via telephone lines. (For more information on the equipment you need for telecommunications, see Chapter 5.) The telecommunications program turns your computer into the equivalent of a large computer system's remote terminal. You type commands, which are transmitted over the telephone lines to a distant computer. The distant computer receives them, processes them, and sends a reply. The replies are displayed on-screen. The effect is much like engaging in a dialog, with the screen showing a record of all transmissions and receptions. With virtually all systems, the whole dialog must be conducted in the standard ASCII character set, which includes upper- and lowercase letters as well as the numbers 0 through 9.

Telecommunications programs perform other tasks in addition to sending and receiving ASCII messages. The best telecommunications packages include features that automate the sometimes tedious task of contacting distant computers, which can involve entering as many as three or four account numbers and passwords. In addition, most programs include telecommunications protocols that enable you to send and receive computer programs, as well as ASCII-based data.

Do you need telecommunications software? Telecommunications applications are often spoken of as if they had tremendous market potential and societal importance, but in fact relatively few personal computer users employ telecommunications applications for serious business purposes. Most of the people who access computer bulletin boards or on-line computer services like CompuServe or The Source are computer hobbyists. Using hobbyist's bulletin boards, moreover, has become dangerous since the advent of computer viruses, which can "infect" your system and possibly wipe out information on your hard disk. Electronic mail services like MCI Mail have been slow to gain acceptance; despite the inconvenience of tracking down someone by telephone, it's still easier—and more personal—to pick up the phone and call the person you need to talk with.

If your business's profitability depends on getting direct access to information that is highly time-sensitive, however, it might make sense to consider subscribing to an on-line information source that makes such information available. The Dow Jones News/Retrieval Service, for instance, offers on-line access to a wide variety of investment and financial data that is constantly updated throughout the day.

Some businesses use telecommunications applications to stay in touch with branch offices or agents in the field. Insurance companies, for instance, find it economical to have agents in branch offices send completed insurance applications to the main office via telecommunications rather than the U.S. mail, which is slow and increasingly unreliable. The growing use of facsimile (FAX) machines, however, has cut into the growth of telecommunications applications for such purposes.

You can choose among several commercial telecommunications packages. Many high-quality programs, however, are available as public domain or shareware programs. If you need many copies of a telecommunications program for branch offices or agents in the field, consider using a public domain program.

Integrated Packages versus Integrated Software Environments

The 1984 debut of integrated packages for the IBM Personal Computer was thought at the time to herald a new age in personal computing. After all, integrated packages such as

Symphony and Framework combined all four basic computing applications (word processing, spreadsheets, database management, and telecommunications) in one program, and what is more, the package's integration of all these features facilitated the easy transfer of data from one module to another. However, it soon became apparent that, for the most part, the individual modules within such packages did not compare favorably to their stand-alone counterparts. Although Symphony's spreadsheet is actually superior to most stand-alone spreadsheet programs, its word processing and database management modules are of inferior quality. Not wanting to sacrifice program functionality and features for the sake of integration, most buyers continue to prefer high-quality stand-alone programs.

The Macintosh's integrated software environment achieves a high measure of software integration without sacrificing program functionality. It accomplishes this feat by means of a feature-packed internal memory, which includes basic screen display and keyboard features. All Macintosh programs may make use of these features, which means that most Macintosh programs employ virtually the same user interface. Once you have learned the keyboard commands, scrolling techniques, and menu-manipulation commands in one program, you can extend your skills readily to other Macintosh programs. What is more, you can easily copy and paste data between applications. In the Macintosh environment, you readily can paste a spreadsheet into a word processing document. You can do the same thing with an IBM-compatible system, but only if you choose your software with such applications in mind.

Accounting Packages

If the personal computer is a great tool for small businesses, then you might think that accounting packages account for a very large share of the PC software market. They don't. Sales of accounting packages for personal computers lag far behind those of other applications—so much so, in fact, that it is virtually impossible to obtain venture capital funding for accounting package development.

The owners of small businesses shy away from accounting software for some very good reasons. For one thing, these people aren't in the accounting business. Any serious small business needs the help of a professional accountant, and most small-business owners are quite happy to leave the accounting to their accountant. A second reason for the slow acceptance of accounting packages is that most of the early ones were designed for the use of accountants, not owners of small businesses. Why computerize your books if you need a degree in accounting to understand how to use the software!

Some equally good reasons, however, might lead to predictions of a coming boom in PC accounting applications. It's quite possible to computerize one's accounts without having much accounting knowledge, as long as the software you're using is well-conceived and designed for the use of people without accounting backgrounds. You have good reason to do so, too. Even if you don't scrutinize your reports and perform analyses of the information they contain, you still need to maintain a ledger that shows all the transactions you complete so that your accountant can have something to work with. You might as well take advantage of the new, powerful accounting packages that enter point-of-sale information directly into the general ledger and accounts receivable modules—without your having to perform the update manually! In addition, this software is capable of performing the analyses you normally receive from your accountant, and you have no long wait. Instead of receiving monthly or quarterly financial reports about your firm's position and progress, you can receive them every week—or every day, if you want.

> If you're thinking about computerizing your firm's books, do so with the help and advice of your accountant.

Checkwriting Programs

One of the hottest-selling programs in the personal computer marketplace is Intuit Software's Quicken, which is available for the IBM and Macintosh environments. The program is usually thought of as a personal financial manager and checkwriting program, but as many as half of its users are putting it to work to keep records for small businesses. Using Quicken, you can code all the deposits or withdrawals from a bank account by category. Like a database management program, Quicken can search your account and select just those transactions whose characteristics you specify. For this reason, Quicken can be very useful for creating periodic reports. You can even use the program to handle a small payroll.

Modular Packages

Modular accounting packages are essentially computerized versions of traditional accounting practices, in which a firm keeps several ledgers—one for accounts receivable, accounts payable, and a general ledger. Updates to the general ledger are made in batches at periodic intervals after the hard copy is carefully proofed for errors. Modular packages are generally sold with several essentially separate programs for each of these functions, and you must undertake special procedures periodically to update the master ledger.

Most modular programs are personal computer versions of mainframe or minicomputer programs, and they were designed for use by professional bookkeeping firms—not for untrained users in a small business. These programs, however, are usually far more flexible than integrated accounting packages (which are discussed in the next section). You can purchase additional modules as your business expands, including inventory control, payroll, order entry, job costing, and professional time billing. All these modules are equipped to post transactions to the general ledger program at regular intervals.

One major advantage of modular packages is that some are available in multiuser packages designed for local area networks. You can set up this kind of system with several point-of-sale computers equipped with bar-code readers to automatically record each item's price, and, via the network, each transaction is automatically posted to the accounting modules. A Macintosh program capable of this multiuser application (including point-of-sale terminals) is Flexware (Microfinancial Corporation); a similar program for IBM-format computers is Excalibur (Armour Systems, Inc.).

Integrated "All in One" Accounting Packages

An integrated, or "all in one," accounting package combines accounts receivable, accounts payable, and general ledger functions into one integrated program. Unlike modular programs, updates to the general ledger are made actively as you use the program—there's no periodic "batch" updating of the ledger to worry about. For this reason, integrated packages are usually much easier to use than modular programs. Many integrated packages are designed for small business owners who want to save money by performing accounting and bookkeeping functions themselves. Furthermore, these programs are designed to replicate as much as possible the way small business books are actually kept on paper.

An example of an integrated "all in one" package is Plains and Simple (Great Plains Software). Available for the Apple Macintosh, Plains and Simple presents ledgers, checks, and other forms on-screen the way you are accustomed to seeing them on paper. Instead of writing entries in a journal, you type them on your Macintosh. The information is then automatically passed to the appropriate accounts in the general ledger, accounts receivable, and accounts payable modules, which are fully integrated in the program. A variety of report functions makes it possible at any time to answer questions such as, How much is my business worth? Who owes me money? How much cash do I have on hand? You can print balance sheets, cash flow projections, income projections, and many other reports.

Accounting Package Pitfalls and Prospects

One major drawback of computerizing your firm's books is that it's hard to predict your future needs. What's going to happen if your firm grows out of its accounting software? Make sure that any package you purchase is capable of adjusting to your firm's growth. A package that lets you define only 1,000 customers isn't going to be of much use when Customer No. 1,001 walks in the door! Will the same firm's more powerful modular package make use of your current program's data files? Probably not.

> Make sure that any accounting software you buy can handle the future growth of your company.

If you decide to use an integrated "all in one" package, you may be sacrificing a great deal of the functionality that is available in modular packages, which offer many "bells and whistles," including point-of-sale entry, payroll, inventory control, and professional time billing.

There is no single, "right" method of accounting, and chances are you have developed a unique method that's just right for your business. If you're thinking about computerizing your books, be sure to choose a package that's flexible enough to accommodate the way you do business. Remember one of this book's cardinal principles: don't let a computer force you to change the way you do business.

As you shop around for accounting packages, make sure that you choose one that has the features and capacities you need. When shopping for an accounting package, ask yourself the following questions:

- ❑ How many vendors can I define with this program?
- ❑ How many customers can I define?
- ❑ What's the maximum amount of each transaction?
- ❑ What's the maximum amount of all transactions?
- ❑ Will the program print checks?
- ❑ Does it help me reconcile the checking account?
- ❑ What reports are available?
- ❑ Does the accounts payable module allow you to track accounts by due date?
- ❑ Does the accounts payable module allow for partial payments?
- ❑ Does the accounts receivable module calculate sales tax?
- ❑ Does the accounts receivable module calculate finance charges?
- ❑ Does the program let you define customer credit limits?
- ❑ Does the program permit one-time customers?
- ❑ Does the program enable you to track sales by salesperson?
- ❑ Does the program figure sales commissions automatically?

If you're a spreadsheet whiz, you may want to choose a package that exports data to popular spreadsheet programs, where you can use it as grist for the "what if" mill.

If you're a professional person, a physician or dentist, for example, find out what your colleagues are doing to computerize their books. They doubtless have experiences, both good and bad, with packages specifically designed for your line of work. Attend professional conferences and read professional journals; they are likely to contain advertisements for vertical-market suppliers whose products remain, and will forever remain, completely unknown to salespeople at computer stores.

Desktop Publishing

One of the hottest new applications in personal computing is desktop publishing, which is more accurately described as desktop typesetting and layout. If you equip your system with a PostScript-compatible laser printer, you can produce newsletters, illustrations, brochures, and forms that will appear as if they were prepared by graphics professionals.

The section on word processing (earlier in this chapter) introduced page layout programs like PageMaker, as well as form-designing programs like SmartForm Designer. For illustrations, choose a PostScript-compatible package like Adobe Illustrator (for the Macintosh or IBM-compatible) or Aldus Freehand (for the Macintosh). Avoid "paint programs," which, although fun to play with, produce low-resolution images that do not approach professional standards.

You can save a great deal of money by producing your own forms, brochures, and illustrations—anyone can learn to use this remarkable new genre of software. Not everyone is a graphic artist, however, and the growth of desktop publishing has seen a concomitant growth in poorly designed documents. If you're unsure about your graphics sensibilities, get some professional advice before risking damage to your firm's image.

> If you decide to produce a newsletter, brochure, illustration, advertisement, or other graphic document for public distribution, get a graphic artist to critique it before you release it.

At the high end of desktop publishing is computer-aided design (CAD) software, which provides computer tools for technical design and drafting.

Project Management Packages

Use project management software to track projects that include many tasks and many types of resources (for example, people, equipment, space). A good place to start might be your computerization project. With project management software you can assign tasks to people, establish deadlines (called *milestones*), and document the tasks that are dependent on the completion of other tasks. With this information, you can identify those critical tasks that, if not completed on time, result in delays for the entire project.

For IBM-compatible systems, consider the following programs:

- Super Project (Computer Associates)
- Project (Microsoft)
- Timeline (Symantec)
- ViewPoint (Computer Aided Management)
- Micro Planner for Windows (Micro Planning International)
- Project Outlook (Strategic Software Planning Corporation)

For Macintosh computers, consider these project management programs:

- MacProject II (Claris)
- Micro Planner Plus (Micro Planning International)
- Manage That (Varcon Systems)

Statistical Analysis Packages

Statistics focuses on the organization and interpretation of numerical data. Methods of statistical analysis are used in scientific studies, business decisions, and in the analysis of raw data elicited by questionnaires. If you send questionnaires to a large number of customers, entering the results into a statistical analysis package enables you to cross-tabulate data so that you can view it from many different angles (for example, family income, sex of the respondent, and so on). The look and feel used by statistical analysis packages and the types of analyses performed vary significantly from one package to another, so research this category carefully before making a choice.

For IBM compatible computers, consider these programs:

- ❏ Systat (Systat Inc.)
- ❏ Statgraphics (STSC Inc.)
- ❏ PSPP/PC+ (SPSS, Inc.)
- ❏ Minitab Statistical Software (Minitab, Inc.)

For the Macintosh, consider Fastat from Systat, Inc.

Time-Billing Packages

Attorneys, accountants, psychologists, and other consultants sell time—their own time—as their primary product. Time-billing packages keep track of the time spent on an individual client. That time may be incoming or outgoing telephone calls, time at a client site, court appearances, postage and copying costs, secretarial costs, and so on. These packages enable the user to set up lists of clients and services and enter the time spent for each one. Several different reports can be generated, including an actual bill that you send to the client. In addition, these packages track the payments that are received from your client. Some time-billing packages can run in the "background" so that they are always just a keystroke away. Running a program in this resident fashion enables the consultant to start a stopwatch to time telephone conversations.

For IBM-compatible systems, consider Timeslips III (North Edge Software Corporation).

For the Macintosh, consider these time-billing programs:

- Timeslips (North Edge Software)
- Professional Time Billing (Professional Systems)
- TimeMinder (Aatrix Software)

Chapter Summary

This chapter surveyed the application software packages available in today's software market. You learned why it's usually a good idea to choose a full-featured word processing program. You learned why spreadsheet programs are so useful for "what if" analysis, and why you should be suspicious of spreadsheets that have not been thoroughly audited for errors. You also learned why relational database programs are most useful for business, and you learned why many businesses use public domain or shareware telecommunications programs. When you considered accounting software, you learned that you must choose between modular programs (which require accounting expertise) or integrated "all in one" programs, which are easy to use but may not have the upward expandability your business may require. You learned that desktop publishing can save you money in typesetting and graphic arts fees. In the next chapter, you will learn how to identify the hardware you need.

CHAPTER 5

Making Hardware Purchasing Decisions

As you learned in the last two chapters, it's crucial that you find the proper software solutions for your business before considering hardware. You should make one hardware decision before finalizing your software choices, however: whether you should opt for a multiple-user network system or settle for single-user machines. Some software is not available in multiple-user versions or performs poorly on a network. You need to consider whether networking is for you before proceeding.

After you have made a decision on the network issue, it's time to investigate your hardware purchasing options. This chapter counsels you to start small, taking the process one step at a time. As you will see, Mark and Marian, the couple whose computerization project is being tracked in this book, began by computerizing their custom-order department before computerizing their inventory. Even though you should start small, you should work with a comprehensive, final plan in mind. If Mark and Marian need a network version of a database management or accounting program to accomplish their goals, they will waste money if they start by buying a nonnetworked version of the software. Start small—but think big.

> Create your own system step-by-step, but make sure that all your purchases will function together effectively in the final system.

Hardware versus Software

Many people who begin learning about computers are confused by the difference between hardware and software. The difference is made quite clear if you can remember a simple rule.

> If you drop it and it breaks, it's hardware.

Software, on the other hand, is information recorded on a storage medium like a floppy disk, a tape cartridge, or an optical disk. Sure, you can drop your hard disk and break it, but the software, because it is just information, cannot break.

Your computer can be made up of thousands of electronic and mechanical components. This chapter, however, looks at the larger operational components of your system.

Single versus Multiuser Systems

Personal computers were consciously designed as stand-alone, single-user machines, but for two very different reasons. The "countercultural" people involved in the personal computer's development were reacting against the impersonality and centralized authority of mainframe computer systems and sought to create a machine that would bring computing power to ordinary people. When IBM developed its Personal Computer, the company emphasized the single-user theme so that the new PC would not compete with its more expensive (and profitable) 3270 minicomputer terminals. Business experience has shown, however, that there are many advantages to linking computers together. Before proceeding with your planning, you should decide whether you want to take advantage of the new networking possibilities with personal computers.

What's the Difference between Single- and Multiuser Systems?

If you are like most people, single-user computing is the environment with which you have become familiar. In the single-user environment, each computer stands by itself: the only way two computers can simultaneously share the same data file is to carry a floppy disk from one computer to the other (see fig. 5.1).

In a multiuser system, programs and data files are stored on a designated device and can be shared among all the computers connected to the file storage unit.

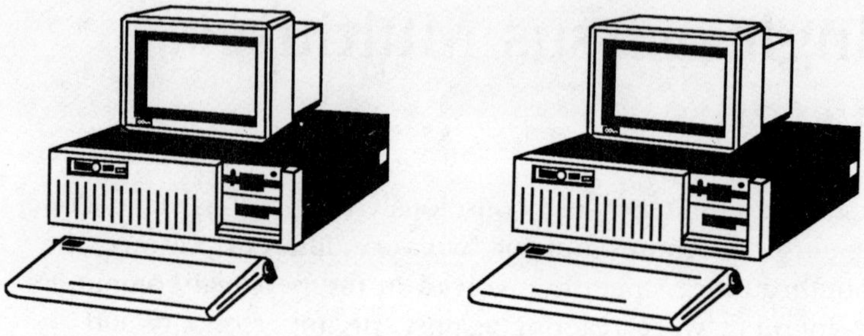

Fig. 5.1. *Single-user computers cannot simultaneously share data.*

Two arrangements exist for file sharing. The first consists of a central computer to which terminals are connected. The terminals have no processing circuitry. All processing takes place in the central computer, and the terminals are simply devices through which the operator can send data to or retrieve information from the central computer. Large corporate mainframe computers operate on this principle, and this arrangement has been scaled down to small systems for businesses of almost any size. Each terminal (called a dumb terminal) has no processing capability of its own, so all processing is performed by the central unit. However, a catastrophic failure in the central unit renders the entire system useless.

The second arrangement, personal computer local area networks (LANs), have achieved great popularity over the last several years. Central file storage is accomplished on a specially configured personal computer (usually with no keyboard or display) or a high-performance device called a *file server*, or *network server* (see fig. 5.2). Instead of dumb terminals, each user is equipped with a fully functional personal computer that, with appropriate software, can process raw data from the server. A LAN, in other words, combines all the advantages of multiuser systems and stand-alone workstations.

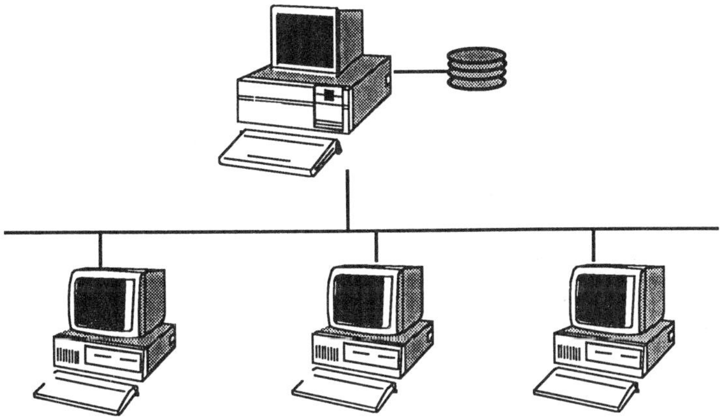

Fig. 5.2. Setting up a local area network.

Should You Consider a Multiuser System?

Are multiuser systems dead? Not according to the big computer manufacturers, whose ads show owners of small businesses sitting proudly next to their business minicomputer as they say disparaging things about personal computer LANs. The truth is that both approaches have advantages and disadvantages.

Disadvantages of a Multiuser System

As you already know, a multiuser system relies on the central processor for all the system's power. Dumb terminals can only display what is sent from the central unit; they cannot interpret, reformat, or compute. When the central processor is out of service, so are all the terminals connected to it. Local area networks distribute processing power among all the computers connected to the network. If the file server goes down, your staff can continue working on their stand-alone workstations until the server is repaired.

Another disadvantage of multiuser systems is their expense. Most such systems employ minicomputers, the prices of which begin at approximately $10,000 to $25,000. The software for such systems is also more expensive than programs designed for personal computers.

Advantages of a Multiuser System

The three key advantages to a multiuser system are the simultaneous access to data by all authorized users, consolidation of data, and the high quality of the software designed for multiuser business systems. Each advantage is discussed in the following paragraphs.

- *Simultaneous Access to Data.* With a multiuser order entry system, for example, all operators can enter orders at the same time. Simply put, that means more orders can be entered during each day, with all the order information in one central location.

  Suppose that you run a furniture store and you have in stock three sofas of a particular style. Each time a sofa is sold, the inventory available figure must be reduced. With multiuser access, anyone can see how many sofas are available; without multiuser access, you may not know that another sales associate just sold the last sofa.

  Not all LAN software provides simultaneous access in this sense. With some inventory-control systems, each workstation uploads the day's transactions in a batch mode process, meaning that the central database may not contain up-to-date information.

- *Data Consolidation.* Suppose that you have five point-of-sale terminals in your furniture store. When you want to know how business was last week, it's unlikely that you care which articles were rung up on a particular terminal. You need a report that consolidates all the information collected at individual terminals. Because all the terminals in your store are saving their sales transactions to a master file of all transactions, processing that data to produce a consolidated sales report becomes a simple task.

In a LAN using personal computers, some software requires that the operator deliberately upload transactions to the file server at periodic intervals. If he or she forgets, the data picture you get is inaccurate—but you do not know it.

- *Quality Software.* Multiuser computer systems are designed for business use, so the companies that install them and create software for them have accumulated many years of business experience. Although bad software can be found in any computing environment, the software created for multiuser systems comes from firms that focus on creating multiuser systems for businesses. Many of these network software developers have been in business for a decade or more. Personal computer software firms, in contrast, are just beginning to get their toes wet in the LAN marketplace, and it is possible that they may not fully understand what small businesses require in software performance.

Should You Consider a Local Area Network?

Local area networks have some advantages and disadvantages when compared to multiuser systems—although if you choose your LAN software carefully, you can avoid some of the disadvantages. The best LAN software, for instance, permits simultaneous access to data and automatically handles data consolidation tasks. Keep these kinds of issues in mind as you shop for software.

You should bear in mind another perspective as you consider this issue: the advantages and disadvantages of a LAN versus two or more nonnetworked personal computers. First, examine the LAN issue from this point of view.

Local Area Network Benefits

As against purchasing several stand-alone PCs, LANs have the following benefits:

- *Improved Data Security.* You have better control over the security of your data because it is centrally stored and access is granted only to authorized employees. If individual PCs are not equipped with disk drives, your employees cannot make unauthorized copies.

- *Improved Data Integrity.* Centrally stored data can be backed up easily to a tape drive for safekeeping. Keep at least eight days' worth of data backed up, and make two copies: one for storage on-site (but away from the network server) and the other in a secured location far away from your business.

- *Improved Data Consistency.* Imagine for a moment that you have no network and a customer list is maintained on each of your computers. How long do you think it would take for the lists to become dissimilar? Probably less than a day. With a network, you have only one list, and it is available to anyone authorized to use it.

- *Reduced Software Expense.* Buy five individual copies of a word processing program at $495, and you spend $2,475. Purchase instead the network version of the exact same product with a license for five workstations, and you spend about $1,500. The savings here is obvious and substantial.

Local Area Network Disadvantages

Local area networks do have their negative side, compared to buying several stand-alone PCs. Drawbacks include the following:

- *Initial Expense.* It is expensive to install a LAN. You need network operating system software, a file server, and network adapters for each computer, and you must run cable to connect each computer to the server. The cost for the network itself, not including the individual computers or any application software, can be several thousand dollars.

- *Ongoing Expense.* Someone in your business must be trained to administer the network. Simply put, that means starting up the system every day, backing up daily files, adding and deleting users from the system, and assigning different security access levels to individual users. Expertise of this sort is best learned from classes conducted by the vendor from whom you purchased the network.

Local area networks can pay handsome dividends by enabling your employees to work in a single cohesive computing environment. Remember, however, that you are a business executive, not a computer whiz. Getting a LAN to work properly isn't easy—bugs multiply like mosquitoes on a summer night. More than a few businesses have suffered delays of up to six months in implementing LANs—and some have given up entirely.

> Local area networks are not for the do-it-yourselfer. Seek professional advice and purchase a network only from people officially certified by the network manufacturer.

Selecting a Personal Computer Hardware Platform

If you decide to go the LAN route, you have several additional purchases to make besides the computers themselves. For now, however, it's time to grapple with another basic issue. For most readers of this book, the multiuser versus LAN issue is moot; the real choice is between stand-alone PCs and a PC-based LAN. The big issue: will your hardware platform consist of IBM-format or Apple Macintosh computers?

IBM-compatible computers are built around the microprocessor chips from Intel Corporation, and the Macintosh is designed around the Motorola 68000 chip. IBM computers run under the MS-DOS/PC DOS or OS/2 operating systems, and the Macintosh comes with its own proprietary operating system. Each type of computer represents a different hardware platform.

IBM Computers

Though Apple was on the scene several years earlier, it took the mighty IBM to legitimize the personal computer for business. IBM did so by introducing its own entry in 1981. The first IBM Personal Computer, based on the Intel 8088 microprocessor, was equipped with two 5 1/4-inch floppy disk drives (no hard disk) and only 64K of RAM! The 8088 ran an internal speed of 4.77 MHz, blindingly fast for its day. Today's top-of-the-line IBM-format personal computers, based on Intel's 80486 microprocessor, run at speeds of up to 33MHz, contain hard disk drives of up to 320M or more, and can be outfitted with up to 16M of RAM!

Is an IBM Compatible Right for You?

Buying IBM became a way of life for data processing executives in large corporate environments. Most data processing shops became true blue—all IBM—no matter what the cost.

This way of life filtered down to the personal computing world. In 1981 you probably would have purchased an IBM Personal Computer, IBM display monitor, and an IBM printer (built by Epson, which, of course, no one had ever heard of at the time). Your disks? IBM. Your operating system? IBM's PC DOS. Word processing? IBM's DisplayWrite. You get the picture. There was one exception: *everyone* bought 1-2-3. After all, that was the reason for buying the computer in the first place!

A couple of years later, COMPAQ Computer Corporation of Houston came along with its portable computer, and suddenly people everywhere discovered a high-quality, competitively priced IBM alternative. The maxim had been shattered, and the world of personal computing has not been the same since.

Mixing manufacturers is not only safe; it's unavoidable, and it makes excellent business sense. Your modem manufacturer doesn't build laser printers, and your monitor manufacturer doesn't build disk drives.

The larger question, of course, is the computer itself. There are literally hundreds of companies marketing computers that claim to be 100 percent compatible (usually called a *clone*) with IBM's XT or AT systems. As long as you stick with a reputable, well-known, well-established company, you should have no problems. Very few IBM PS/2 clones exist, and there are no Macintosh clones at all.

Why buy a clone? You can save many hundreds of dollars by buying a clone. And many clones feature performance that outshines IBM's best. When considering compatibles, pay careful attention to the length of the warranty, what the warranty covers, and the arrangements for service. Some companies provide on-site service, but others expect you to pack up the computer and ship it back to the factory *at your expense*.

Advantages and Disadvantages of IBM-Format Computing

Whether made by IBM or some other manufacturer, IBM-format computers dominate the personal computer marketplace. As a result, there is a huge variety of software available for IBM-format computers. If you decide to go the IBM route, you will find yourself in quite a crowd. Many people, including business people you know, use and understand IBM-format computers and software. You will find it easy to find programmers, technicians, and maintenance people who have experience in the IBM environment.

Another advantage of choosing IBM-format computing is the low price of clones and peripheral equipment. You can purchase a high-quality but very basic IBM clone for as little as $750—and the price includes a 20M hard disk! If you opt for the Macintosh, you find yourself paying considerably more for the computer and peripheral equipment.

Despite these and other advantages, however, IBM-format computing has one major disadvantage. Designed back in the days when internal memories were severely limited due to the high cost of memory chips, the operating systems of these computers do not include user interface features, such as defining which key you press to delete a line of text or to quit the program. These features are provided by the individual program you use. The trouble is that each program creates its own, unique user interface. For example, whereas you press F1 for help in 1-2-3, you press F3 for help in WordPerfect. In a more critical example, in one program you might press Ctrl-X to delete a line of text—but in another program, the same key quits the program without saving your work! This inconsistency in user interfaces can cause you and your staff serious problems as you attempt to learn two or more completely different packages, and you often find yourself looking up basic commands in reference books and manuals.

IBM-format computing would be greatly aided by standardization of user interface features. This standardization was precisely the goal of Microsoft Corporation in introducing Microsoft Windows, which is a graphic user interface quite similar to the operating system of the Apple Macintosh. But Apple has sued Microsoft, alleging that Microsoft violated Apple's copyright on its user interface technology. Partly as a result of this suit, and also because Windows was slow to gain acceptance in the marketplace anyway, relatively few software publishers have developed applications that take full advantage of the Windows user interface standards.

Macintosh Systems

Apple calls the Macintosh "the computer for the rest of us." Although the machine is the computer for *some* of us, it has a long, long way to go to catch up with the millions of IBM PCs that cover the earth.

The Macintosh was Apple's second attempt at a computer based on what it called a user-friendly, graphical user interface. (The first, the Lisa, was a technical triumph and a marketing disaster.) The idea was simple: instead of staring at an IBM screen with only the DOS `C:\>` prompt facing you, the Macintosh displays pictorial representations (called *icons*) of various options. Where IBM would have you type *del mydoc* to erase the word processing file MYDOC, the

Macintosh asks that you drag the image of a sheet of paper labeled `MYDOC` to a picture of a trash can. Millions of users have become accustomed to this new way of doing things, but millions of others say it's much faster to type *del mydoc*.

The original Macintosh, equipped with 256K of RAM and one single-sided 3 1/2-inch disk drive, was drastically underpowered, slow, and unsuitable for sophisticated business use (as was the original IBM Personal Computer). Several years and models later, the Macintosh IIx with its Motorola 68030 microprocessor delivers the performance wallop that today's database management or desktop publishing applications require.

It is not correct to say that the Macintosh is better or worse than the PC. It's different. But that difference has enabled people who would never otherwise touch a computer to jump right in and develop considerable expertise.

If one single factor has provided the high level of comfort, it's the Macintosh's consistent user interface—the manner in which the user interacts with the machine. Virtually all Macintosh software is written to a standard interface. The theory is that if you learn to use one Macintosh program, you're on your way to learning them all. Although that statement may be somewhat exaggerated, you do not find the glaring discrepancies between programs that are evident in the PC world.

Your need for color becomes a major factor in which Macintosh model you choose. The all-in-one models, such as the Macintosh SE, include a black-and-white monitor that cannot be replaced by a color display (although you can add an external color display). To choose color from the beginning, you must invest in the Macintosh II, IIx, or IIcx, which employ a design like the IBM PC in which the central processor and display are housed separately.

IBM or Macintosh?

Your choice of a hardware platform should be dictated by software availability. But what if the same program, or very comparable programs, are available in both environments? In favor of IBM-format computing, you probably can assemble a system at approximately 20 to 30 percent less cost than a comparable Macintosh system. In favor of the Macintosh, you will spend less on training your staff.

Operating Systems

Choosing a hardware platform is a task that rightfully involves a look at software—specifically, the operating system. An essential program for day-to-day work with the computer, the operating system is designed to work only with one hardware platform. If you choose IBM-format computing, you get MS-DOS or OS/2. If you choose the Macintosh, you get the Macintosh System. These programs vary markedly, and because none runs on a different hardware platform, they are rightly considered as you face the IBM versus Macintosh decision.

MS-DOS and PC DOS

MS-DOS is an acronym for Microsoft Disk Operating System. Microsoft provides licensed versions of MS-DOS to every computer manufacturer that wants to be IBM compatible. Each manufacturer is free to make modifications to its version of MS-DOS as it sees fit. Each computer maker's rendition of MS-DOS is unique, even though the systems may carry the same version number.

IBM elected to market its own unique version of MS-DOS under the name PC DOS. The bottom line is that PC DOS is

IBM's version of MS-DOS. In this book, all these individual versions of MS-DOS are collectively referred to simply as DOS.

DOS was perfect for the early personal computer, when one operator was performing a single task. The capacities designed into DOS were more than adequate for those days. The original 1981 IBM PC shipped with a grand total of 64K of RAM! Who could have thought that wouldn't be enough? Yet DOS could address 640K of RAM—far more than would ever be required—or so it was thought.

And what about disk space? The original IBM PC/XT shipped with a 10M hard disk drive that didn't even come close to the DOS upper limit of 32M. Today, the only place you're likely to find a 10M hard disk drive is in a museum.

Despite limitations, DOS remains a powerful and completely viable operating system. Hundreds of thousands of programs have been written to run under DOS, and they are not about to disappear overnight or over the next several years. DOS cannot break the 640K RAM barrier, however, and consequently, DOS software cannot compete with Macintosh software for overall user-friendliness. DOS is cheaper than OS/2, and IBM-format clones are cheaper than Macintoshes, but opting for DOS almost certainly results in higher training costs.

OS/2

Microsoft's next generation operating system, Operating System/2, is truly a quantum leap over the constraints imposed by DOS. Whereas DOS limits you under normal conditions to 640K of RAM, OS/2 can access up to 16M of RAM, an amount beyond anyone's wildest imagination just a few years ago.

In addition, OS/2 is designed to be a true multitasking operating system: you can load several programs and have them all computing simultaneously. Imagine having your word processor, accounting system, and database management system all running at the same time!

Any local area network operating system built around Microsoft's LAN Manager product (such as 3+ Open from 3Com Corporation) requires OS/2.

OS/2 raises two questions. First, should you buy OS/2 if you already have IBM-compatible computers running DOS? In a word, no, because you already have invested in DOS and it's unlikely that you can justify the cost of buying OS/2 versions of all your software programs (if you can find them at all).

Second, if you are buying computers for the first time, should you buy OS/2 instead of DOS? Again, the recommendation for standard business applications is to stay with DOS. Very few programs have been translated into OS/2 versions, and those translations are quite a bit more expensive than their DOS counterparts. OS/2 itself is several hundred dollars more expensive than DOS.

Finally, whereas DOS runs under 640K of RAM, OS/2 requires a minimum of 2M, with 4M being a more realistic entry amount.

There is little doubt that OS/2 is the operating system of the future. But most people agree that for the average computer user, the future is several years away, because OS/2's progress has been very, very slow—to the surprise of Microsoft, which predicted that OS/2 would have by now almost completely replaced DOS.

The slow acceptance of OS/2 is understandable, however, when one considers the bind in which it places software publishers. Because there are still so many millions of 8088-based IBM Personal Computers and clones still in use, software manufacturers are reluctant to create programs that cannot run under DOS. The problem is that taking advantage of the new technical possibilities of the OS/2 environment requires just that: creating programs that cannot run under

DOS. The result is that many new programs are being released that run under OS/2 *and* DOS—which means that they aren't taking full advantage of OS/2's potential. Because that is the case, few users see any real advantage to switching to OS/2. If ever there was a vicious circle, this is it.

Where does that leave you? If you have opted for IBM-format computing, you can protect yourself by purchasing a system with a microprocessor that's OS/2-ready. Run DOS now—and switch to OS/2 after this difficult transition period runs its course.

For more information on microprocessor options, see the section titled "The Microprocessor," later in this chapter.

UNIX/XENIX/AIX

The UNIX operating system, developed by Bell Laboratories, is a true multitasking operating system that has gained much deserved praise in the minicomputer world. Microsoft markets a version of UNIX called XENIX, and IBM markets a version under the name AIX. Perhaps the most popular implementation of UNIX is a multiuser operating system called SCO XENIX from the Santa Cruz Operation. In addition, the VINES local network operating system from Banyan Systems is designed around UNIX.

UNIX operating systems provide power and capabilities not available in single-user DOS, but dealing with them requires consultants specializing in UNIX. Don't let that scare you, however; UNIX is the proper solution in many multiuser business environments.

The Macintosh Operating System

In discussing the Macintosh operating system, you must distinguish between the user interface features that are built into the Macintosh's *firmware* (its permanent internal memory), the software that is called the System, and the utility that is called the Finder.

The Macintosh's internal firmware contains many basic routines for displaying windows on-screen, manipulating the cursor, scrolling, and supplying other fundamental features of the user interface you see on-screen. When you write a program for the Macintosh, therefore, you don't have to worry about adding these features to your program. You just include "hooks" that put these built-in user interface routines into motion. This programming convenience is the reason that most Macintosh programs employ a common user interface.

The System contains the portion of the Macintosh's operating system that is kept on disk, and the System is subject to frequent revision. (New versions are made available at a nominal fee or free of charge.) System 7.0, scheduled for release in early 1990, will feature embedded support for searching external mainframe databases using the structured query language (SQL), dynamic data-sharing across applications, a new printer driver that will achieve better results on non-PostScript laser printers, and better hard disk organization. With System 7.0, top-of-the-line Macintoshes (the Macintosh II family and the SE/30) will accommodate up to 128M of physical RAM, or sections of a hard disk that have been configured to act as extensions of RAM.

The Finder, which most people mistakenly think is the Macintosh's operating system, is actually a utility program that you can replace, if you want, with a different one. Several commercial alternatives to the Finder are available, and you can use any one of them with any Macintosh program. Some of these commercial alternatives give you better ways of organizing and finding files on a very large hard disk.

MultiFinder is a version of the Finder that permits you to place two or more programs in memory at once. If you ever find it necessary to move information from one program to another (for instance, from a spreadsheet program to a word processing program), MultiFinder is so convenient that this utility alone may sell you on the Macintosh. To move from one program to another, you click an icon in the right corner of the screen. Unlike the true multitasking capabilities of OS/2, however, MultiFinder does not run these programs simultaneously; when you switch from one program to the next, the first program's operation is suspended until you switch back.

Understanding Hardware Terminology

With the general issues of multiuser versus LAN systems and hardware platform choices behind you, it is time to delve deeper into all the mysterious terms—such as *system units*, *microprocessors*, and *RAM*—that you encounter as you shop for hardware.

System Units

Consider an IBM-compatible personal computer or a Macintosh II. What do you see? Almost always, you see three components: a monitor, a keyboard, and a large chassis called either the system unit or central processing unit (CPU).

The system unit does many things. First, like the skin on your body that holds the organs inside, the system unit is a cabinet that contains many subsystems, such as disk drives and the ports to which you connect your printer or other peripherals. Besides providing a convenient resting place, the system unit contains the microprocessor chip that provides your computer's computational power and the memory chips that hold data to be processed by the microprocessor.

In addition, the CPU contains a *bus*, a complex series of electronic pipelines that route data from one component or subsystem to another (from the keyboard to the screen or from your disk to the printer). If you look inside your computer, you may see a series of *expansion slots* into which you can insert *expansion cards*, or circuit boards, that provide additional capabilities, such as more memory or local area network connections. Each expansion slot is connected to the bus.

The Microprocessor

The microprocessor, a tiny sliver of silicon, is the heart and brains of your entire computer. The microprocessor contains the computational power needed to run this complex system, to arbitrate hundreds of simultaneous signals flowing across the bus, and to tell all other components of the system what to do next.

Different microprocessors are used in different computers, sometimes resulting in incompatibilities.

The IBM family, designed to be backward-compatible from one generation to the next, is built around microprocessors manufactured by Intel Corporation. The original IBM PC and the soon-to-follow XT employed the Intel 8088 as their processor. The 8088 (and its cousin the 8086) was a powerful microprocessor in its day, but once the public became hooked on personal computing, the 8088 just didn't run fast enough. Along came the IBM PC AT, built around Intel's next generation microprocessor, the 80286. The 80286, or 286 as it is usually called, remains to this day a powerful processor and is used in most PCs bought today. With the introduction of IBM's PS/2 family and the COMPAQ Deskpro 386 came the Intel 80386. With a 386-based computer you can have, for under $10,000, the same computing power that a million-dollar IBM mainframe computer provided about ten years ago.

Although many 286 machines are still available and represent an excellent value, 386-based machines are dropping in price rapidly. You also have solid technical grounds for preferring 386-based machines over their 286-based predecessors. The 80386 chip represents a major technological advance over the 80286 chip, resulting in vastly superior performance. Unlike the 286, the 386 can take full advantage of applications written specifically for OS/2 and the special processing capabilities of 386 and later chips. New to the IBM-format marketplace are machines based on the 80486 chip, which is even faster than the 80386. Unlike the 80386 chip, however, the 80486 is only an incremental advance over its immediate predecessor. With 486 machines leading the high end, 386 machines will become an excellent value.

In shopping for an IBM-format computer, you hear a great deal about *clock speed*, or the number of cycles per second at which the microprocessor cycles. Clock speeds are usually expressed in *megahertz* (abbreviated MHz), or millions of cycles per second. The original IBM PC's 8088 chip ran at a speed of 4.77 MHz, a glacial pace by today's standards. (You can buy 8088 chips now that run at 10 MHz, and they are considerably faster than the 4.77 MHz chips.) Be forewarned, though, that clock speed is not the only determinant of system speed—the microprocessor's capability to shuffle data around internally, and the speed of other system components and peripherals all play a role. For this reason, a 286 machine running at 10 MHz is considerably faster than an 8088 running at 10 MHz. Use clock speeds to compare speeds among machines with the same microprocessor, not different microprocessors.

Among 386 machines, you can find models that run at 16 MHz, 20 MHz, 25 MHz, and even 33 MHz. The faster the clock speed, the more expensive the machine. Only part of the price increase is attributable to the greater expense of the faster chip; much of the increase is explained by the higher cost of other system components, which also must be fast if they are to meet the speed of the microprocessor.

Should you opt for a superfast clock speed? For most business applications, you have little to gain by purchasing the fastest machine you can find. Clock speed is most evident in operations that do not involve peripherals, such as the disk drives, but most application programs go to disk frequently. As a result, you don't gain much performance by going for a 33 MHz machine as opposed to a considerably cheaper 25 or 20 MHz model, which will prove less temperamental.

The Apple Macintosh employs microprocessors based on the Motorola 68000 chip and its descendants, and much the same picture applies. The 68000 running at about 8 MHz powers the Macintosh Plus and the Macintosh SE, which are—like the 8088-based machines in IBM-format computing—obsolete. The newer chips in the family, the 68020 and 68030, run at 16 MHz and deliver superior performance. These chips power the Macintosh IIx, the very popular IIcx, and the compact SE/30. Not only are these chips faster, they also include the virtual memory management features that, when used with System 7.0, enable you to configure part of the computer's hard disk as if it were RAM.

> If you're using an IBM-format computer, choose a machine with the 80386 or 80486 microprocessor. If you're buying a Macintosh, choose a machine with the 68030.

RAM and ROM

Although your computer contains memory chips that perform a variety of tasks, there are only two types of memory: random-access memory (RAM) and read-only memory (ROM).

Random-access memory is necessary because the accounts payable program and data stored on your hard disk, for instance, cannot be used in that stored form. To run the program, it first must be read from the disk and copied into RAM. The same applies to the data. The copies loaded into RAM do all the work. The copies on your disk remain there undisturbed, until you save your updated data back to the disk. You need to store data and programs on the hard disk, because RAM is *volatile*, or temporary; load a program or data into RAM and it remains there until you shut off the power (or erase the program or the data). RAM and ROM are both measured in kilobytes (abbreviated K) and megabytes (abbreviated M). One kilobyte equals approximately 1,000 characters (letters or numbers), and one megabyte equals approximately 1,000,000 characters.

More RAM means more room for larger amounts of data and larger, more complex programs. For example, early versions of the IBM version of the WordPerfect word processing program ran in 192K of RAM, but Version 5.0 of the same program requires a minimum of 512K (although 640K is recommended). As RAM is occupied by ever-growing programs, the amount of memory remaining for data decreases.

How much RAM do you need? For DOS machines, 640K—the maximum—is virtually required. For OS/2, you need at least 2M, but 4M improves performance considerably. For the Macintosh, you need 1M at the minimum; 2M enables you to run System 7.0. You need 4M for superior performance.

Read-only memory is very different. Unlike RAM, which allows data to be written in and read from it, ROM chips are manufactured with permanent data or programs that remain intact even when the power is shut off. ROM is said to be *nonvolatile*. The programs contained in ROM assist the operating system software to communicate with the actual hardware of your system. For example, your accounting system may request the loading of a data file from disk. The operating system processes the request, but cannot directly communicate with the disk drive. A special program called the BIOS (Basic Input/Output System) gets the processed request from the operating system to the disk drive itself.

It's very unlikely that you need to be concerned with your computer's ROM.

Ports

To communicate with the surrounding world, your computer is equipped with a series of ports, jacks, or sockets that you can use to connect external devices. Your keyboard is attached to a keyboard port, and your monitor is attached to a display port. If you have a mouse, it, too, is plugged into a port.

Usually, however, *port* refers to the parallel or serial ports to which you connect printers, modems, external data storage devices, plotters, typesetters, and so on.

Parallel ports, called LPT1, LPT2, and so on, in the IBM-compatible world, carry that name because they can send eight bits of data simultaneously—eight separate wires carrying one bit each. Eight bits equal one byte, which is equivalent to a single character. Serial ports, on the other hand, must send one byte at a time over a single wire, hence the name *serial*.

Most of today's printers are configured for parallel operation. Parallel data transmission is faster than serial operation under normal operating circumstances, and parallel devices are much easier to install. Simply connect your parallel cable to the printer at one end and to the port at the other end. Once you tell your application program what brand and model of printer you are using, you can begin printing right away.

Serial ports are used for all other devices (and some printers, too). Equipment like modems and plotters require serial data. Configuring serial devices is more complicated than installing parallel devices. You need to provide several pieces of information to your application. In addition to the brand and model of the device, you must supply several other values. The speed at which your computer sends data to the port, called the baud rate, must be entered. You must enter the value for error-parity checking as even, odd, or none. The characteristics of the data itself require that you specify the number of stop bits (1 or 2) and the number of data bits (7 or 8). Finally, you may need to say whether the XON/XOFF communications protocol is to be used. The values that you enter for these parameters are always printed in the owner's manual for the piece of equipment you are connecting. Refer to the manual when configuring serial devices for your computer.

Storage Options

Without permanent storage, your computer is virtually useless. You need storage to save data (a memo, for instance) so that you can edit it a week later, and to store the program that you use to perform the editing. Technology doesn't stand still for long, and new storage devices with ever-increasing capacities seem to appear frequently.

Disk Drives

Where would you be without at least one disk drive? All the software you buy is furnished on disks, so you need a disk drive capable of reading the information stored on disks, as well as capable of writing updated information to your disks. Don't overlook the best feature of *floppy disks*: they're portable.

Two disk sizes are available for modern personal computers: 5 1/4-inch and 3 1/2-inch disks. The larger and older 5 1/4-inch size was popular with early Apple home computers and was adopted by IBM for its original PC line. The IBM machines use a double-sided, double-density disk that holds about 360,000 bytes (360K) of data. With the advent of IBM's AT computer, the company switched to double-sided, quad-density disks that hold 1.2M of data. Special quad-density disks are required, and disks using the 1.2M layout cannot be used in a machine that understands only 360K.

To complicate matters, IBM's PS/2 series of computers not only switched to 3 1/2-inch disks, but two densities were introduced here also: 720K for the models 25 and 30, and 1.44M for the models 50, 55, 60, 70, and 80.

The Macintosh environment shows a little more upward compatibility. From the beginning, Macintoshes have used the 3 1/2-inch disk format to the exclusion of all others. The first Macintoshes used single-sided, 400K drives, but with the Macintosh Plus came double-sided 800K drives (which could still read the older 400K disks). New on the scene is a high-density 1.4M drive that, in addition to being able to read 400K and 800K disks, also can read and write to MS-DOS format 3 1/2-inch disks.

The moral for you? Choose a disk format and stick with it. If you elect to go with IBM-compatible equipment, consider the 1.44M 3 1/2-inch drive as your standard. Fitting 1.44M on each disk means you have fewer disks to keep track of, and 3 1/2-inch disks in their hard plastic cases are far more durable than the older 5 1/4-inch floppy disks. One additional recommendation: consider equipping one of your IBM-compatible computers with both a 3 1/2-inch and 5 1/4-inch drive. Why? Because at some point you will need to exchange disks with clients who have only 5 1/4-inch disks and because you may buy a software package that is not yet available in the 3 1/2-inch size.

Hard Disk Drives

If the floppy disk represents portability at the expense of capacity, the *hard disk* (or *fixed disk*, as IBM calls it) is just the opposite. Like the floppy disk, a hard disk stores data, but it stores a lot of data. It is commonplace to see hard drives with a 60M (60,000,000 bytes) capacity installed in a PC. At mail-order prices, you can do that for well under $500.

Hard disk drives are almost always permanently installed in the computer. Because they use rigid aluminum or glass platters instead of thin sheets of mylar, they are far more durable than floppy disks. Their rigid construction makes them able to spin at higher speeds (3600 rpm versus 300 rpm for floppy disks) and therefore transfer data more quickly.

Here is an easy rule of thumb. Every computer you buy, unless it is for connection to a local area network, should be equipped with a hard disk. Especially in a business environment, there is no excuse for scrimping on disk storage. Computer life without hard disks is not fun.

If your computers are connected to a local area network, the network's central file server is the repository for all the network's data files. That being the case, there may be no need for a hard disk at each workstation computer. In fact, you can buy workstation PC's with no disk drives at all.

Like microprocessors, hard disks vary widely in their speed—some are sluggish, but others are lightning fast. The speed of a hard disk is determined by several factors, including the width of the data pathway linking the drive to the CPU and the speed of the disk's internal machinery.

For IBM-format computers, hard disks for 8088-based machines are limited to an 8-bit data pathway, rendering their performance sluggish at best. The 80286 and later chips employ a 16-bit pathway, resulting in considerably better performance.

The internal speed of hard disks is rated in several ways, but the most common measure is the time it takes the disk to access recorded data (the *access time*), which is measured in milliseconds (abbreviated ms). The lower the access time, the faster the drive. A drive with an access time of 60 ms is very slow; a drive with an access time of 20 ms is very fast, all other considerations being equal.

Beware of a computer "deal" in which the access time of the hard disk isn't specified. Many apparent "bargain" 286 and 386 machines saddle you with a sluggish disk drive, wiping out the speed benefits of the microprocessor.

Optical Drives

The advent of the audio compact disc (CD) has brought several new storage technologies to the computer world. You can buy discs called CD-ROMs (compact disc read-only memory) that are the same size as and look exactly like their audio counterpart. The ROM designation means that, like an audio CD, you can only read from these disks. Several companies now market CD-ROMs that contain huge databases of information. For example, the entire Grolier encyclopedia is available on a single CD-ROM disc.

Another technology is a disc called WORM (write once read mostly). With the proper drive and applications software, you can save data to these discs once. Data written to a WORM disc is permanent; it cannot be overwritten by other data. These discs are wonderful for periodic archival storage of your customer databases, month-ending data from your accounting system, and so on.

The newest, and most expensive (about $6,500), technology is the *rewriteable optical disc*. This is similar to a WORM, but it allows the optical disc to be used over and over, much like a standard floppy disk. With their 650M capacity (650,000,000 bytes!), these drives are used mostly for daily file backups in a local area network.

Tape Drives

Tape drives for the personal computing environment are like the cassette deck you have in your stereo system, except that special high-quality data cartridges which store up to 60M are used. Tape drives are commonly used for backing up data in a networking environment. Are you thinking about a network? Then you positively must plan for backing up all files at least once a day. For you, a tape drive is required equipment.

Display Monitors and Resolution

The earliest home computers did not use special display monitors; you simply connected the computer to your television set and played games to your heart's content. How things have changed! Today you start by choosing monochrome or color. But that's only the beginning.

In the IBM world, you can choose monochrome displays that render your data in either green or amber. You can add a display card to your computer that enables you to display monochrome graphic images (graphs, charts, and so on) in addition to the text-based data from your word processor or accounting program. Of course, you need programs that are capable of displaying graphics. Monochrome is quickly fading as color technology improves. In fact, most displays sold now are color. A significant exception to the rule lies in the realm of desktop publishing, where "paper-white" monitors—displays that show black text against a paper-white background—are increasingly common. After all, if you are designing text or graphics that is to be printed in black and white, it makes good sense to view a graphic representation of the page as it will appear when printed—and a paper-white monitor does precisely that.

You have good reason for choosing color, however, for business applications, apart from word processing or desktop publishing. At a point-of-sale or order entry terminal, your staff will find it helpful if on-screen headings and data fields are displayed in distinctive colors. The colors help guide the eye around the screen.

Choosing color for your IBM-compatible machine means still more decisions. Which standard should you choose? In 1981, IBM introduced the Color Graphics Adapter (CGA). *Adapter* refers to the video logic circuit board located in the computer. In 1984, CGA was succeeded by the Enhanced Graphics Adapter (EGA) and the Professional Graphics Adapter (PGA). EGA provided a crisper, higher-resolution image than the old CGA did and quickly became the new standard. PGA never caught on due to its expense. With the new PS/2 line in 1987 came another standard: Video Graphics Array (VGA). VGA provides yet better resolution and has emerged as the new standard.

> If you're buying an IBM-format computer, purchase a paper-white VGA display for desktop publishing or word processing. Purchase a color VGA display for database management, spreadsheet, and accounting applications.

With the arrival of "open architecture" Macintosh systems, such as the SE/30 and the Macintosh II, you have many display options. Standard Macintoshes use a crisp but small (9-inch diagonal measurement) paper-white monochrome display. With the SE/30 and Macintosh II, however, you can opt for a full-page or two-page paper-white display for desktop publishing or a 14-inch color display. Expect to pay about 30 to 40 percent more for Macintosh external displays and video cards than you would for their IBM-format counterparts.

Output Options

You cannot use information that you cannot see. Once you have entered data and your programs have processed that data into information, you need a way to view the results.

Although the video display qualifies as an output device, there are others, including printers, plotters, modems, and facsimile devices.

Printers

Not too many years ago, a parade of visionaries and futurists predicted the dawn of the "paperless society." Well, don't believe it for a minute! The type of printer (or printers) you choose depends on your printing requirements and your budget. Printers fall into three main categories: dot-matrix, daisywheel, and laser.

Dot-Matrix Printers

Dot-matrix printers use a series of thin wires (usually 9 or 24), arranged, more or less in a vertical column, to strike a ribbon, which, in turn, transfers ink onto the paper. As the printhead moves across the paper, only the pins necessary for a dot at a particular position are "fired." The resulting array of dots creates the printed characters on the page. Most dot-matrix printers are capable of delivering several modes of output, from high-speed, low-quality "draft" mode to low-speed, higher-quality "near letter-quality" mode.

Because dot-matrix printers use an impact technology, they are an excellent choice for forms that you print in duplicate or triplicate on carbonless paper. Dot-matrix printers are inexpensive: a good quality printer can be purchased for less than $500.

On the down side, the noise made by a dot-matrix printer can be very irritating. Consider an acoustic enclosure for your printer.

Daisywheel Printers

This type of printer is characterized by the molded plastic print wheel or thimble that contains a complete set of fully formed characters. The print wheel rotates to the proper position, where it is struck by a small metal plunger or hammer. The print wheel strikes the ribbon, which, in turn, transfers ink in the shape of the character to the paper. The result looks exactly as if it were typed on an electric typewriter.

Daisywheel printers, because they use fully formed characters, produce extremely high quality output that even today is preferred in many executive suites. They are excellent for multipart forms, but are extremely slow, very noisy, and have an unending appetite for ribbons. In addition, daisywheel printers can be expensive and are generally not capable of printing graphics images.

If a daisywheel printer is right for you, buy one now because their heyday has long since come and gone. As laser printers have dropped in price, so has the selection of daisywheel printers.

Laser Printers

Laser printers produce output so high in quality that it is commonly called "near-typeset." These devices print quickly, generate almost no noise, use standard 8 1/2-by-11-inch sheets of paper, and can even print envelopes. The variety of typefaces and sizes of type is seemingly endless.

Laser printers (and their cousins, the light-emitting diode printers) just about do it all. These printers, however, do have disadvantages that you should consider before making a major hardware investment.

Laser printers do not print with impact technology. As a result, they cannot print multipart forms. Neither can they accept continuous pin-fed forms. Also, if the software you use does not provide adequate support, your laser printer may produce strange or possibly no results.

For desktop publishing or other graphics-intensive applications, consider a laser printer that understands the Adobe PostScript page description language. PostScript-compatible software is capable of very complicated graphic effects and can scale text to any size or rotate it to any position. The Apple LaserWriter family of printers is one example of a PostScript-compatible device. For less complicated graphics or for standard text-based applications, the Hewlett-Packard laser printers, which employ HP-PCL (Hewlett-Packard Printer Control Language) should suffice. If in doubt about which you need, check the system requirements for all the software packages you plan to use. A PostScript-compatible printer generally costs $2,000 more than a similarly equipped non-PostScript compatible device.

Before forking over big bucks for a Macintosh PostScript printer, however, remember that Apple Computer sold off its stock in Adobe Systems (the creators of PostScript) and in mid-1989 announced that it would create its own "clone" of PostScript. In the meantime, the Macintosh's new operating system, System 7.0, includes system support for many PostScript-like features, making it possible to produce excellent-quality output on less expensive laser printers. In the Macintosh world, the future of PostScript is unclear at this writing, so exercise caution.

Plotters

A plotter is like an automated draftsman that can produce extremely accurate, multicolored, highly detailed technical plans and drawings. Many plotters support up to eight colors, which you choose by inserting different colored plotter pens into a holding device. Your software instructs the plotter to choose one of the pens, move to a specific location on the paper, and begin drawing.

If you choose a computer-aided drafting and design (CADD) software package, you need a plotter to produce your architectural drawings and plans. In addition, virtually all charting software (programs that create graphs from your data) support the use of plotters.

You are not limited to using paper in a plotter. You also can use a transparent drawing medium to create professional-looking overhead transparencies.

Plotters are expensive. Prices average around $1,500 for high-quality standard plotters to several thousand dollars for models that handle large sheets of paper.

Unless a plotter is a requirement for your business, consider this item to be a luxury.

Modems

Modems enable you to connect your computer to another computer over telephone lines. If you have equipped your computer with telecommunications software, you can access on-line database services, electronic mail services, and computer bulletin boards, and you can share data with other, similarly equipped computers.

As explained in the preceding chapter, telecommunications applications are of little business value unless they can be linked intelligently to an overall business strategy. On-line databases are useful if accessing them gives you time-sensitive information that you can use to profitable advantage. The hobbyist's services, such as The Source and CompuServe, however, are far more likely to become an unproductive drain on your resources than they are to increase your business's profitability, and the same goes for computer bulletin boards. Although you can obtain public domain software and shareware from bulletin boards, you also can buy it via mail order from a variety of mail-order ventures, all of which advertise in computer magazines.

> Stay away from telecommunications unless you can envision a specific application that will increase your business's profitability.

A Profitable Application of Telecommunications

One of the country's largest manufacturers of pharmaceuticals recently issued battery-powered laptop computers to its entire worldwide sales force. Each computer is equipped with a built-in modem. As each salesperson travels, notes from client meetings and purchase orders are typed into the computer. Each evening, the salesperson connects the computer to the telephone in his or her hotel room and transmits the day's data to the company's headquarters through a global electronic mail service. Nothing gets lost in the translation because there are no messages or purchase orders to be transcribed manually. The purchase order information is fed directly into the company's corporate mainframe order-processing system. Your business need not be a Fortune 500 company to employ an electronic mail system. Companies with as few as two employees can make excellent use of electronic mail.

A less well-known use for a modem is remote operation of a computer. Leave your office computer on overnight (you can turn off the display). If your office and home computers are connected by modem, you run programs on the office computer and view the results at home. You can even stay home and print reports on your office computer system.

Modems are rated in terms of how many bits per second (bps) they are designed to transmit. You see modems rated at 300, 1200, 2400, 4800, 9600 bps, and as high as 19.2K bps. The faster a modem can send, the more money it costs. Because modems are needed at both ends of the telephone line, your expensive 9600 bps modem is mostly wasted if the other modem cannot communicate faster than 1200 bps. Remember, too, that on-line database services charge premium prices for higher speed communication.

A faster modem is not always a good solution. If your telephone lines are noisy, you may encounter data transmission problems. To ensure error-free transmission, some modems use built-in hardware-based error checking such as Microcom Networking Protocol Class 5 (MNP), and all data communications software uses file-transfer protocols like XMODEM and Kermit to sense errors and retransmit garbled packets of data.

The 2400 bps modem costs only a few hundred dollars and is a good solution for businesses with moderate data communication requirements. Businesses with continuous high-volume requirements should consider 9600 bps modems. They cost more than a thousand dollars but can make quick work of your data communications tasks. Remember that you need a compatible 9600 bps modem at the other end.

Facsimile

Stand-alone facsimile (FAX) machines have taken the country by storm. With a FAX you can send virtually any paper image to anyone else with a FAX machine. Why use a thousand words when a picture will do?

FAX has arrived on the personal computer, too. You can use your computer in several ways to take advantage of FAX technology.

First, the major electronic-mail (E-mail) services, (MCI Mail, CompuServe, and so on) accept any ASCII text file (a file containing only printable characters) and route it to the FAX destination of your choice when you specify the FAX machine's phone number. This technique is a real time saver because you eliminate the need to print your document first. No special equipment other than your modem and subscription to an E-mail service is required. You pay a dollar or two for a standard eight-page transmission.

Other FAX techniques require the installation of a FAX board in your computer or a FAX server on your network. With a FAX board in your computer, not only can you send text files, but you can send almost any graphics image and also receive FAX messages sent to you. FAX documents you receive are stored on your hard disk for viewing or printing at your convenience. You don't need to walk down the hall to send or receive a FAX, and you don't even waste paper printing out an incoming FAX. A FAX server is similar to a FAX board, but the server supports any computer connected to the network and has additional capabilities to support directly the specialized file formats of many word processing and graphics programs. Plan to spend $600 to $1,000 for a FAX board and several thousand dollars for a FAX server.

If you want to FAX paper originals through your computer, you need to add a scanner (examined in the next section, "Input Options").

A FAX board in your computer can improve productivity if you buy the right type of board. Make sure that the board you are considering is capable of "background operation." In background operation, the software that controls your FAX board is loaded, but it sits dormant in the background while you run your word processor or accounting system. When an incoming FAX is detected, the program you are using may be put on hold while the FAX is being received. Tomorrow's more sophisticated multitasking system may be able to receive the FAX and continue your program simultaneously.

Input Options

Input is simply getting data *into* your computer. The most prominent of these methods is your keyboard. Other input options are also output devices (disks, tapes, modems, FAX) and have already been examined. What's left are the not-so-common alternative input technologies.

Mouse

Wouldn't it be nice if you could just point to an area of the display instead of pressing a series of keys to move the cursor? That is the idea behind the mouse, which was popularized by the Macintosh. The mouse is simply a pointing device that consists of a rolling ball encased in a plastic case, connected via cable to the computer. An alternative mouse technology reduces the number of moving parts by employing a pair of light emitting diodes instead of the rolling ball. You move the cursor on-screen by moving the mouse across your desk.

The mouse that comes with the Macintosh has a single button on top of the housing. You choose options in your program by pressing the button once (called *clicking*) or two times in quick succession (*double-clicking*). Mice for the IBM have either two or three buttons.

All Macintosh software uses the mouse. Choosing a mouse for IBM-compatible computers is completely optional, but as more graphical interface-based software becomes available, the need for a mouse will become almost mandatory. If you plan to stick with text-based business software, a mouse is unnecessary. Mouse prices are generally between $100 and $200.

If desk space is too precious, consider the trackball, a cousin to the mouse. A trackball is like an upside mouse—the plastic housing is stationary but the large upward-facing ball is designed to be manipulated directly by your fingers. Buttons on the trackball housing enable you to click menu choices on the screen.

Scanners

Suppose that you are producing a newsletter and you want to include a photograph of your employee of the month. You could print a single copy of the newsletter and take it, along with the photograph, to a print shop. The printer would make printing plates and then print your newsletter on an offset press. You achieve the highest production quality this way, but the cost is also comparatively high, and you may have to a wait a week for the job to be completed.

Now imagine that your office is equipped with a scanner, a device similar to your office copier. The scanner translates your original photograph into a special file format on your hard disk instead of making copies on sheets of paper.

A scanner is convenient, but it will set you back around $2,000 and can be temperamental with photographs that contain a wide range of shades between bright white and solid black. The best use for a scanner is to create graphics files that you subsequently manipulate with other software to fine-tune the image. Products for the Macintosh, like Digital Darkroom from Silicon Beach Software, can combine elements from different photographs, change shading and contrast, and move objects to create different perspectives. Although some results of these capabilities may be unethical in journalism (like photos of couples in the supermarket tabloids that never actually met each other), scanners may be exactly what the doctor ordered for an advertising agency doing creative work.

Sharing Peripherals

Laser printers are expensive. Their prices range from $1,800 to more than $10,000, depending on capabilities. Sharing a laser printer among several computers is a far more cost-effective solution than purchasing one for each computer. Consider just how often a printer connected to one computer is actually in use. The printer is probably idle most of the time.

Solutions for sharing peripheral devices (printers, modems, and so forth) abound. They range from expensive (a local area network) to somewhat inexpensive (software-controlled switchboxes that queue print jobs) to very inexpensive (manual switchboxes and several connecting cables).

Choose the solutions that provide the best payback according to your requirements. If your overall solution includes connecting your computers together through a local area network, then you simply connect the printer (or other peripheral device) to the network. On the other hand, if you are installing two computers for just word processing, a manual switchbox placed between the two computers suffices. Although a switchbox solution may be frowned upon as archaic and low-tech, you sleep well at night, comfortable with the knowledge that you provided a total solution at bargain basement prices.

Multiuser Terms

Although it may be true that no man is an island, it was not too long ago that personal computers *were* an island unto themselves. Everyone has seen it: two people need to use the same word processing document, so they run back and forth from desk to desk carrying disks. This method was the earliest form of personal computer networking, dubbed "sneaker-net" by one wag.

The industry has come a long, long way since sneaker-net. Today, personal computers talk not only to each other, but also to minicomputers and mainframes, as well.

Local Area Networks

A local area network is a method of connecting several personal computers. (Local area networks are discussed in-depth earlier in this chapter.) With appropriate networking software, you can even connect IBM-compatible PCs to Macintoshes. The idea behind local area networking is to make the same set of data available to all authorized persons in order to avoid data redundancy, and, what is often a greater concern, to prevent several sets of the same data from becoming dissimilar.

Many pieces must come together for a network to function properly. These pieces include the individual computers (called *workstations* or *clients* in a networking environment), servers, the cabling system, the network operating system software, and the application software.

Once your network is running, you need someone to perform administrative tasks, such as adding and deleting users, assigning user passwords, and performing general housekeeping (keeping hard disks from becoming cluttered with unused files, for instance).

Installing a local area network is a job that you should not undertake on your own. Seek the expertise of someone *authorized* by the manufacturer of the network operating system.

Servers

The server is either a specially configured personal computer or a proprietary machine that operates as the heart of the network. The server is the central repository for all data files and program files. The network operating system software is kept on the server. The server is equipped with high-capacity hard disks (a minimum of 150M is usually recommended) and a huge amount of RAM (at least 4M, although your software will love you if you install 16M). The server controls all network activity, including the loading of individual applications (like your accounting package) and directing print jobs to any printer you indicate.

Workstations

As mentioned previously, the individual computers connected to the network are called workstations or clients. More and more, workstations are equipped with no disk drives at all. This configuration gives the user full personal computing power, but withholds the means to copy sensitive or confidential files from the network to a disk that may "walk" out the door. If security is a concern, consider diskless workstations.

Network Operating Systems

The network operating system is the software that enables communications between the various components connected to the network. The network operating system controls the security of files and the overall operation of the network.

Network operating systems actually have two parts. First is the operating system itself, which is loaded on the server. Sometimes this software runs in conjunction with the regular operating system (DOS or OS/2 for IBM-compatible PCs), as in the case of 3+ Open (3Com Corporation), and sometimes this software completely replaces the standard operating system, as in the case of NetWare (Novell Corporation) or VINES (Banyan Systems). For the Macintosh, the major players are TOPS (Sun Microsystems) and AppleTalk (Apple). Novell supports Macintosh connectivity within IBM-compatible local area networks.

The second piece of the network operating system is a small program, or "shell," that is resident in the individual personal computer workstations. This program, which you load after loading the regular operating system (DOS or OS/2 for IBM PCs), provides the remainder of the link among the devices connected to the network.

Some network operating systems provide *fault tolerance*, a mechanism that stores two copies of every file in different locations to protect against hardware failure. Fault tolerance is recommended for so-called *mission-critical applications*, those without which the business would come to an immediate halt.

Network operating system software is expensive. Depending on the capacities (number of workstations, total disk capacity), security features, fault-tolerance mechanisms, and operating characteristics, you can pay anywhere from $1,500 to $10,000.

Cabling

Although wireless networks are just beginning to appear, virtually 100 percent of network installations use various types of cabling to connect all the network devices.

Ethernet, Arcnet, token-ring, and StarLan are common types of cabling arrangements. Each arrangement, sometimes called a *topology*, has its own advantages as well as shortcomings. This book lacks the space for a detailed analysis of topologies, and your business may be suited for one topology over another. This choice is another reason for finding a consultant who specializes in local area networks. For more information on networking computers, refer to Que Corporation's *Networking Personal Computers*, 3rd Edition, by Michael Durr and Mark Gibbs.

Here's an extra hint: local area network experts usually do not work for a storefront retail operation. You find these experts situated in office building suites or industrial parks. Why? The storefront retailer is more concerned with "pushing boxes"— selling computers. The nonstorefront local area networking expert specializes in getting those boxes to *interoperate*, that is, to talk to each other.

Network Adapter Cards

Like any other device to which you connect your computer, the network cable must have a port to which it can be attached. Making this connection requires a special circuit board called the *network adapter card*. Different cards are required for different topologies (Ethernet, token-ring, and so on) and different variations are used, depending on your computer. The PC and XT use one card, the AT uses another, and the PS/2 still another. Every workstation requires one card and the server requires one or more, depending on the total number of workstations being connected. Plan to spend about $500 per card.

Accessories

Do you remember buying your last new car? Did you settle for the stripped-down basic model, or did you load it with options? Computer systems are no different—there are plenty of accessories to complement your basic shopping list.

Surge Protectors

Surge protectors protect your equipment from sudden voltage surges in the electricity supplied to your business. A common occurrence, most voltage surges are too small to have any effect on your equipment. But if the "big one" hits, it could fry the delicate electronic components that populate the many circuit boards in your system. Lightning storms are a frequent cause of voltage surges, as is the period when power is restored following a total outage.

The surge protector contains circuitry designed to "smooth out" these momentary peaks. Plan to pay just under $100 for a surge protector.

Cables

Cables aren't glamorous, but they certainly are necessary. You need cables to connect printers, modems, external disk drives, plotters, and other peripheral devices to your computer. Some computer retailers toss in cables for free, whereas others charge for them.

Even though cables are inexpensive ($15–$50), buy the best quality you can find. Cables labeled *shielded* contain a metallic inner wrap that protects the cable from electromagnetic interference that may corrupt data as it travels through the cable.

Cables are equipped with different connectors, depending on the peripheral device and computer port to which they are being connected. Serial ports (those used for modems, plotters, and some printers) require either a 9-pin or 25-pin D-shaped connector at the computer and a 25-pin connector at the device. Cables for printers connected to a parallel port use a 25-pin connector at the computer and a 36-pin Centronics connector at the printer end.

Cabling for a local area network is in a different league. Depending on your requirements and your physical plant, a consultant runs either special cable or uses the same *unshielded twisted pair* cabling that your telephone system uses. Again, there is no right or wrong choice; every situation calls for an on-site decision by a qualified professional.

Switch Boxes and Buffers

Suppose that your business computing requirements are modest—two computers and one laser printer—and that the work to be done is a combination of word processing and accounting. Wouldn't it be nice if the two computers could share the printer without resorting to the high expense of a network? It can be done, and it can be done very inexpensively.

A switchbox costing about $25 is the budget-minded solution. Connect cables from each computer to the switchbox and then a single cable from the switchbox to the printer. Simply turn the switchbox's dial to *A* or *B* to indicate which computer you want to print from. For about $75 you can buy a switchbox that lets you connect up to four computers to a single peripheral device. (It could be a modem instead of a printer.) The only problem is that whoever is about to print needs to check with everyone else to make sure that it is all right to turn the dial, lest another print job be interrupted. Virtually every computer supply mail-order catalog offers a selection of switchboxes.

The next step up the ladder is so-called smart switchboxes, which are equipped with RAM. These devices, sometimes called buffers (because they act as a buffer zone between the computers and printer), sense when a computer is attempting to send a print job to the printer. If the printer is available, the job prints immediately. But if the printer is in use, the new print job is sent to the device's built-in RAM. When the printer becomes available, the stored (or buffered) print job is released to the printer. Depending on the amount of built-in RAM and the number of ports for computer connections, you can pay from $500 to $2,000 for this type of switchbox. Most mail-order catalogs offer these devices. Another product worth investigating is the $700 Logical Connection from Fifth Generation Systems.

How To Talk to a Salesperson about Hardware

Although it's probably not true that today's computer salespeople were yesterday's automobile salespeople, most people shopping for a computer act as if that were the case. You need to be prepared when you go out looking for your computer system.

When you shop for hardware, you should be prepared to discuss your requirements in detail with the salesperson. It isn't enough to say that you want "a computer for the office." The salesperson needs to know what applications you intend to run, whether you need a color display, and how much money you are willing to spend. Additionally, you should explain your data communications or networking needs, your printing, disk storage, and backup requirements, and the type of physical environment where the equipment will be installed. The last point is important, because equipment designed for office use may not be appropriate for use on a shop floor.

Mark and Marian developed, with the help of their consultant, a written list of hardware requirements that provided the information needed by the salesperson. Figure 5.3 shows their list of hardware requirements.

Number of computers: 5; 4 as workstations, 1 as a local area network server. (3 workstations will be deployed on the sales floor, 1 will be in Mark and Marian's private office)

Monitors: color on the workstations, monochrome on the server

Applications: word processing, accounting, custom order-entry system. All programs will be network versions.

Special equipment: bar code readers for 3 workstations, bar code printer at 1 workstation, cash drawer at 3 workstations

Disk Storage: 3 workstations require no disk storage, 1 workstation (the one in Mark and Marian's office) should have hard disk and floppy disk drives as an alternative to the server. The server should have a high-capacity drive to store all programs and associated data for all users.

Tape Backup: A tape backup device should be located at the server for daily backup of the hard disk drive.

Printers: Dot-matrix printers at each workstation to print multipart customer receipts, a dot-matrix printer in Mark and Marian's office to print multipart purchase orders, one laser printer (to be installed in a location to be determined) for printing high-quality correspondence and bar code labels.

Networking: All devices should be linked in a local area network that will allow for additional workstations, hard disk capacity, printers, and other peripheral devices as dictated by company growth.

Communications: The computer in Mark and Marian's office should be equipped with a modem.

Other: The server should be equipped with an uninterruptible power supply. All workstations should be equipped with surge suppressors.

Environment: All devices will be installed in a retail store that is air conditioned and kept dust-free. Network cabling can be run inside the suspended ceiling. The network server will be in a locked office.

Fig. 5.3. *Mark and Marian's hardware requirements list.*

With this detailed list in hand, Mark and Marian are able to anticipate the questions that salespersons ask. It's also less likely that Mark and Marian will be talked into purchasing equipment they do not need.

Note what is omitted: there is no mention at all of the hardware platform or brand of computer. Remember, your selection of software dictates whether you go with Macintosh, IBM compatible, or other hardware platform.

As in shopping for software, do not be tempted to make a purchase on your first visit to a retailer. Visit several dealers— traditional storefront retail operations and nonstorefront value-added resellers (VARs). Though price is certainly an important factor, seek a supplier that provides knowledgeable pre- and post-sales support.

> A rock-bottom price with no technical support may be far more expensive in the long run than a more expensive model with technical support.

Starting Small with Hardware

"Starting small" means deploying only the equipment you actually need to get started with the computerization process.

Mark and Marian, whose bed and bath business has been followed through this book, decided to computerize only the Custom Orders department and wait several months before proceeding to the inventory portion of the business. Their decision is appropriate for the following reasons:

- First, installing one facet of the overall solution significantly lowers the initial capital outlay—less equipment bought is a lesser expense.

- Second, concentrating on a single aspect of the business prevents Mark and Marian from diluting their efforts or otherwise spreading themselves too thin.

Sample Configurations

The configurations presented in this section are suggestions that you can use as starting points. Your business may require a larger or smaller configuration. These suggested setups overlap—no matter what business you are in you probably want word processing software.

A Retail Store Configuration

For a retail store, you can configure a personal computer with a cash drawer, customer display, and bar code reader for use as a point-of-sale (POS) terminal. With appropriate software, this setup can record all sales transactions and consolidate the data on a daily, weekly, monthly, or other periodic basis for reporting purposes.

If your store requires several POS terminals, you can connect them in a local area network so that data collected by any individual terminal is stored in the network's central server.

For daily backup of your files, a streaming tape drive installed at the server is essential. This device, which uses special tape cartridges slightly larger than a standard audio cassette, is life insurance for your data. Rotate daily backups over at least eight cassettes so that a minimum of one week's worth of data is always available in case a catastrophic failure demands restoration of data. Keep these backups in a safe place away from your computer. After all, if a water pipe bursts and destroys your computers and your backups, you have nothing with which to carry on your recordkeeping.

An Accounting Office Configuration

With more than 300 accounting software packages on the market, you should have little difficulty finding a solution compatible with your business. The hardware approach you choose becomes an important factor in the success of your project.

Whether you select the IBM or Macintosh environment, pay particular attention to the ways in which you handle data. Consider connecting all your computers together in a local area network so that files can be shared among appropriate employees. With all data files centrally stored on a network server, sharing, security, and the critical daily backup process are more easily managed.

To ensure the security of your data, consider deploying diskless workstations, essentially computers with no disk drive at all. With no disk drive available, individual employees cannot copy sensitive data to disks.

Accounting offices generally install a laser printer for preparation of reports and tax forms, but also require a printer capable of handling multipart continuous forms, such as W-2 Wage and Tax Statements. An accounting office can perform daily file backups with the procedures and equipment described in the preceding retail store configuration.

A Word Processing Configuration

Word processing is the most ubiquitous of all personal computing applications and is involved in more than 85 percent of all PC use. Almost every business can improve productivity with the addition of a computer for word processing.

You need not start big to achieve the productivity gains that word processing software offers. One computer equipped with a hard disk and a monochrome monitor provides sufficient capabilities for most common business writing. Depending on your budget and the quality of output required, you can print your documents on a dot-matrix, daisywheel, or laser printer.

The entire manuscript for this book was written on an IBM PC XT (purchased in 1984 and still running strong, although generally said to be obsolete), using WordPerfect Corporation's WordPerfect software and printed on a Hewlett-Packard LaserJet Series II laser printer.

A Spreadsheet Configuration

Use spreadsheet software to perform analyses of numeric data or to create budgets that you can modify easily, with the results displayed immediately.

The computer system described in the word processing configuration works equally well for average spreadsheet requirements. For very large spreadsheets, and depending on the software you use, additional RAM may be required.

A Desktop Publishing Configuration

Desktop publishing is a market carved out and defined by the Apple Macintosh, which still claims the lion's share of professional level publishing and related software. Although software products for the IBM environment continue to come to market, the breadth of Macintosh-compatible software makes the Macintosh the hands-down winner.

A high-end single-user system typically consists of the Macintosh II computer equipped with an oversize display for previewing full pages. Depending on the kind of work you do, you select various types of software: word processing to create your text, illustration to create complex drawings, and page layout software to put it all together. You need a library of Postscript-compatible fonts and a laser printer or typesetter for generating camera-ready output. If you work in color, you need programs that support either the CMYK (cyan, magenta, yellow, black) or Pantone PMS color matching systems. You need a scanner and appropriate software if you plan to include photographs in your work. In addition, you can buy utility software that kerns (adjusts space between characters) type for a pleasing appearance or produces special effects like shadowing or stretching lines of type. Of course, you need accounting software to keep track of your business.

Environmental Considerations

The physical setup of your computer is important for the well-being of both your employees and the computer equipment. The wrong environment can make it difficult for your employees to see the computer screen clearly, a situation that can contribute to eyestrain and fatigue in the computer operator. A dusty or poorly ventilated environment severely shortens the life of your computing equipment. You must provide the proper working conditions for your staff and your equipment—both will serve you better in the long run. Consider the following environmental specifics.

Furniture

Although you are correct in concluding that furniture does not make or break your project, you should pay a certain amount of attention to the special requirements of your employees.

Working Surface

Desks and tables are generally too high for comfortable computer operation. As a rule of thumb, the computer operator's arms should be parallel to the floor when typing. Inexpensive computer desks are available at many office supply houses and furniture stores. Depending on style, size, and finish, prices range from fifty dollars to several hundred dollars.

Chair

Your back takes a great deal of punishment when you are sitting at a keyboard for long periods of time. Invest in a chair that provides proper lumbar support for your computer operator's lower back. Most of the companies that manufacture office seating have adjustable chairs for just this purpose. Your staff will be forever grateful. Better yet, let the person using the chair pick it out. Be prepared to spend $200 to $400.

Electrical Concerns

You cannot do business with a computer unless you are sure power will *never* be interrupted. Power surges and failures can have catastrophic consequences if you don't protect your system.

Power

Today's more powerful desktop computers need to be supplied with adequate power to ensure proper operation. Ideally, you should have your computer equipment on a separate 20 ampere circuit breaker, but this is not a requirement. Be sure not to use equipment that causes electrical interference on the same circuit as your computing equipment. Such equipment usually contains electric motors; drills and vacuum cleaners are common examples.

Surge Protection

One absolute requirement is to protect your equipment from momentary electrical surges with a surge protector, a device that plugs into a power outlet. A lightning strike to a power transmission line can cause electrical surges powerful enough to destroy your computer's delicate electronic components. The cost of a surge protector, typically less than $100, is a small price to pay for such important protection.

Uninterruptible Power Supply

What happens when the power fails? Without electricity, any data stored in your computer's memory is lost. Files on your disk in the process of being updated may be corrupted beyond repair. The only sure-fire way to protect against power loss is with an uninterruptible power supply (UPS). A UPS is essentially a battery backup for your computer that provides enough power (10 to 15 minutes) to let you perform an orderly shutdown of the system, including closing all files and exiting from any programs currently in use. A UPS is like buying life insurance for your business—you hope that you never need to use it, but it is always there just in case.

> A UPS is not designed to allow continued operation for extended periods of time.

Individual computers performing noncritical operations like word processing do not need UPS protection, but individual machines working with data critical to the business (mission-critical data) should be protected. If you connect several computers together in a network, it is imperative that you provide protection to the file server, because it acts as the central data repository for all computers on the network. Depending on the amount of power needed (in watts) and the length of service (in minutes) you require, the cost of a UPS for desktop-size computers can vary from a few hundred dollars to about $1,500. If that sounds like too much money, compare it to the several hundred thousand dollars a UPS for a corporate mainframe can cost.

HVAC Concerns

Treat your computer equipment as you would treat your employees—the heating, ventilating, and air conditioning (HVAC) requirements are about the same. Too high or too low a temperature shortens the life of electronic equipment, as does too little or too much humidity. Avoid high humidity, long periods of time with temperatures over 80F, and, most importantly, never use computer equipment designed for office use in a dirty or dusty environment. Keep a small vacuum handy and use it often on keyboards and ventilation louvers.

Lighting

Situate your computer screen to prevent glare from fluorescent light reflection on the screen. Indirect even lighting is best for general computer use. You also should provide additional task lighting for the paperwork that your computer operator handles.

If screen glare cannot be eliminated, consider purchasing a glare screen. A specially treated glass or mesh overlay for your computer screen, glare screens cut glare and improve contrast. Just about all the mail-order computer supply houses stock a selection of glare screens for about $100.

Static Control

Humidity that is too low also can cause problems. A jolt of static electricity can corrupt data stored on disks or tape and can destroy the processing and memory chips inside your computer. If you live in a cold winter climate and you create static electricity sparks by touching metal after walking across a carpet, then you should raise the humidity by installing a humidifier. Keep the humidifier's mist away from the computer equipment, however—the idea is to raise to overall humidity, not to get the equipment wet. You also can purchase special desktop mats (about $40) that safely discharge static electricity when touched.

Sound Control

Today's computers are reasonably quiet; it's the printers that make all the racket. Dot-matrix and daisywheel (typewriter-like) printers print by striking a ribbon with either a series of metal pins or a printwheel. Both are extremely noisy and irritating. Put these printers in an acoustic enclosure designed for cutting down on printer noise. Depending on your printer's size, plan to spend from $100 to $250 for an enclosure. Laser printers generate virtually no noise. If your budget and the tasks you are automating allow, a laser is the best way to go.

Workspace Considerations

People need to work. Allow enough desk space for working papers to be spread out. Skimping on desk space can reduce productivity by forcing the operator to juggle paperwork, inevitably resulting in errors.

Traditional personal computers place everything on the desktop: keyboard, monitor, and central processing unit. Some newer systems use a "tower" design in which the central processor is housed in a floor-mounted, upright cabinet. Tower systems have both pros and cons.

The tower can free up valuable desktop real estate for other uses and sometimes simplify running cables. On the down side, towers are more expensive and do not necessarily provide additional functionality. They may be kicked and may pick up dust and dirt from the floor. The recommendation? Buy a floor-mount system when it is the only machine that will do the job. Otherwise, stick with the desktop models.

Chapter Summary

This chapter covered a great deal of territory. In this survey of hardware, you learned the difference between hardware and software. Next you learned about hardware platforms, which are the different types of personal computers that might address your specific business requirements. Along with hardware platforms, you read about the operating system software without which your computer can do very little. Then you took a tour of many of the hardware components that, when taken together, constitute a working personal computer. These components include the microprocessor, two kinds of memory, and three kinds of disk drives and tape drives for data storage. You learned about display options, and output options, including several types of printers, plotters, FAX devices, and modems. A brief discussion of input options led to a close-up look at local area networking, including servers, workstations, network operating systems, cabling, and adapter cards. An overview of accessories and switching devices rounded out the tour.

Finally, armed with this information, you developed a list of hardware requirements for your business and learned how to use that list to communicate effectively with a computer salesperson.

You learned how hardware can be adapted to several different purposes, and you learned how to shape the computer's environment so that the computers stay in good working order.

If all the information in the previous chapters seems overwhelming, you have plenty of company. That's the reason many business people turn to consultants at this point. The next chapter shows you how to obtain the help you need if you cannot go it alone.

CHAPTER 6

Getting Help from a Consultant

No one is an expert at everything.

Would you computerize a dairy farm? No? Well, think again. Agribusiness automation is a fast-growing segment of the vertical market software industry. To understand the farm's financial position at any moment, the dairy farmer must know how much feed each cow consumes in relation to the amount of milk produced, be able track the actual milk production of each cow, control inventories of feed, schedule milking times, and much more. When the dairy farming industry discovered that computerization can lead to better herd management and, ultimately, increased profits, the need for the dairy farming consultant was born.

What Can a Consultant Bring to the Project?

Everyone is a consultant of sorts. The customers in Mark and Marian's bed and bath accessories store seek their advice 20, 30, or more times per day. Do those customers pay for that advice? You bet they do! The cost of that advice is built into the prices of the products sold in the store. Just what is a consultant?

> A consultant is a person who sells experience, advice, or service in a specific field, industry, or other area.

A consultant brings with him or her a successful track record for the specific tasks you are undertaking.

Where To Find a Consultant

Consultants abound. After all, everyone loves spending someone else's money. (The authors can say this—they, too, are consultants.) Because you are the person seeking expert advice, you need to separate the wheat from the chaff and find the one consultant perfect for both you and your business.

The local Yellow Pages is not the place to go to find a consultant. Where do you look?

- *Trade Groups*. Every industry has trade organizations. For retailers, it's the New York City-based National Retail Merchants Association; for attorneys, it's the American Bar Association. Organizations of this type maintain lists of consultants for referral purposes. Your membership in a trade group usually guarantees you access to these lists at no charge. Keep in mind that the consultants listed in these referral services have probably paid a fee to the trade organization in exchange for the listing and any referrals generated by the listing. That situation is not bad, but it does mean that the names you receive may not include all consultants in your geographic area.

- *Trade Shows and Conventions*. Just about any business can find a trade show or seminar series that relates to the business. If you own a shoe store, you probably travel to the National Shoe Fair of America. Dentists in the northeast can visit the Yankee Dental Conference each January. Even the American Bar Association holds an annual convention.

  Trade shows are an excellent place to find products and consultants. Representatives of hardware and software firms usually are spread throughout the exhibition space.

- *Trade Publications*. If you own an office supply business, you read *Modern Office Technology* or *Office Products Dealer*; if you are in the telemarketing business, you read *Inbound/Outbound*. Trade magazines like these are good places to find advertisements for computer systems and consultants.

- *User Groups*. Join a club. In New England, the Boston Computer Society sponsors special interest groups (SIGs) for people involved in the legal, accounting, retail, real estate, medical/dental, church/synagogue, desktop publishing, construction, and even consulting professions. A club may be where you find the motherlode. Go to a meeting and listen; it will not take long to find out who is worth consideration.

- *Your Competition*. Perhaps others in your line of business have computerized already. Everyone enjoys showing off a new system and your competitors are no different. Remember, though, that you are there to observe, not to gain an unfair advantage.

- *Advertising.* You may see advertisements for consultants in the business section of your Sunday paper or you may receive a direct mailing. Although consultants who advertise should not be disparaged, most consultants find that business comes to them in the form of referrals.

Evaluating a Prospective Consultant

Before you place your future in the hands of a total stranger, be sure to do your homework.

- *Look at a number of candidates.* Consider evaluating more than one consultant. You may find that each consultant, although expert in your industry, carries a different mix of skills, but only one expert is a match for your particular business. Finding a consultant does not cost money, so it makes good sense to examine several possibilities.

- *Get a resume.* The prospective consultant should be prepared to discuss his or her employment history. Where has the consultant worked? Are the skills learned at those companies transferable to your project and your business? Why did the consultant leave his or her employer and start a consulting practice? If the answer is "because I couldn't get along my boss," then find yourself another consultant. After all, for this project you are the boss.

- *Get a list of clients.* Whom has this consultant consulted? Your candidate should provide a complete list of clients (excluding only those who decline to be listed), along with dates, the scope of the work performed, and the client's name and phone number. Call as many of these references as possible. Even though the names were provided by the consultant, you will be amazed at how candid some of these clients can be. Ask what was done, whether it was completed on time and within budget. Find out what the client liked and disliked about the consultant. Ask to visit a former client's site to see first-hand what the consultant accomplished. Most important, ask "Would you hire this consultant again?"

- *Interview the prospective consultant.* Although most consultants offer a no-cost initial consultation, make it clear that you are conducting a search for a consultant and that this meeting does not constitute the initial consultation. Interview the candidate as you would a prospective employee. Determine whether you can get along with each other on a personal level. After all, the greatest consultant in the world does you no good if you intensely dislike each other. Ask about business philosophies. Does the candidate subscribe to your business theories? Opinions that differ from yours can help to shed new light, but don't hire a consultant with whom you violently disagree.

After you have completed the evaluation process, you are ready to hire your consultant.

How To Hire a Consultant

The golden rule of hiring a consultant is, *Get It In Writing.* You must have a legally binding contract with your consultant, that spells out precisely what will be done, who will do it, when it will be finished, how much it will cost, what happens if it costs more than planned, and what to do if it does not work.

> Always negotiate a written, legally binding contract with your consultant.

What You Can Expect To Pay a Consultant

Consultants usually charge by the hour and the prices vary widely. Factors that determine pricing include location (a New York consultant charges more than a similar consultant in Montana), the scope and complexity of the work being undertaken by the consultant, and the consultant's need to show a profit based on his or her overhead (rent, salaries). In major metropolitan areas you should be prepared to pay from $75 to $150 per hour for consulting fees, plus expenses.

Negotiating a Consulting Contract

A contract is an agreement between two or more parties, that is enforceable by law. Your contract must be in writing and signed by an authorized agent of your business and the consultant.

Negotiating a contract is no place to save a few dollars. Your attorney should be fully involved in the process.

Execute at least three copies of the contract: one for you, one for your attorney, and one for the consultant.

Because the consultant has been through the negotiating process many times, he or she has an advantage. In fact, you should expect the consultant to provide a contract that you can use as a basis for negotiations. That sample contract should never be signed—remember, it was written by the consultant to favor the consultant. Strive for a balance of protections and benefits for all parties.

> Use the contract presented by the consultant as a starting point for negotiations. It was not meant to be signed by you.

The contract should spell out, in detail, what work is to be performed, the deliverables (reports, for instance), the fees and payment schedule, and penalties if any aspect of the contract is not kept.

A sample contract for consulting services can be found in Appendix B.

Managing a Consultant

When you hire a consultant, you are the boss, the consultant is not. Because the consultant is essentially an employee, he or she must be managed as you would manage anyone else. Managing your consultant is critical to getting the job done.

Require a periodic status report from your consultant. This written report should tell you what the consultant did during the reporting period and is so important that it should be a contractual requirement. The report should explain, in detail, what activities were performed, the dates and amount of time expended, and people with whom the consultant talked. The report should also indicate the planned activities for the next reporting period.

If you have questions regarding anything in the report, hold a private meeting with the consultant to learn the details. Remember, though, that the consultant's meter will be running.

You also need to be aware of issues or questions that arise during the course of the consultant's research. Some consultants prefer to discuss issues in person, others prefer to write a memo, and still others include issues in the status report. The preferred method is to write a separate but brief memo about each issue, because you want to document everything done by the consultant. Keep yourself available for discussion, too—the consultant needs timely answers to important questions.

Getting a Second Opinion

If your physician diagnoses a severe illness and counsels a major operation, you get a second opinion. Why not do the same with the advice you're getting from a consultant? After all, it's your business that's at stake. Although it's not much fun to think about, many physicians perform unnecessary operations—and many consultants recommend unnecessarily complex or expensive computer solutions. When your consultant has given you a complete proposal, take it to another consultant—or someone whose technical expertise you have reason to trust—and ask for critical feedback. Then go back to the original consultant and ask for justification for his or her approach. If you don't find the response convincing, it's time to change consultants.

Custom Software Developers

If both you and the experts with whom you are working (consultant, computer salesperson or dealer, and so forth) all agree, after conducting an exhaustive search, that no prepackaged software solution meets your business requirements, three alternatives exist: you can (1) modify your requirements, (2) purchase software that includes the program listings (source code) so that you can hire programmers to make changes, or (3) contract for a custom-developed system. The trade-off is simple: spend less money and get a system that may be a less-than-perfect fit, spend a great deal of money and get a one-of-a-kind, custom-developed system, or find a solution somewhere in between.

In Chapter 1, you saw a figure that related risk and payoff. You learned that low risk and high payoff is far more desirable than high risk and low payoff. You also saw that high risk and high payoff could be the road to ultimate success. A similar scenario works for software (see fig. 6.1).

Cost			
	Section 2 High cost Poor fit	*Section 4* High cost Good fit	*Section 6* High cost Excellent fit
	Section 1 Low cost Poor fit	*Section 3* Low cost Good fit	*Section 5* Low cost Excellent fit
		Fit	

Fig. 6.1. *Graph plotting software costs and fitness for use.*

Section 1 shows a low-cost/poor fit scenario. Would you purchase a complete accounting system for $59 if it did not fit your business? Of course not. Software that is incompatible with your business should be avoided no matter how much of a bargain it might be.

Section 2 shows the worst of all possible scenarios: spending a great deal of money for an improper software solution. It's doubtful anyone would pay $5,000 for an accounting system that doesn't fit his or her business.

Section 3—finally, a reasonable alternative! If that $59 accounting system meets 85 percent of your business needs, it deserves serious consideration. Ask yourself how much more you would be willing to pay for the 15 percent functionality this particular solution does not provide. If you are willing to pay much more for the 15 percent, you fall into section 6 of this chart.

Section 4, high cost with only a good fit, shows no more reasonable a solution than did section 2. If you plan to spend a great deal of money, you should expect a solution tailored to fit your business.

Section 5, of course, is the best of all worlds: a low-cost solution that is an excellent fit for your business. If the $59 accounting system meets 99 percent of your needs, you ought to stop there. Remember the price/performance ratio? You will never get more "bang for the buck!"

Section 6 is the solution of last resort. Come here only when no other solution can be found. Here you find either large, complex, software solutions that meet all your business needs, or one-of-a-kind, custom-developed software solutions.

Getting Help from Programmers

If a custom software solution is what you need, programmers to design the system and then write the software become part of your project team. Ask your consultant to provide a list of programmers who have done similar work in the past, and make sure that you see these systems in operation and talk with the people who use those systems.

You are better off letting your consultant hire the programmers after you indicate the acceptable choices, for several reasons. First, the programmers become the consultant's responsibility, not yours. You still have a business to run, and managing another group of outsiders only causes more distractions. Second, a contract between your consultant and the programmers, because of the consultant's knowledge, tends to place more stringent performance requirements on the programmers than you might stipulate yourself. Third, and perhaps most important, your consultant remains responsible for all deliverables—if the programmers do not deliver on time it becomes your consultant's problem, not yours.

The programmers need access to your business. Like the consultant, they may need to observe your business practices, interview you or your employees, and ask for other information.

Expect to pay at least $40 per hour for programmers.

Before permitting your consultant to engage a programmer, however, ask the consultant to demonstrate why off-the-shelf application software cannot meet your needs. If the consultant proposes to hire a programmer to write an application from scratch, insist that he or she demonstrate why the problem cannot be solved by using an application-specific language, such as the several available for dBASE. Usually, customizing an existing application is cheaper than writing a new one.

How Technical Writers Can Help

Technical writers, those trained in the craft of developing user manuals and other documentation, are important to the success of your custom software project. After all, if your employees have questions and the documentation does not answer them, what do you do?

Any technical writing resources required for your custom programming project probably will be selected by the programmers. That's fine, because the programmers and technical writers probably have worked together before and understand each others' needs.

You have every right to expect clear, easy-to-understand, accurate documentation. Develop questions about your system and check the documentation for several items. Can the information be found at all? Did you use the index? If so, how complete is it? Is the documentation accurate? Is it complete? Does it go far enough in anticipating other questions?

Technical documentation may be your last resort in getting answers to questions. If you are not happy with the documentation in any way, make that very clear to your consultant, in writing. It then becomes the consultant's problem.

Learning from the Competition

Is your business in a class by itself? Is there no other business like it anywhere? You can expect that other businesses similar to yours exist. If these businesses have undertaken automation projects, they may have come up against the same issues you are now facing. Your competition—the very people you are out to beat—is a veritable gold mine of information.

You probably know your competitors. Visit them and ask for a tour of their system. You will be surprised at how many are willing to show off! Set up a time when you will cause the least interruption, and come prepared with a list of questions that you have memorized. Don't take notes! You certainly do not want to come across as a spy! Ask your questions, commit the answers to memory, and remain observant. When you get back to your car or office, you can do a "brain-dump" and write everything down.

Find out whether your competitor is satisfied with the system he or she installed. Although few people willingly admit to a failure, you should be able to tell from the enthusiasm level how well the system has been received. What software does the system use? Who was the consultant? How difficult was it to get the system installed and running? Although you can ask about cost, you may not get an answer, and if you do, it may not be directly applicable to the configuration you require.

Chapter Summary

This chapter looked at the possibility of bringing a consultant into your project to add expertise and experience. You learned what a consultant is. You also learned about the procedures for finding and evaluating a consultant and negotiating a contract for services (including timetables, division of responsibilities, and deliverables). Next, you saw that low-cost prepackaged software that fits your business is the best solution from a price/performance standpoint, but that high-cost, custom-developed software may be required if no other satisfactory solution can be found. You learned about dealing with programmers—let your consultant do it. You saw that technical writers, those who develop your instruction manuals, also should be managed by the consultant, but you should retain final approval of the documentation. Finally, you paid a friendly but educational visit to your competition.

CHAPTER 7

Deciding Where To Buy Your Computer Equipment

Think back to your last new car and the strategies you adopted in acquiring it. Did you buy the car in the first showroom you visited? Not likely. Did you pay the full sticker price? Also not likely.

What did you do? You probably visited several dealers and negotiated a price using the sticker as a reference—a point of departure. The dealer wouldn't meet your price so you expressed your disgust and walked out in a huff. Sure enough, the dealer called you at home, offered a better deal, and begged you to come back.

Believe it or not, buying a computer system can be a similar experience. You should be prepared to shop several locations and even different kinds of vendors—those who operate from a storefront and those who do not.

You need to find a dealer you trust, a price you can live with, a warranty that protects you, and a service policy that allows you to keep your business up and running.

Types of Vendors

Where you buy your system is an important decision that you should consider carefully. Each source of equipment has advantages as well as disadvantages. One outlet may offer terrific prices but little in the way of technical support, and another may provide round-the-clock service paid for with higher prices. Find a source that specializes in features that match your purchasing priorities. The following list shows the various sources of new computing equipment:

- ❏ Retail stores
- ❏ Independent vendors
- ❏ Value-added resellers
- ❏ Mail-order companies
- ❏ Mass merchandisers
- ❏ Warehouse and office-supply superstores

Retail Stores

The most visible source for personal computing equipment is the storefront retailer. You have seen them—ComputerLand, BusinessLand, Inacomp, Nynex Business Centers, Sears Business Centers, The Computer Factory, Valcom, and many more.

These stores are a very safe place to buy name-brand products. The problem is that equipment not on a store's list of "approved" items may not be available. Expect to pay more at storefront retailers because their fixed costs, or *overhead*, are high. These expenses include rent and the royalties they must pay to the corporate parent.

Storefront retailers are in business to sell equipment. As a result, some chains are weak when it comes to technical issues like system designing, local area network consulting, or finding the perfect software package for the job.

Another disadvantage to the retail channel is the "good-bye syndrome": the sales associate loads your newly purchased equipment into your car and waves good-bye, hoping never to see you again. Although this characterization surely does not apply to every computer storefront retailer, it is a fact of life.

What are the advantages of buying equipment from a storefront retail operation? That question is difficult to answer. Prices are high and post-sale support tends to be meager. Even the reassurance of knowing that a big chain will always be around may be more serendipity than fact. The business of selling computers fluctuates with the economy. When the economy becomes soft, so too does the demand for computing equipment. As a result, computer chains may disappear or merge. A few years ago, even IBM withdrew from the storefront retail computer business when it sold its IBM Business Centers to Nynex Corporation.

Although this book may not champion retail operations, you should visit several in your area and decide for yourself. Some storefront retailers offer a wide selection of products at reasonable prices. Retailers carry sales literature by the carload, and they have floor models of equipment that you can try. Many chains also offer excellent classroom training.

Caveat emptor: These chains speak in glowing terms only about the equipment or software they carry in their standard inventory. Training at your site is difficult if not impossible to obtain from a retail store.

Independent Vendors/VARs

The marketing channel known as value-added retailers (VAR) or resellers (or sometimes systems integrators) has virtually no resemblance to the storefront dealer other than the core business of selling computing.

VARs almost never operate out of a retail storefront. Instead, they are usually found in a suite in an office building or sometimes in a light industrial area. The atmosphere is usually different, too. Don't expect to see fancy backlit glass and wooden display fixtures—many VARs consider them unnecessary. What you may see can vary from professional-looking office space to a shop with workbenches.

VARs concentrate on the technical aspects of personal computing. Need a particular software package? They will find it. Need a local area network? These people are certified by the likes of 3Com and Novell not just to sell, but to analyze your business and to design a networking solution for you. VARs offer training courses, custom application development, and service for your system.

Resellers have a distinct advantage over the retail storefront channel: many of them specialize. Like physicians who specialize in a narrowly focused area of medicine, many resellers have become experts in specific vertical market applications. You can find resellers who specialize in legal office software, medical office management software, or retail point-of-sale applications. You can benefit from the resellers' expertise: they understand your line of business, know all the software solutions available, and can prescribe the best solution for *your* particular operation.

The VAR channel may sound like the perfect solution, but it isn't for everyone. Very few VARs are authorized to sell genuine IBM or Apple computers. If your company mandates buying those two brands, you may be better off going back to the storefront dealer. Although the prices you pay for hardware can be considerably less than storefront prices, the VAR makes up for this difference by charging for consulting, analysis, system design, installation, training, and service. The result? The money you pay for these services could drive the total system beyond the storefront price for the same system. When you buy through a VAR, however, you are buying expertise and a relationship—the two products many storefronts are unable to offer.

Make sure that the VAR is licensed to sell the products you are buying. If you buy a network operating system from a VAR not authorized by the manufacturer to sell it, technical support may be difficult to find when questions arise.

Mail-Order Houses

Mail-order houses have become a major distribution channel for computing equipment. They offer very attractive prices, toll-free telephone numbers for ordering, delivery to your door, and some even offer on-site service through large third-party service companies like TRW, General Electric, or Sorbus. What could possibly go wrong?

Mail-order companies sometimes go out of business between the time they take your order and the time your order is scheduled to be shipped. If you pay by credit card you may be safe, but if you pay by check and the company goes belly-up, you may have to chalk it up to experience and call your attorney.

Some mail-order companies have been known to substitute other products in place of what you ordered. Some claim, for month after month, that the item you ordered is on back-order from the manufacturer or distributor. Also, beware of mail-order houses that charge a membership fee, which is an old technique used to build up capital and to purchase inventory. This type of mail-order company can be dangerous to the well-being of your project.

Who is reputable? Actually, most mail-order houses are reputable. Start with the companies that take out large, color, multipage advertisements, *on a regular basis*, in the major monthly computer magazines, *near the front of the magazine*. Although this method is not an iron-clad test, you often can use it to take the pulse of the company. Color and multipage advertisements are expensive. This kind of advertising is a sign that the company is well-funded. Advertising on a regular basis—every month—usually indicates that cash flow is not a problem. The company is taking in enough money each month to pay its bills. Advertisements near the front of a magazine cost more than advertisements bunched together in the rear.

Read the advertisements *very* carefully. Understand the return and refund policies *before* you place your order. Defective products can be returned, but who pays the freight? What do you do while the defective product is being repaired? Will the company supply a loaner unit?

What about refunds? After a product has been out for repair more than 30 days, do you get your money back, a merchandise credit, or do you have to sit and wait with no money and no product?

Remember, too, that when you buy from a mail order house, you get rock-bottom prices and no more; no expertise in selecting the right application, no installation support or training, and no network design.

When you buy from a mail-order house, you first should have shopped elsewhere and know precisely—right down to the make and model—what you want to buy. Also be prepared to undertake installation and support by yourself or to contract for it locally.

Mass Merchandisers

Several large discount chain stores and even toy stores have begun selling computers. Though you may be able to pick up word processing or spreadsheet software at a reasonable price, it's very unlikely that you can get the equipment needed for a commercial business environment. If you do find IBM-compatible equipment, you may find it underpowered or not equipped with enough disk storage for your needs.

Warehouse and Office Supply Superstores

Like mass merchandisers, warehouse stores (which may require membership) and the new office supply superstore chains sometimes carry IBM-compatible personal computers. These stores are good sources for supplies. They often sell diskettes, laser printer toner cartridges, printer ribbons, and continuous-form paper at low prices.

Good buys on computers can be found, but carefully research the equipment before you buy. Any IBM-compatible equipment you buy should be AT compatible—built around the 80286 or 80386 microprocessor. Computers designated PC-, XT-, or PC/XT-compatible, although very inexpensive, represent an investment in obsolete technology that provides a limited growth path.

Should You Buy Used Equipment?

Did you ever buy a used car? Probably. Was it a good investment? Maybe, but then again, maybe not. Buying used computing equipment is much like buying a used car. Sometimes you can find good buys that last a lifetime, and sometimes you don't.

The intent of this section is not to scare you away from purchasing equipment—quite the contrary. The market is huge, with hundreds of thousands of satisfied customers.

How Does Used Equipment Enter the Market?

Used equipment comes into the marketplace because it has outlived its usefulness to the owner. Depending on the owner, "usefulness" can mean different things. The following are sources of used equipment:

- ❏ Individuals
- ❏ Computer exchange organizations
- ❏ Storefront retailers
- ❏ Value-added resellers
- ❏ Auctions

An individual who owns a computer may simply yearn for the newest, sleekest machine on the market. The used equipment may be the most desirable of all—maintained lovingly in the home by a single owner. Used only by a hobbyist, it is often "low mileage," well-maintained, home-based equipment that may be in like-new condition. Many times, too, home-based equipment has been souped-up with the addition of high-capacity hard disks or several additional megabytes of memory.

Large companies sometimes trade away older equipment when it no longer is able to provide the processing punch needed by newer, more powerful applications. In the past, these machines were pushed down to the secretarial level for simple word processing, but as we enter the 1990s, even the secretarial base is becoming saturated with computers.

Other companies get rid of equipment simply because it has been fully depreciated and the accountant says it is time to start the depreciation process all over again.

Companies that lease computer equipment may find that equipment obsolete when it's returned by the lessee at the end of the lease term.

Sources of Used Equipment

If you look hard enough, you can find a virtual cornucopia of sources for used equipment.

Individuals selling a single machine tend to place classified advertisements in a Sunday newspaper, computer user group newsletter, or even in one of the national periodicals that are essentially listings of equipment for sale. You can find national periodicals in the computer magazine section of almost any full-service bookstore.

Equipment often finds its way to organizations that buy and sell used equipment much like a stockbroker buys and sells securities. These companies, the Boston Computer Exchange being the largest, match equipment buyers and sellers and, like a real estate broker, they charge a percentage of the price as a service fee. Prices for a particular kind of computer vary, sometimes substantially, from week to week, based on supply and demand, and the introduction of new models that make even more obsolete the equipment being offered for sale.

Another source of used equipment is storefront retailers and value-added resellers. Sometimes they accept trades from a customer as a service to help secure a large order. Many times the retailers have no use for this used equipment. You may find a good deal here.

Pros and Cons of Purchasing Used Equipment

Like buying a used car, there are risks associated with buying used equipment. Unfortunately, computers and printers are not equipped with odometers, so it's difficult to determine how much a particular piece of equipment may have been used.

Used equipment is often very inexpensive for obvious reasons. New, more powerful computing equipment is constantly being brought to the marketplace. As these new models, which command premium prices, arrive, they force the prices of less powerful computers (or printers) downward. As new technologies supersede the old, and as manufacturing techniques and miniaturization of electronic components improve, the downward pressure on prices becomes greater.

This downward pressure eventually ripples through every tier of computing and printing power. The longer you wait, then, the better the price. Yet by waiting, you also are putting yourself farther away from the leading edge of technology.

Although it's impossible to generalize, you can follow a few rules of thumb. Equipment owned by a hobbyist has probably been subjected to few hours of use (evening) and the best environment (in a house). Equipment used in a home-based business, such as freelance word processing, may have a great deal of mileage, but benefits from having been used in the home, a clean environment. Computer equipment used in an office building environment may have been used constantly and may have been operated in a dusty environment. Finally, equipment used on a shop floor, warehouse, outside, or in some other hostile environment is the least desirable of all.

If possible, arrange to try out the equipment for a couple of days. If you do buy that used equipment, be sure to get *in writing* a 100 percent unconditional money-back guarantee for a period of at least 30 days. During that 30-day trial period use the equipment constantly and leave it running all day and night. Run hard-disk diagnostics to see how many clusters are marked as "bad" and therefore unusable. After this stress test, you need to make a judgment call about keeping the equipment.

Auctions

The sad fact is that companies do go out of business. Do you know what happens to a company's physical assets when the company is being liquidated? Many times the assets are sold at public auction. A list of auctions is as close as your nearest Sunday newspaper. Although you may feel a certain coldness about attending an auction (one regular attender compares people attending auctions to vultures circling their prey), remember that your purpose in attending is to conduct a business transaction—and no more. Business is business, right?

Consider a recent *Boston Sunday Globe*. It listed two auctions of particular interest. A retail computer outlet that had been in bankruptcy was liquidating its entire inventory of used *and new* computing equipment. A private college in foreclosure was liquidating everything at its two campuses. Items included everything from pencil sharpeners to drafting tables to automotive equipment, not to mention more than 300 genuine IBM PS/2 personal computers, Hewlett-Packard LaserJet printers, software, and more.

If you plan to attend an auction, contact the auctioneer ahead. See whether a complete list of the items to be auctioned is available. If so, have a list mailed to you. Mark the items that interest you and establish the price you are willing to pay. Stick to your price! Licensed auctioneers are trained professionals—their job is to get the highest price for each item. If someone outbids you, it just wasn't meant to be.

You must pay a cash deposit at the door of the auction. At that time you are asked to fill out a registration card, and you receive a bidding card with a number. You hold up that card to place a bid. If it's the first time you have attended an auction, watch the pros in action before you jump in. Be prepared to pay for your find immediately with cash or a bank check; personal checks and credit cards are not welcome. Remember, too, that all sales are final and everything is sold *as is* and *as shown*. There are no warranties or refunds.

Auctions are fun. If you exercise reasonable care, you can walk away with some great bargains.

What Is Included in the Price?

No matter where you buy your equipment, understand exactly what you are getting for each dollar you spend. With long equipment lists and options, it's easy for small (and sometimes not-so-small) things to be overlooked. Ask for, and receive, in writing, a list that contains a detailed configuration for each piece of equipment purchased.

Consider part of an advertisement that recently appeared in one of the leading computer magazines: "A perfect budget-priced home computer. A solid, reliable, compatible performer." The price sure seemed like a bargain, it was just $549!

But the next line of the add, set in smaller type, said, "Base system with single floppy, no video." So what exactly would you get? Just an 8088-based IBM PC-compatible clone with no display capabilities and virtually no storage.

By the time you equipped this spartan PC with a VGA display card and monitor, and a 32M hard disk, it would cost up to

$1,478, according to the ad. Is that a bargain? Probably not, because an 80286-based AT-compatible also with the same VGA display options and a 32M hard disk is $1,898, only $420 more.

Buying new equipment is like buying a new car. You have a base price and a list of options. The base price of your computer may seem like a bargain, but the total system price, including all the options, is what really matters.

For example, when you buy a printer, is the connecting cable included? If not, plan on spending up to another $50. When buying a computer, know exactly what options are included. How much internal memory is included? (You should not settle for less that 640K.) Is a hard disk included? If so, what is its capacity? You should expect at least 32M; most mail-order houses now carry hard disks that are 60M and larger.

What display options are included? If the display is monochrome, are graphics capabilities included? If the display is color, which specification is used: CGA, EGA, or VGA?

Other factors in pricing include system design and installation. Mail-order houses and many storefront retailers offer neither of these services; you purchase the equipment and then either install it yourself or contract the installation with someone else. A value-added reseller usually will come to your site, determine what you need (perhaps in conjunction with your consultant), and install all the equipment. These services are not free.

Consider your local area network. You have bought the workstations, the network server, and the adapter card to link each device to the network. You spent some serious money for the actual network operating system software as well as network versions of your software applications. Who is going to run the cable to connect all these devices together? It takes a pro to design a network configuration, install the cabling without disrupting your business operation, and install the software on the server and workstations. This expertise is expensive but essential for a successful project.

Support Considerations

The word *support* means different things to different people. Some equate support with answering questions about the operation of a specific software program. Others see support as the physical repair of disabled equipment. Still others view support as operator training.

However you define support, understand what the supplier of your equipment is and is not providing. Equipment you buy at auction comes *as is* with no support of any kind. Equipment you purchase from a hobbyist may be delivered and installed by the seller to make sure that the equipment is operating properly in its new home. A storefront retailer or value-added reseller is obligated to support manufacturers' warranties for defective equipment, but probably charges extra for software support or training.

Leasing versus Buying

Most large corporations lease their mainframe computers but usually purchase their personal computing equipment. No matter how small your business, you should review lease versus buy options.

Advantages of Leasing

Leasing affords two clear advantages: protection from obsolescence and payments spread out over time.

Imagine that in 1984 you decided to buy several personal computers. (At that time, just about the only game in town was IBM's original dual floppy disk PC or its sibling the XT equipped with a 10M hard disk drive—in those days 10M was an incredible amount.) You plunked down several thousand dollars apiece for your new machines, and they performed flawlessly. Even today they may still be performing, but those machines are obsolete. They have only a small fraction of the power of today's most powerful desktop computers, and that 10 megabyte disk drive is woefully inadequate. Today, for half the money, you can buy a system that processes data five times as fast and includes a high-capacity, 60M drive. If you had leased that first computer, you could swap it for a bigger, better, faster model at the end of the lease term. When leasing, you never need worry about being stuck with old, slow, low-capacity machines.

The other advantage in leasing equipment (you usually cannot lease personal computing software) is the way in which funds are paid out. Unless you arranged for bank financing, those five computers you bought in 1984 may have cost a total of nearly $20,000, which you would have had to pay at the time of purchase. With a lease, you instead make monthly payments for the life of the lease. Even though you probably pay out more total dollars through a leasing arrangement, the sting of needing $20,000 up front is eliminated.

Disadvantages of Leasing

The problem with leasing is that you have no tangible assets to show for all the money you have spent. Depending on your business situation, that can be good or bad. See your accountant. Almost surely the total funds paid out over a lease term for any given piece of equipment is much more than the retail price for the equipment when it was new. The leasing company is in business to show a profit, isn't it? That profit is built into the lease.

Leasing Arrangements

Two kinds of leases are commonly used today: the closed-ended lease and the open-ended lease. With the closed-ended lease, you simply return the equipment to the leasing company at the end of the lease term. With the open-ended lease, you are given the option to buy the equipment at a price stipulated in the lease itself.

By walking away from the equipment at the end of the lease term, you put the burden of disposing of the equipment on the leasing company. If the equipment is obsolete to you, it surely is obsolete to the leasing company. They may end up junking some equipment, selling it to a company that deals with used equipment, or placing it on the auction block. When signing a leasing agreement, who knows what the equipment will be worth a year or more down the road? For that reason, the leasing company must build in a cushion in case the equipment turns out to be worthless. What that means is that you pay more per month to cover losses the leasing company may experience when it comes time to get rid of the equipment.

On the other hand, by your agreeing to purchase the equipment at the end of the lease period, the leasing company can protect itself against a severe drop in the value of old equipment. *You* now assume that risk. If you agree to pay $1,500 for a two-year-old, $4,000 system, and then a new, more powerful model debuts a week before the end of the lease, you may find yourself paying $1,500 for a box worth $500. Because you, not the leasing company, assumes the risk, the leasing company can afford to lower the monthly rental fee.

Which is better? There is no clear answer. If you can deploy those old obsolete PCs at stations for secretaries with modest computing needs, you may be better off going for the reduced monthly payments and owning the equipment at the end of the lease. If you work for an engineering firm that must always have the latest, most powerful systems, it probably makes sense to pay more each month, knowing that you will never be stuck with old, underpowered equipment.

Tax Considerations

The best tax advice this book can give is to see your accountant and to do so before you make any buying decision. Your business is unique, and the decision to lease or buy your computing equipment can be heavily swayed by the advice of your accountant.

Payments that you make for the leasing of equipment are, of course, deductible as a business expense. However, purchasing equipment also enables you to depreciate the equipment you own, an attractive advantage, especially if you have purchased a large amount of equipment.

Finding Vendors

These days it seems as if everyone sells computing equipment! Finding vendors who meet your needs, whether it's providing adequate support or offering the lowest price, requires an investment of your time. The following sources can be very helpful in finding computer equipment vendors:

- ❑ Telephone book Yellow Pages
- ❑ Sunday newspaper
- ❑ Computer magazines
- ❑ Computer newspapers
- ❑ Trade groups

- ❑ Software manufacturers
- ❑ Your competitors
- ❑ Consultants

The Yellow Pages

If you choose to shop with your fingers, then the Yellow Pages of the local telephone book is probably your best bet. Unfortunately, with so many aspects of computerization, the number of categories in the Yellow Pages has exploded.

Here's a list of categories from the Yellow Pages of one large metropolitan area: computer graphics, computer room installation and equipment, computer dealers, computer renting and leasing, computer service and repair, computer software and services, computer supplies and parts, computer system designers and consultants, and computer wholesale and manufacturers.

That's quite a list. The categories that make the most sense are dealers, software and services, and system designers and consultants. You find a great deal of overlap, so study each carefully.

Read the display advertisements. Look for phrases like "authorized dealer," "authorized sales and service," "authorized distributor," or "authorized reseller." Manufacturers are very restrictive in allowing dealers to use these phrases in their advertising. The absence of these phrases does not imply that a dealer is not authorized, but their presence means that the dealer has the blessing of the manufacturer. Still, *you* must determine whether the dealer is deserving of your business.

You will recognize the names of the large retail chains, but pay particular attention to the smaller advertisements. These ads usually belong to the value-added reseller or nonstorefront dealer who is equipped to provide a more focused range of services than a large retail operation offers.

What you have accomplished by reading the telephone book is merely to come up with a list of names. You still need to check out those dealers who make your list.

The Sunday Newspaper

The business section of the Sunday paper is almost always full of businesses selling computing equipment and services. The rules that apply to finding names in the Yellow Pages apply here as well.

One key advantage to the Sunday paper is that you see actual products and prices being advertised. These prices are certainly negotiable once you get into the store, but they provide an excellent barometer of what the local market is demanding or, in case of drastically reduced prices, what *isn't* selling.

Computer Magazines and Newspapers

Mail-order houses advertise heavily in just about every computer periodical aimed at users. A walk into any local bookstore yields an armful of magazines aimed at IBM and Apple users, owners of laptop computers, and even those who run a home-based computerized business.

The magazines with the largest circulation bases are *PC Magazine*, *PC World*, *PC Computing*, and *Personal Computing* for the IBM-compatible world, and *MacWorld* and *MacUser* for the Apple Macintosh world. If you are interested in desktop publishing, look for *Publish!* and *Personal Publishing*.

The computer newspapers are more difficult to find because they are not aimed at the retail over-the-counter market, but at "the trade." When visiting computer dealers, ask to see copies of *PC Week*, *MacWeek*, *InfoWorld*, *Computer Reseller News*, and *Macintosh News*.

Trade Groups

Many times the trade association for an industry reaches an agreement with a particular dealer who agrees to offer a special suite of services or sell systems at a reduced price in exchange for the referrals generated by the trade organization.

If the dealer has the perfect business solution for you and is capable of providing the level of service that you demand, then it makes good sense to proceed with the dealer. You may save some money, and the trade organization may be paid a fee by the dealer for the successful referral. If the business solution is not a good fit, however, you should continue your search. Like on-sale shoes that are uncomfortable, a bargain computer system that doesn't address your needs is a bad investment.

Software Manufacturers

Call the manufacturer of the software packages you are considering. Not only will you be referred to a local *authorized* dealer, but you may also be able to get a list of other users in your area.

When you call a software company, start with the sales department. If they cannot provide you with dealer and user information, ask for the public relations department. Always ask for a complete set of product literature. You can add it to your collection of product brochures.

Competitors

You learned about checking out the competition earlier in this book. The principle is repeated here. Your competitor has done a great deal of legwork for you and probably has taken aspirin tablets that otherwise would have been inscribed with your name.

If your competitor's system meets your needs, you may have saved a great deal of legwork. *May* is the key, because other products that are more suitable for you may have reached the market since your competitor's system was installed.

On the other hand, a software package your competitor considered inadequate may have been improved tremendously since your competitor evaluated it.

The lesson to be learned here is that shopping the competition is neither a starting point nor an ending point; it's a step along the way.

Consultants

Perhaps you have chosen to work with a consultant throughout your project. If so, he or she has most likely established a relationship with one or more dealers. That's fine, because the consultant has done most of the weeding out for you, but think back to the contract you signed with the consultant. The contract should say that you are the boss (remember the consultant works for *you*) and that you have final approval for any dealer proposed by your consultant.

As long as the chosen dealer is from the consultant's own list, it remains, subject to the terms of your consultant's contract, the responsibility of the consultant to install an appropriate system.

If you choose a dealer with whom the consultant is not familiar, the consultant may not be willing to accept responsibility for the results.

Evaluating Vendors

With your list of vendors narrowed down to a workable list, you are ready for the next important task: selecting the final candidates. Much of this process is the same as selecting a consultant or choosing software.

First, determine what the dealer is authorized to sell. Sometimes dealers, VARs, and system integrators obtain merchandise through informal agreements with distributors, even though they may not be authorized by the manufacturer to sell that particular line.

Selling merchandise without authorization can result in attractive prices because costs are lower (no training expenses in obtaining authorization or no royalties paid to the headquarters of large computer retail chains); however, it may be difficult or impossible to obtain warranty service if that becomes necessary.

Manufacturers' authorizations are not granted lightly. To obtain that coveted status, dealers must take courses given by the manufacturer (or authorized training center) and pass difficult, often highly technical written tests. Authorization also can be linked to the solvency of the dealer; a well-financed dealer may be more likely to win authorization. Some manufacturers grant authorization for limited periods of time—a year or two—and require that the dealer take periodic refresher courses and pass examinations.

Assessing the Dealer

Once you have found dealers authorized to sell the equipment you need, talk to them and establish a relationship. Considering the amount of money that you are about to spend, it's important to have the dealer in your corner. Make sure that you can get along with your dealer. If you and your dealer are unable to "hit it off," you should consider looking elsewhere.

A dealer's track record is another important factor. How long has the dealer been in business? If the dealer is a retail storefront operation that is a franchisee of a national chain, it's safe to assume that the location is reasonably well financed. If you are dealing with an independent reseller or systems integrator, however, that may not always be the case. Some resellers are so small that commercial banks are unwilling to establish relationships. Many times these smaller resellers are in a position to offer the highest level of technical expertise and personalized service. If you are paranoid about the dealer "being there" a week from Sunday, sticking with a franchisee provides peace of mind (but no guarantees!). On the other hand, a smaller operation may provide a higher degree of personalized service. Smaller operations, with the addition of clients like you, grow into bigger, well-financed operations.

Your dealer should be happy to provide a list of recent clients. Feel free to tell the dealer that it is all right if he or she obtains permission from these customers before handing you the list. If the dealer flatly refuses to provide a list, claiming that it is "not policy," consider continuing your search elsewhere. If the dealer does provide a list, be sure to call the customers on that list!

Evaluating Equipment

Evaluating equipment is difficult at best and impossible at worst. After all, a clone is a clone is a clone and any machine that is a 100 percent functional equivalent of an IBM Personal Computer is just that—equivalent.

There are differences, however. You already have learned about pricing and base configurations, but there are more subtle items that you may not know about.

Ask the dealer to remove the cabinet of the computer you are considering and examine the workmanship. Are wires neatly laid out or are they just stuffed into an available void? Look at printed circuit boards closely. Small "jumper" wires soldered to a board indicate engineering revisions to solve problems that were discovered after the circuit boards were produced. Although jumpers are not indicative of an inferior product and in fact may improve a computer's performance, they are one of many factors that you should consider.

Study the specifications of all equipment carefully. Published specifications are a good barometer of a device's performance characteristics, but remember that these specifications are compiled by manufacturers who want to portray their equipment in the best possible light. Specifications tend to be on the optimistic side.

The best use for specifications is a comparative analysis between similar models from different manufacturers. For example, you may find that manufacturer A's computer, a 12 MHz 80286-based IBM AT-compatible, is equipped with more memory and a larger hard disk than manufacturer B's 16Mhz 80286-based AT clone. Which is the better deal?

Assessing Availability for Questions or Problems

Unless your computing needs are limited to the most simple of configurations, it's likely that you will need to have questions answered from time to time concerning operation of your hardware, methods for enhancing its capabilities, or repair of malfunctioning equipment. Although getting answers to these questions is of paramount importance—after all your business cannot come to a standstill—it's the *accessibility* to those with the answers that really counts.

Ask your dealer who will be answering your questions. Will it be the salesperson who is familiar with your particular configuration but who may possess only a limited technical knowledge, or will it be a specially trained person dedicated to providing technical support? Also, find out how many support people will be available.

Be sure to ask about response time for technical assistance and service. You may not realize it, but there are different kinds of response time: minimum, maximum, and average. All three are important and paint a clear picture of your dealer's ability to serve your support needs.

Minimum response time is the time in which you can expect a response under the best of all possible conditions. A very low (quick) response time may mean your dealer has technical support sitting around waiting for phone calls or that your dealer is located next door to your office or store. For these reasons, minimum response time is not a viable indicator of the level of support you can expect.

Average response time provides a good barometer of your dealer's ability to respond. Most dealers and value-added resellers are willing to quote an average response time of four hours. While that's not bad, it may be unacceptable in your particular situation. If you cannot live with that four-hour response time, you probably are well advised to purchase spare computers and consider installing a redundant server if you are operating in a networked environment. Keep in mind, though, that average response time is just that—average. Average response time is the mathematical average of response times for all support calls responded to by the dealer. That four-hour average response time quoted by your dealer is a combination of one customer's one-hour response and another customer's seven-hour response. The faster response is great, but you cannot expect it, and probably will not live to see it! Average response time is a useful measure, but like minimum response time, you cannot bet your business on it.

Maximum response time is what separates the pros from the also-rans. If your dealer guarantees a maximum response time of four hours you can, assuming that the dealer lives up to his or her word, rest assured that your problem or question will be dealt with in that time frame. Because this method of dealing with support measures the outside, or worst-case, limits of response, you should strive to get your dealer to commit to this figure.

Now that you understand how response times can make dealers, or even software companies, appear to provide better service than they are capable of delivering, one other measure works hand-in-hand with maximum response time: repeats.

That guaranteed maximum response time of four hours looks great on paper but what happens when the problem cannot be resolved in that period? Consider this common scenario. The server on your network fails. You call for service, and the dealer, or whoever you have contracted for service, shows up in a truck within the allotted time. The repairman works with the server and concludes that the problem is a faulty hard disk coprocessor board (a circuit board that optimizes transmission of data to and from the server's hard disk). "That's great," you say, looking at the truck loaded with parts with the expectation the problem will be fixed in minutes. But if the repairman says, "I need to pick up a board at the shop," you are out of luck. Or even worse, the repairman might say, "We need to special order that part because they hardly ever fail so we don't keep them in stock." The dealer has kept his or her end of the deal: a response within the time stipulated in the contract you signed, but that sure seems worthless now, doesn't it?

One last thing you need to learn from your dealer or service provider is the track record on repeat calls. What percentage of problems are dealt with in one call, two calls, and so on? You have every right to expect the vast majority of issues to be resolved in a single call, whether it's over the phone, via electronic mail, or through an on-site visit. What if the dealer isn't willing to share that little bit of history with you? Well, no one is forcing you to do business with the dealer!

> Use maximum response time and number of repeat calls in evaluating equipment dealers.

Evaluating Refund and Exchange Policies

Refund and exchange policies are a difficult area, one that can lead to great frustration if not clearly and completely understood.

While most dealers will exchange a computer, printer, or other device that is DOA (dead on arrival)—not working when it comes out of the box—policies vary wildly beyond that. No dealer will exchange equipment that you "don't like." After all, it is ultimately your responsibility to decide which equipment to buy. No dealer will guarantee that the equipment you purchase is suitable for the job at hand, unless the dealer himself made the recommendations.

The best you may be able to do is return unsuitable equipment for a merchandise credit to be used against future purchases. Don't expect a cash refund.

Your contract with your consultant is your insurance in case you want a refund. Consider including a clause stating that if the system proves unsuitable, the equipment may be returned within 30 days for a full refund. It is your responsibility to make sure that the equipment is undamaged, unmarked, and that all original packing materials have been retained. Your inability, no matter how slight, to repackage the equipment in its original pristine condition may release the consultant (or dealer) from taking back equipment in exchange for a refund.

> Ask about and understand your dealer's refund and exchange policies before you buy anything.

Evaluating Warranties

When was the last time you read a warranty? Can't remember? That means you're perfectly normal! We tend not to read warranties in detail because our expectation when purchasing new equipment is that a failure of that equipment is unlikely. But you do need to bring your car in for service, and that fancy video cassette recorder probably needs a minor tweaking every now and then. Computer software and hardware are no different.

Evaluating Hardware Warranties

Computers can break down for literally hundreds of reasons, because a computer is essentially a cabinet that houses a myriad of subsystems all made by different manufacturers. Your hard disk drive, floppy disk drive, and memory expansion boards were all made by different companies. Even the chips mounted on a single board were most likely made by several different companies.

What does all that mean to you? It depends on how your system was configured and by whom. IBM, for example, sells you a personal computer with the IBM logo on the outside. However, on the inside the computer is assembled with subsystems from various suppliers. Because IBM acted as the *system integrator*, it is IBM (or IBM's authorized dealer) that issues a warranty on the entire computer. A value-added reseller usually takes a different route, configuring systems for you from various off-the-shelf components, each of which is the most appropriate choice for your business needs. Because the reseller is the system's integrator, it may be the reseller who issues a warranty for the entire system. The reseller may simply furnish you with the original manufacturer's warranty for each system component. The best solution is to find a dealer or reseller willing to issue a warranty for whatever you buy, no matter what the configuration and no matter who put the components together.

Warranties are not all the same. They cover varying periods of time and provide different levels of coverage. You should understand the warranties that come with your equipment.

Some manufacturers provide a warranty good only for days, and others provide a full year's warranty. Some pay for both parts and labor; others pay only for parts. Where service is provided can be a major consideration. A storefront dealer may require that you return the equipment to the store for service, but a value-added reseller may be willing to come to you (that is part of the value that's added). In the latest twist, many of the larger mail-order houses will provide service at your site through national third-party service organizations like Sorbus and TRW.

> Warranties are useful only if you read them.

Computer equipment has become so reliable that many dealers consider warranties superfluous. You know better!

Should the warranty dictate which equipment you buy? In a word, no. It is always proper to find the best hardware for the job (remember, though, that comes *after* finding the correct software). The warranty is but one criterion that you can use in choosing among equally suitable equipment, but it shouldn't result in purchasing hardware that is inappropriate for the job.

Evaluating Software Warranties

Warranties for commercially available software packages are remarkably similar. Some companies allow you to return an *unopened* package for a full refund, and you can usually exchange a defective disk, for a modest handling fee, within the first 30 to 90 days of ownership, but that's about it. The manufacturer of the package does not warrant the software suitability for a job and is not responsible for any negative impact on your business due to misuse, or even errors that may be lurking in the software itself.

Software is fundamentally different from hardware because you do not own the software even though you purchased the software package. You are instead granted a *license* by the manufacturer to use that software, but the manufacturer retains ownership and copyright. Because you don't actually own the software, your rights are limited.

Custom software is an entirely different situation, because you negotiated a contract with the software developer. That contract should contain clauses granting you an evaluation period for testing the software. If the software is defective or unsuitable, you should be allowed remedies ranging from modification of the software to outright rejection. Rejections should include a refund of part or all of the money you paid for development.

Ownership and copyright of a custom-written software application are negotiable as well. If you reject the program, the programmer should retain all rights and ownership. If you accept the program, depending on your contract, you may own it all or have shared ownership. If the program has commercial possibilities, you may want to allow the developer to retain the marketing rights in exchange for a royalty on every copy sold or reduced payments to the developer on your part.

Types of Recourse

No one wins when problems cannot be resolved. The best solution, of course, is to do your homework and select the best hardware and software so that problems do not occur. Wouldn't it be nice if things always worked out that way!

When any sort of problem occurs, don't wait for it to go away. Unlike a scraped knee, computers just aren't capable of healing themselves. Document the situation completely, including what programs were running, what specific activities were taking place, the weather (was there a lightning storm at the time?), and what data was being entered, viewed, or modified when the problem occurred. Then pick up the telephone and call your first line of support. That may be your consultant, your dealer or reseller, your custom programmer, or the manufacturer of your software package. Work as a team to resolve problems and be sure to keep a cool head. Would you want *your* customers to come in yelling and screaming about a problem? The golden rule works here, too!

Sometimes issues arise that jeopardize the success of your automation project or even threaten the survival of your business. What if the custom software program you paid thousands of dollars for regularly corrupts the data that forms the heart of your business? What if that expensive file server experiences disk drive problems that just cannot seem to be repaired? Perhaps most common, what if the system works perfectly but simply doesn't do what you expected it to do?

Recourse of some kind is necessary, and there is a range of action you can take, from peaceful settlement through binding arbitration to full-blown lawsuits.

> When attempting to resolve disputes, begin with the least combative method and escalate your efforts to the next level only as a last resort.

The best protection of all is a contract that spells out in detail what is expected, by whom, and to what extent. To make sure that a custom software system performs as expected, you should have included the detailed functional specification as an exhibit in the contract. That way, there can be no question regarding what the system should do, the processing it should perform, the design of display screens, and the layout and content of reports. Work with the other party in your contract to resolve these disputes and be prepared to negotiate. Although you may not get everything you want, a negotiated settlement that brings you closer to that point with a minimum of pain is a far better resolution than a situation where neither party is willing to budge.

If a negotiated settlement between parties cannot be achieved after a reasonable effort, it may become necessary to escalate the issue to the next tier. Arbitration is becoming increasingly popular as a means for resolving otherwise unresolvable conflicts. If you retained a consultant or hired a custom programming house, it makes good sense to include a section in your contract that all disputes relating to the performance or interpretation of the contract, if they cannot be resolved by you and the other party, be resolved through binding arbitration. It is customary to allow either party to request arbitration, and arbitration usually is conducted in accordance with the rules of the American Arbitration Association. To prevent things from getting out of hand, include a clause indicating that arbitration shall be the exclusive forum for any disputes and that neither party shall have the right to file a lawsuit.

Litigation, the filing of a lawsuit, should be pursued only as a last resort when all other avenues of settlement have failed and only if you are not expressly prohibited from seeking legal recourse. Lawsuits take time and attorneys are expensive. Even if you sue and win, the cost in dollars and time away from your business may be too much to bear. Winning your lawsuit while watching your business go down the drain really doesn't accomplish much of anything, does it?

Chapter Summary

In this chapter, you learned about the many places from which you can purchase your computer hardware. These sources include retail stores, independent value-added resellers, mail order houses, mass merchandisers, and even warehouse and office supply stores. You saw that a huge market in used equipment exists and that in some cases buying used equipment can be an economical alternative.

You learned that leasing can be a valuable method for protecting yourself from obsolescence and may provide certain tax advantages. This chapter also taught you how to evaluate vendors in terms of trustworthiness, comfort level, and track record. Finally, you evaluated software and hardware warranties and learned about the avenues of recourse you can take when attempting to resolve disputes.

With your hardware finally in hand, it's on to the next step in the process, installation of your new system.

CHAPTER 8

Implementing Your New System

Take a step back and see how much ground you have covered. You have agreed that there are opportunities to make your business more profitable. You certainly wouldn't have come this far for the sport of it! After a careful analysis, you have concluded that the best method for achieving increased profitability is through reducing errors in the data that drives your business and by increasing the productivity of your employees. After examining several alternatives, all of which would reduce errors and increase productivity, you and your advisors have elected to automate certain aspects of your business.

You have searched for software solutions that meet your prioritized objectives and then looked for hardware capable of running the software you have purchased either off-the-shelf or from a custom software developer.

At this point, the myriad pieces of the puzzle begin to come together. Like a jigsaw puzzle with thousands of pieces, implementing a system cannot be done in one session.

Implementation of a computer is far more than simply unpacking boxes and connecting all the cables. This chapter deals with a variety of topics. They include

- ❑ Preparing the site before the boxes are even opened
- ❑ Setting up the system
- ❑ Devising testing plans to make sure that the system performs its tasks properly and accurately

The chapter also covers how to train your employees and how to deal with unexpected events.

Getting Ready for the Arrival of the System

Much site preparation work needs to be done before the boxes arrive at your business. If furniture needs to be rearranged, now is the time—not when you have so much equipment piled up that just moving is nearly impossible.

Developing a Floor Plan

Where does everything go? When you moved into your home, you at least labeled the outside of each carton with the proper room so that your fine bone china wouldn't be piled in the garage next to the power tools. Your computer system is no different. Several issues need to be considered:

- ❑ Work flow
- ❑ People flow

- ❑ Electrical outlets
- ❑ Cabling
- ❑ Telephone access
- ❑ Lighting

Work Flow

Imagine that you have three individuals manually processing purchase orders that come into your office from customers. Patrick opens the envelopes and logs the purchase orders. When he's done, the purchase order is passed along to Mary, who checks to see whether the inventory is in stock and instructs the warehouse to fill the order. Finally, Mary passes the filled purchase order to Larry, who types a packing slip and invoice.

You will agree, of course, that Patrick, Mary, and Larry should be seated in that order so that the flow of paperwork is a straight line rather than a series of criss-crossing loops.

Your computer system is no different. If you are situated in an office environment, this time is the best opportunity you will ever have to arrange your employees and their furniture for the most efficient flow of work. Simply create a list of the work flow as it is today (the manual flow) and a list of the work flow as it will be after your system is implemented (the automated flow).

You will find that many manual tasks (like Larry's typing of packing slips and invoices) simply disappear and are replaced by a computer with a printer. But you will also find that new tasks have been created. For example, if you are running an accounts payable system, the old method of typing checks one-by-one is replaced by new tasks: filling out voucher forms; bundling, or *batching*, them together; and entering data through the keyboard into the system. Even from this simple example, you can see that work flow can change dramatically.

So get out your pad of graph paper and ruler and begin rearranging the furniture to suit the flow of the work. Focus on the tasks rather than on the individual employees who will be performing the work.

Get your employees involved in the planning. These are, after all, exciting times for your business. Separating Amy and Tara after fifteen years together may not be that big a deal to you. Yet to them, the one-third of their lives spent behind those desks is everything. If they need to be separated, get them involved early. Present the case to them so clearly that they (not you) conclude that moving apart is the proper solution. If separating old buddies continues to be a problem, consider re-distributing tasks among your employees so that old friends can remain together. Remember that valued employees are indeed a precious commodity. Installing the new system will create enough trauma; there is no need to cause additional stress when it can be avoided.

Electrical and Cabling Work

Arranging the work flow—and with it the location of desks and other furniture—is crucial. You will need to make sure that the components of your system can be easily installed.

Each piece of equipment requires electrical power. (Power specifications are covered elsewhere in this book.) You must make sure that adequate power is available within a reasonable distance of each electrical component. Avoid using long extension cords. They constitute a fire hazard and are easily tripped over. They could result in injuries to employees—or even customers—and would almost certainly cause data corruption or loss when power-to-system components are interrupted.

If electrical outlets are not within a few feet of each component, hire an electrician to install additional receptacles in accordance with the amperage requirements of your hardware. There is simply no alternative.

Cabling for your local area network, if you are installing one, should be done at the same time. Depending on your particular environment, you can go the easy and inexpensive route, the better looking but more expensive route, or the high-tech but incredibly expensive route.

"Easy and inexpensive" means simply stringing cables behind desks and along the floor baseboards to run the network from one computer or printer to the next. The result may not look pretty, but it will certainly operate with no problems. The dangers are similar to the dangers of exposed electrical extension cords. Although these low voltage coaxial or twisted pair cables provide no electrical shock hazard, they are easy to trip over. (The sight of a $3,500 computer crashing to the floor is not pretty!)

The best solution for cabling is to run it through walls and ceiling and terminate each connection with a wall plug. You can then run a short length of cable from your computer to the wall plug. The cost is much higher than simply running exposed cable, but the hazards are greatly reduced. In a public show room, office, or retail store, you may have no other choice from an aesthetic standpoint. Running the cables inside your walls, however, does not make the components perform better.

The final choice is strictly for the science fiction fan. Several companies are now offering wireless local area networks. This type of network is perfect for historical buildings where local ordinances may prohibit drilling holes to run wire. The wireless network is also ideal in food processing factories where the cost of stainless steel conduit pipes would be prohibitive. Wireless local area networks eliminate the need for most wires, but they can be very expensive—up to $1,500 per workstation—and they tend to operate slowly. Their time has just not yet come.

If additional electrical outlets are required, any local electrician can handle the job. The work is straightforward, and you can probably get the job done by the low bidder. However, having an electrician cable your place of business for a network may be unwise.

Installing cable for a network requires special expertise and goes hand-in-hand with the design of the network. Many factors must be taken into consideration. The network designer will need to know the required number of servers and workstations, their physical placement, and the lengths of cable needed to connect them. Each branch (or segment) of the network may have restrictions regarding the number of devices that can be connected and the total length of cable allowed. Unless your electrician is experienced with this type of work, have your consultant, dealer, reseller, or network designer recommend a reputable cable installer. Believe it or not, some companies do nothing but install cables for computer networks—large and small.

Telephone

It certainly makes sense to have a telephone within easy reach of every computer you install. However, your communications requirements will probably go well beyond this. If you plan to install modems, you may want to consider installing separate telephone numbers, with separate jacks at each modem location. This installation prevents data transmission calls from being routed through your main telephone system. Going through a main switchboard can be a problem when you are trying to dial into a modem from a remote computer. Another benefit of separate telephone numbers is that you can transmit data to a remote location and simultaneously hold a conversation with the operator of the remote system. If you do order a separate telephone number for a modem hookup, be sure to have the telephone company classify the number as unlisted. Make sure that it's not listed in the telephone directory and unavailable from directory services. Would you believe it? The phone companies charge extra to *not* print the number!

If you are installing a network, consider the purchase of a *modem server* (sometimes called a *communications server*). A modem server is a single modemlike device that can be reached from any workstation on your network. If your communications requirements are modest and you probably will never have several data communications sessions running simultaneously, a modem server can save money because you buy just one device and pay for only one extra telephone line.

Lighting

Lighting is covered earlier in this book. Simply make sure that there is enough light and that it does not cause glare on the users' screens. If you see a glare on the screen, try moving the light or the equipment if possible. If moving doesn't work, as a last resort, purchase an antiglare screen for the video display.

Ensuring Security

Security comes in two flavors: physical and data. Physical security is a way to make sure that your expensive hardware, software packages, and documentation stay where you want them to stay. Data security, the protection of your data files from corruption, illicit copying, and occasionally even malicious harm, is by far the more important of the two. A stolen laser printer can always be replaced. But the protection of your business's most valuable asset, its data files, should always be your top priority.

Physical Security

You have probably already thought about data security, but what about the physical security of your hardware? It has been said that personal computers and printers have legs—they seem to disappear when the boss isn't looking. If you're in the retail business, you are surely familiar with shrinkage. Shrinkage is a polite word for stealing. Your hardware and supplies are subject to the same problem.

You can drill holes in your desktops and bolt the equipment down, and you can even chain your equipment to the legs of a desk. A determined thief will still find a way to abscond with the goods. The best you can ever hope to do is to deter the person who steals only when the opportunity presents itself. Make it difficult for that person, and virtually all your shrinkage problems go away.

Many mail-order companies sell inexpensive devices that will stop the "borderline" thief. These devices consist of a metal or plastic plate that is coated on one side with an industrial-strength, pressure-sensitive adhesive. Attached to the plate is a plastic-coated, stranded, steel cable similar to the locks popular with bicyclists. With the kit you also receive smaller adhesive-backed plates with metal loops or hooks through which the cable can pass. You attach the big plate to your desk and the small plates to each piece of equipment, and run the cable through the loops, finally attaching the free end (usually equipped with a combination lock) back to the main plate. For under $50, you have an effective security system. Of course, removing the plates from the desk or devices is just about impossible!

Some pieces of your system are nearly impossible to protect from theft. Floppy disks may disappear by the carload. Computer paper seems to disappear at twice the rate at which you print reports. Even printer ribbons seem just to fly away.

If you install a network, consider installing the server in a secure location. You do not want unauthorized personnel gaining access to the server. They might possibly destroy your crucial data files, remove applications, install unauthorized applications, or otherwise interfere with the operation of the network. The secured location shouldn't be a broom closet, however. Your network administrator (maybe that's you) will need regular access to the server to add and delete authorized users, perform general system maintenance, and do occasional fine-tuning. The best location is an office that can be locked when the administrator is not there.

Data Security

Data security is the protection of your data. Your data files are the lifeblood of your business. Allowing those files to get into the wrong hands can spell disaster. Imagine that you are an attorney and that a paralegal working in your office copies your entire client file. When that paralegal passes the bar and hangs out his own shingle, a list of highly qualified leads is suddenly in the hands of the competition.

What can you do about protecting your data from theft? Any computer with a disk drive is a tool for making illicit copies of data. It's important, therefore, to keep data files secured so that copies cannot be made.

One way to protect data is through encryption. Encrypted data is transformed, by using a mathematical formula with a secret numeric "key," into illegible and incomprehensible gibberish. To decrypt the data into a usable form, you need both the formula (sometimes called an *algorithm*) and the key (which serves as a password). For example, most large banks with automated teller machines (ATMs) encrypt your personal identification number (PIN) right at the ATM machine by using the United States Government approved Data Encryption Standard (DES). This encryption is done so that anyone tapping into the telephone lines between the

ATM and the bank's computers cannot see your PIN in its unencrypted state.

A few application programs encrypt data before storing it on disk. Of course, to make use of that encrypted data, your application program does the reverse—it decrypts the data at the moment the data is in use. In this case, data making an unauthorized trip outside your business would have to be accompanied by a copy of the application program—certainly not an impossible task. The third element needed is the encryption key; for without it, decryption of the data is, for all practical purposes, impossible.

You can lock up data kept on floppy disks, but what happens when an employee needs to come in on a Saturday morning to catch up on some work? Are you going to get up and come in with the key and then stick around all day to make sure that the disks are locked up? No way! So you give the key to a trusted employee, who may pass it along to someone else. Sooner or later the key gets lost or no one bothers to use it. You can see that this method doesn't work particularly well either.

You can also purchase a removable cartridge. Cartridges are like hard disks, but because they are removable, they encounter the same secured-storage problems as disks.

What is the ideal solution for secure storage of data? Imagine a corporate mainframe computer for a moment. Every bit of data is kept on giant disk drives or tape volumes at the computer's central site. Individual users have no physical access to the actual media on which the data is stored. The terminals connected to a mainframe computer are rarely equipped with floppy disk drives.

In the world of personal computing, the local area network once again comes to the rescue. With a network, you can duplicate the security of a mainframe system.

A perfect local area network has the file server located in a secure, locked environment. The server has a disk drive for loading new software programs and making copies of files and should also have a cassette-like streaming tape drive for making daily backups of data. The other personal computers on the network (which are called workstations in a networking environment) actually have no need for disk drives. Without disk drives, copies of data cannot be made. So it shouldn't come as a surprise that the hottest new piece of equipment in personal network computing is the "diskless workstation."

You can use a data communications program to transmit a data file over the telephone to a remote computer, which can store the data in question. However, it remains the responsibility of the network administrator to ensure that access rights into the network are correctly configured to prevent such occurrences.

Lack of data security can be a threat to your business. Plan ahead to make your data as secure as possible.

Installing Your New System

Finally, the time for installation has arrived. If your system is modest, you can probably accept delivery of all the components and install them in a day or two. But if you are installing a system with many computers, printers, and other devices, the large quantity and bulk of shipping containers may be overwhelming. In that case, consider accepting several partial deliveries.

Setting Up Your Hardware

Devise a plan for installing hardware. Do you want to start at one side of the business and work your way across to the other side, or does it make more sense to target specific work areas for early installation? If you are in a retail store, do you want installers walking around while customers are in the store? If you are a physician or dentist automating your medical practice, you will need to have full access to your current patient files.

What about the disruption of your current business practices? Do you have hardware devices that must be installed first because nothing else will function without them? These are questions to consider when planning your hardware installation.

Here is what Mark and Marian did in their bath and bedroom store. Remember that they decided to install a small local area network and that the special orders department was the first phase of their overall project.

Once the cabling for the network and the electrical work for new hardware had been finished, Mark and Marian arranged for the network server to be installed first. They had several good reasons for doing this.

First, the server is the most critical device in the entire system. Even though the server is nothing more than a specially configured, high-performance computer with high-capacity disk storage, it is the nerve center for the entire system. All the programs and data will reside here. If the server isn't working properly, the workstations located on the sales floor won't work either.

Second, the server can take several days to be installed and configured. Depending on the network operating system used and the number of employees who must be defined to the system with their log-in identification names and passwords, the process can take several days. Once that step is finished, the loading of application programs and creation of data files, if necessary, can take another several days. Some networking resellers will also install a workstation next to the server so that the operation and interaction between workstation and server can be viewed from a single vantage point.

Other devices connected to the server must be tested. If you purchase a tape or optical disk backup system for making daily backups of your data files, it must also be installed, properly configured, and tested.

Installation is not complete without also installing the software. Although this book is divided into two sections, hardware (this section) and software (the next section), in reality, hardware and software travel hand-in-hand. The only way to tell whether any computing device (a server, workstation, or other personal computer) is functioning properly is to turn it on and see whether it runs. Of course, that test means loading the operating system software. Both sections apply simultaneously.

After the server is up and running, it's time to connect the first workstation. Experienced network resellers almost always recommend hooking up just one workstation and putting it in operation before moving on to the next. If you have 10 workstations and you connect them all only to discover a problem, how will you know where to look?

Once the workstations are connected, the remainder of the equipment (including printers, cash drawers, modems, FAX boards, and other devices) can be connected. The amount of time required for connecting each device can vary significantly. The uncrating and installation of a laser printer can take from 10 minutes to over an hour. The time depends on how often you have done the task before.

Setting Up Your Software

Like setting up hardware, setting up software is an area where installation time and effort can vary widely, depending on the size of your system and the number and complexity of your software applications.

Installing a word processor on a single computer should take about one-half hour for someone experienced. Yet installing a network version of that same program could easily take a half day or more. Installing a word processor on a network is an involved process. Network installation includes creating private subdirectories on the server's hard disk for each user's files, assigning passwords and granting access rights, and defining printing devices connected to the network.

Most single-user software programs (software designed to be used on a non-networked, stand-alone computer) can usually be installed by anyone with a modest amount of computing experience. If you have the time and the inclination, fine, but remember that you have a business to run and that a good manager knows how to delegate. If your consultant, reseller, or dealer will not install the software, you should choose someone from your ranks. The person who volunteers for the job can become a valuable asset as you move through the computerization process.

> When installing software, read the instructions from start to finish *before* beginning the installation process.

You will need certain supplies when installing software. Usually, these supplies consist of several formatted blank disks with labels and sometimes a pad of paper for taking notes about configuration options you may be required to enter during the installation process. For example, many accounting packages ask you, during installation, for the number of customers, number of suppliers, and the part numbers required in your business. Although these limits can be raised when your business grows beyond these bounds, questions like this are not unusual.

Follow the installation instructions exactly. When you see a step about which you are unsure, pick up the telephone and call the technical support department of the software's manufacturer. Making an error in installation will probably not do any serious damage to data. However, a phone call may save you from having to repeat the entire installation process.

More and more software packages include an installation utility program. An installation program, if included, guides you through the installation process by telling you which disks to insert in the computer and which keys to press. Software packages that do not include an installation utility usually come instead with more extensive printed instructions requiring you to pay closer attention.

> If a given software package does not include an installation utility program, DON'T use one from a different package. They are not the same!

Some software packages are shipped on disks that are *copy protected*. The files on a copy-protected disk cannot, under ordinary circumstances, be copied to another disk with your computer's COPY command. Copy protection was instituted in the early days of personal computing to prevent illicit copies of software. In other words, if you have two people using a spreadsheet package on two different computers at the same time but you purchased only a single copy, someone is using an illegal copy. Today copy-protected software is rare. Even the last of the big holdouts, Lotus Development Corporation and Ashton-Tate Corporation, have dropped copy-protection from their products.

Most software packages strongly recommend that you make a working copy of all the disks in the package and store the originals in a safe, dry, secured location. If the working copy is destroyed or becomes corrupted, you can always make another working copy from your safely stored originals. Most hard disk systems do not need a working copy of disks because the program is installed directly on the hard disk.

> Even though software without copy protection can be physically copied, it is illegal to do so except for the purpose of making archival backup copies that will be used only in the event of the accidental destruction of the original copy or working copy.

Be fair to the companies who manufactured your software, whether you have one-of-a-kind custom software or the millionth copy of a popular word processing program. Making illegal copies of software is stealing. In principle, illegal copying is no different from shoplifting from Mark and Marian's bathroom accessories store.

Testing Your Equipment

Testing your equipment simply means asking, "Does it start when you turn on the switch?" You are still not at the point of running a formal system test to see whether the results are what you expect. But then again, you're not that far away either!

Depending on your particular computer and how it was configured by the dealer, you may be instructed to start the computer by using the disk containing the operating system software. The reason for this instruction is that your hard disk, if you have one, may not have been *formatted*, or prepared for use. Check with your dealer. He should deliver your machine with the hard disk already formatted and a copy of the operating system installed. If not, you will need to go through the process of formatting the hard disk before you can use it.

Formatting is a process that prepares your hard disk by writing test data to every possible location on the disk. When the data is written, it is immediately read back. If the written data and the data read back are exactly the same, the operating system assumes that this location on the disk is suitable for use. If the data read back is not the same as the data written to that location on the disk, the operating system assumes that this specific location on the disk is defective and not suitable for data storage. The operating system creates a *map* of your hard disk, keeping a list of locations that must never be used for data storage. High-capacity hard disks may have as much as two percent of their total data storage area marked as unusable. This percentage is normal and should create no concern.

Floppy disks are also formatted for use in a similar manner.

Once the hard disk is formatted, you can begin installing files.

> The first files you should install on a hard disk are the operating system files.

The operating system files enable the computer to start up (or *boot)* from the hard disk. The operating system for IBM computers consists of three files: IBMDOS.COM, IBMBIO.COM, and COMMAND.COM. IBMDOS.COM and IBMBIO.COM are not shown on a directory listing of your root directory.

With individual computers, once the operating system software is installed, you can simply follow the instructions for a first-time boot up. If you have reached this point, your computer is working just fine—you have cleared the first hurdle.

If you have installed a printer, turn it on and try printing. With your IBM-compatible computer and a printer connected to the parallel port, type the command:

```
dir > lpt1
```

If everything is connected properly, you should send a copy of the directory listing of files to the printer. That test is the second hurdle. If the command doesn't work, your printer may be connected to lpt2, the second parallel port, or to com1 or com2, the first and second serial ports, respectively.

Testing a networked installation is best left to your network reseller. Not only must the installer test the server, workstations, printers, disks, tape backup, and other devices; but the installer will probably take time to fine-tune the performance of the system for optimum performance.

Deciding What To Implement First

Consider Mark and Marian's project. They chose to automate two areas of their bed and bath store operation: the regular retail portion of the store, where customers purchase inventory directly from display units, and the Custom Orders department, where customers place orders for merchandise that arrives several weeks later.

After performing their analysis, Mark and Marian agreed to split the project into two phases. Their analysis revealed that the logical first step was tackling the Custom Orders department because most of the errors were attributable to mishandling of orders and error-prone manual procedures.

But what about your business? The managers of a small accounting firm that provides accounting services for 200 individual physicians had several options in deciding what to implement first. They could have installed a network with a network accounting software system to handle the core business. They could have installed a commercial tax-preparation package that not only calculates and fills out commercial and personal tax forms but also prints the completed forms on a laser printer using special downloaded soft fonts. They could have installed a word processor for correspondence. After much discussion, the staff agreed that the application that deserved to be installed first was the time-billing package that prepares the monthly invoices for each client and tracks moneys received in paying those invoices.

Why did the staff make that choice? First, no network was required. The decision deferred a major expense, and the actual accounting was getting done—albeit manually. Second, the company had virtually no requirement for word processing. The occasional reports that needed to be produced were being typed manually, and a word processor did not offer an immediate opportunity for a large gain in productivity. The staff did recognize, however, that automating the word processing would be second. Preparation and laser printing of tax returns was being subcontracted. Even though this represented an avoidable expense, the work was being returned on time and without error. This procedure would also be brought in-house at a later time.

But the failure to generate timely invoices had a severe impact on the cash position of the accounting business itself. The invoices were always several weeks late and usually contained omissions that resulted in services being provided free of charge. When the time to prepare the invoices came, two clerks spent an entire weekend manually preparing the invoices. The office manager manually logged payments in a three-ring binder.

The requirements for automating were modest: one personal computer, one laser printer to print the invoices, and a software package designed for time billing and invoice preparation with tracking of payables.

> Install first the part of the system that provides the best payback for the least money with the least effort.

The time required to install this small configuration was about 4 hours. The training for the software package took 3 days. Data entry of all the client information took about a week. And the positive results were immediate. Instead of 6 person-days required to compile and type the invoices manually, the program allowed each client's invoice to be previewed on the screen for accuracy and completeness. Total time for 200 clients at an average of 3 minutes per client was 600 minutes, or 10 hours (1.25 person-days figuring 8 hours per person-day). Next, the invoices were printed on the laser in about a half hour. Total time for both operations was about 10.5 hours, or roughly 1.3 person-days (8 hours = 1 person/day). With the old method, envelopes were manually typed. Figuring 2 minutes per envelope, that task totaled 400 minutes, or 6.67 hours. The new solution uses window envelopes so processing of envelopes is completely eliminated. Folding invoices and stuffing envelopes is still done manually—for now. But that step will change with the purchase of a $300 electric folding machine.

Table 8.1 compares both methods.

Table 8.1
Sample Comparison of
Manual and Automated Procedures

Task	*Manual Hours*	*Automated Hours*	*Savings Percentage*
Compile invoice data	30	10	67%
Type (print) invoices	18	0.5	97%
Type envelopes	6.67	0	100%
Fold invoices	1	0.5	50%
Stuff envelopes	0.8	0.8	0%
Total hours	56.47	11.8	79%
Clerk Costs*	$1,468.22	$306.80	79%

*Clerk costs ($20 per hr. plus 30% benefits resulting in a figure of $26 per hr. for calculations)

Clearly a total investment of about $5,000 has been a good investment. This choice was right for the first automation project. Remember that this chart represents just one month. The savings in clerk wages of $1,161.42 each month represents an annual savings of $13,937.04. Discounting the initial learning curve of the system, the $5,000 system paid for itself in just over four months. All the savings after that go directly to the bottom line. And there were other benefits too. Because the invoices went out earlier, the payments came in sooner. Because receivables were being tracked on the system (and this chart doesn't even include the time savings realized), late payers were automatically identified and follow-up invoices were generated by the system.

Risk and Payoff

As you saw earlier in this book, a delicate balance between risk and payoff must always be considered. The two extremes are low risk with a low payoff and high risk with a high payoff. Everything else lies somewhere in between.

What's best for you may not be best for everybody. Low risk usually implies a comfort factor. If your project doesn't fare as you had hoped, you can change your mind while keeping losses to a minimum. But high risk almost always brings with it greater chances for success.

Low Risk and High Payoff

The time billing example in this chapter is a clear-cut case of low risk and high payoff. With a minimum amount of funds invested (about $5,000), this client was able to institute a simple technological solution (one computer, one off-the-shelf commercial software package, and one printer). With a modest amount of personnel training, the system produced sensational savings in time, resulting in hours freed up for other work and in far superior control of the invoicing process, which is actually the only genuine revenue-producing activity in the entire company. Choosing a high-cost, high-risk project, such as installing a networked accounting system, would have yielded dividends; but an analysis showed they would not have been as dramatic. Would you start out with a high risk with low payoff project?

High Risk and High Payoff

Certainly more compelling than a high risk with low payoff alternative is high risk with a high payoff. Think of Donald Trump or Microsoft Corporation's Bill Gates, and you will immediately understand the concept of risking "it all for the big score."

Mark and Marian found themselves in a similar—but much scaled-down—situation. Their bed and bath store had no need for time billing, so that low-risk solution was out. They did very little word processing. That easy project was out too. They agreed that automating the Custom Orders department was the single most important factor in determining whether their business would sink or swim. This was the project that *had* to be done. And as you have surely heard, if a job is worth doing, it's worth doing right.

The solution for Mark and Marian was high-risk and high-cost. They installed a local area network with each workstation configured as a cash register. They hired a consultant to develop objectives, priorities, and plans. They sought out value-added resellers who specialized in solutions for retailers and who were authorized to install networks. Mark and Marian hired a custom programmer and held many meetings with employees, customers, and the all-important vendors with whom the custom orders were ultimately placed. Now *this procedure* is high risk.

The payoff, you will recall from an earlier chapter was a carefully charted expectation of reduced errors that could be measured over a specific period of time. To Mark and Marian, their accountant, and the bank that financed the start-up of their business, these expectations represented a payoff big enough to justify the high cost and risk of this phase of their project.

The Nature of Your Business

The nature of your business will have a substantial bearing on which application you bring up first. While an accounting system may be your ultimate goal and is at the heart of virtually every business, the installation, training, and conversion of your current manual systems may be too big a project to undertake initially.

As you saw with the example of the small accounting business, the managers elected not to install an accounting system even though accounting services are the actual service they provide to customers. Instead, the staff decided to implement a small application that required minimal effort, training, and conversion.

> Your first application should be one that guarantees success and sets a positive tone for the remainder of your computerization projects.

No one wants to fail. So why take a chance on an application that requires huge amounts of preparation and training? Instead, proceed in tiny steps and be assured of each step's success. This approach is better than taking a giant step and stumbling. Success breeds a desire for more success and creates an environment where morale will most assuredly improve.

> Set your employees up for success, not for failure.

Logical First Choices

What you see in this section are common choices for a first software application. As you have just seen, these choices may not be the correct choices for *your* business. The examples do merit your consideration, however. They can help you understand that each of these applications represents a modest step assuring success. If none of these applications applies to your particular business environment, develop a list of first choices that are small in scope and modest in terms of difficulty.

Accounts Receivable

For those not familiar with accounting, accounts receivable is a piece, or *module*, of an entire accounting system. The accounts receivable module tracks the money owed to you by your customers. Without money coming in, you wouldn't have much of a business, would you? Other modules in a complete accounting system may include

- ❏ Accounts payable
- ❏ General ledger
- ❏ Payroll
- ❏ Inventory control
- ❏ Purchase order management
- ❏ Sales analysis

With accounts receivable you keep track of individual customers: who they are, how much they owe, what they bought, and—perhaps most important—their track record for paying on time. Receivables systems usually include a feature called *aging*, which analyzes each customer's records to determine whether invoices older than 30, 60, 90, or 120 days remain unpaid.

Receivables systems perform other tasks: preparation of invoices and statements, calculation of finance charges, application of cash receipts to the account as a whole or sometimes to specific invoices, and generation of mailing labels. Your receivables module will print many different types of reports, including aging, cash flow, and sales reports. You may be able to sort sales reports by customer, salesperson, or product. Many systems include a *report writer* feature, which lets you create custom reports to meet your unique needs.

Any accounting module requires time to install. Perhaps the biggest job ahead of you is the data entry of your customer information. For every customer you want included in the system, you will be entering at least the following information:

- ❑ Customer identification number
- ❑ Name
- ❑ Address
- ❑ Telephone number(s)
- ❑ Contact names
- ❑ Tax rate
- ❑ Tax identification number
- ❑ Discount percentage
- ❑ Discount days

- ❏ Credit limit
- ❏ Monthly finance charge rate

You may have other entries, depending on your business. Many systems let you print messages at the bottom of a statement. The messages may vary according to the number of days the statement is overdue. For example, statements without overdue balance may print, "Thank you for your business." Statements 90 days overdue may print, "Your account is seriously overdue and will be referred to a collection agency if payment is not received in ten days." These features, and many others, are available in most accounting systems and individual modules.

Time Billing

Time billing is the application that the small accounting firm chose to implement first. Time billing is actually a specialized type of accounts receivable application: it keeps track of money owed to you by clients and generates invoices and statements. Time-billing systems differ primarily in the type of product for which they are designed to charge. In an auto parts business, you charge for parts—which is merchandise, or inventory.

Professional services many times do not deal with inventory. Attorneys, accountants, and consultants charge for their *time*. Time-billing programs understand how these different kinds of businesses operate. The systems contain features for items like hourly rates for specific services, flat-rate billing with maximums and minimums, and tracking of retainer fees paid up front by clients to be drawn against as services are provided by the professional. Retainers are standard operating procedure for many attorneys and consultants. As a rule, a time-billing program is more straightforward to use than a full-featured accounts receivable module. Of course, you will still need to invest time to enter customer information into the system.

Word Processing

Try to imagine a business that doesn't write letters, memorandums, reports, or other typed documents. Imagining a business that wouldn't benefit from word processing is difficult. Word processing isn't always perfect (addressing a single envelope will be done faster with your trusty old typewriter); but any document, once created and stored on disk, can be retrieved, edited, and printed thousands and thousands of time. Because you don't need to retype the material, each subsequent use of that particular document file saves you additional time.

Some businesses depend on word processors. An attorney's office today is at a distinct competitive disadvantage without word processing to create contracts, briefs, and other legal documents. Books like this one would take far longer to produce if an author's manuscript were submitted on stacks of printed paper instead of on floppy disks.

As for your business, your needs may be quite different. An auto body repair shop uses pre-printed forms that are filled in by hand. However, the shop may have an occasional need to send correspondence to an insurance company. Even Mark and Marian concluded that their bed and bath store had little need for word processing. Their typewriter still worked and was suitable for the one or two letters they typed each week. Because they opted for the custom-order entry system, they thought it best to wait before tackling word processing.

Word processing is the most horizontal of all personal computing applications. This description means simply that word processing has appeal to everyone, no matter what the business. That aspect is quite different from narrowly focused vertical market software that is designed for highly specific uses (like crop rotation management software). More computers are bought for word processing than for any other purpose.

Database Management

In a sense, many software packages manage a base of collected data. The data may be numbers (accounting) or words (word processing). True database management systems, like Ashton-Tate's dBASE family of products, provide powerful engines for the creation of databases, the entry and validation of data, and the generation of reports about the data. But simply buying a database management system (DBMS) may not be the best first choice.

A DBMS offers an environment in which you can write application programs to control the input, output, and processing of data. You could write an application that is a complete accounting system, a card catalog and lending application for a public library, or a personnel system for a large company's human resources department. Of course, you can also buy commercial applications or contract for custom programming for almost any data management need. In fact, Mark and Marian's custom-order entry system was written in a database management language.

If you plan to write programs in-house, you can buy a DBMS. You can also buy a *compiler*. This special software package takes the programs you have written and generates programs that load and run without the need for the DBMS package. In the IBM-compatible world, for example, Clipper, QuickSilver, and FoxBASE+ are built on the generic dBASE language but add their own extensions to the language and greatly improve performance. These compilers create a stand-alone customized database application, which simplifies the complexity of using a DBMS.

Does this information make you think twice about choosing a DBMS for your first application? Your choice depends on your needs. If you need the database management capabilities that other programs can't deliver, perhaps your best alternative is contracting with a custom software developer who will deliver a finished, professionally written, software application. This choice would free you from having to buy a DBMS package.

Chapter Summary

In this chapter, you have learned that implementing your system is more than connecting your hardware and installing software. Even before the hardware arrives, a significant amount of planning is necessary—from developing a floor plan to analyzing the flow of work. Your office or store must be prepared to receive the equipment you have spent so much time choosing. This preparation may involve moving telephones, installing new lines for modems, ensuring that adequate electrical power is available at the appropriate location, and providing adequate but glare-free lighting. You learned that the physical security of your equipment and, more important, the security of your data are an essential part of the planning process.

Installing hardware includes examining it for obvious physical damage, cabling for your network (if that's appropriate), and finally connecting each device with a cable. You saw that loading software is a crucial step and that you should carefully follow the software manufacturer's instructions for the best results. Finally, you turned the equipment on and performed some simple tests or started an application software program to make sure that your hardware was functioning properly. You haven't done any software testing, though. That comes later.

You decided what software program to implement first. In some cases—if you buy only one application—you will have no choice. In most other cases, however, you can implement a simple application that shows quick positive results. A happy ending for your first application will whet everyone's appetite for more. Or you can install a complex application that requires a substantial training of your staff. That's a higher risk, but if the payoff in better productivity, reduced errors, or improved profitability justifies the initial risk, that choice may be the best choice for you.

All through this book you have seen that there is not one right way to approach computerization. What is best for you may not be appropriate for someone else—even someone else in the same business. Every individual business has its own unique manner of operation. If all dental practices were alike, there wouldn't be a need for over 40 dental office management software packages.

With your hardware fully installed and tested, it's on to the next step: developing a plan for testing the software on which your business will depend.

CHAPTER 9

Testing Your System

By now your hardware is installed, and you have installed and probably experimented with one or more software applications. Before you entrust your business to a new computer system, you must put the system through rigorous testing to ensure that the system performs exactly the tasks for which the software was designed.

Not all software needs to go through rigorous testing. If you are working with a word processing program, you need not perform extensive testing because commercially available, mass-marketed software has already been thoroughly tested (although obscure glitches are occasionally found). It is also unlikely that you will suffer a data loss so catastrophic that your business is placed in jeopardy. The same conditions apply to most commercial software: spreadsheet, communications, desktop publishing, and others. The exception to this generalization is accounting systems. An off-the-shelf accounting system is probably error free, but you must still test to make sure that the system performs as you expect it to.

What you must test are the systems that are *mission critical*. That term means simply that any software program essential to the survival of your business must be thoroughly tested to ensure that it performs the tasks you expect, in the manner and with the results you expect, and, most important, that the program's management of data, computation of results, and presentation of output are one hundred percent accurate.

You have reached a point where errors can be hunted down and corrected. Many people enjoy the process of testing and finding errors in logic, that were inadvertently built into a software program.

The most important and most rigorous testing is reserved for custom software, which does not have the advantage of having been tested by thousands of previous users. Because this software was developed specifically for your business, you and your consultant, programmer, and other team members must put the product through its paces. Mark and Marian were aware of this fact, and they set aside several weeks for the testing process.

Testing your system incorporates a healthy side benefit—training. As you and your staff move through the testing process, you will also be training yourself to use the system. For more about training, see Chapter 10.

Testing the Right Stuff

What do you want to test? Sure, you want to test your new software package, but in what way? For example, Mark and Marian's custom-order entry system was designed to produce, among other things, order sheets by vendor, for all the custom orders placed within the last seven days. They wanted to test that aspect of the system for accuracy to be sure that all the orders placed were correctly sorted by vendor, and that no omissions or double processing of data could occur. In short, Mark and Marian wanted the printed reports to reflect exactly the orders entered into the system. That goal is commendable and presents no problems, at least not yet.

Mark and Marian did make one error in judgment. They decided to compare their computer-generated order sheets with the hand-written order sheets they had painstakingly compiled for years. Do you see their error? The computer reports and the manual reports will *never* reconcile because manual reports are hardly ever error-free to begin with. This particular test can never run successfully.

The better method, at least initially, is to use test data and manual reports that have been checked by several people and are known to be accurate. If you are testing a general purpose accounting system, your plan of attack should be no different. Test data that produces a known result forms the basis for all software testing.

Developing the Testing Scheme

Testing your system includes these steps:

- ❏ Devising a test plan
- ❏ Creating a test script of transactions
- ❏ Entering any necessary data into the system
- ❏ Performing the test transactions
- ❏ Running any programs required to process the transactions and generate reports
- ❏ Analyzing the reports

Each step has specific goals and is dependent on the step that precedes it. For that reason, you should perform all these procedures.

Devising a Test Plan

What do you want to test? The accuracy of printed reports? The layout of data entry screens? The speed at which your software performs its designated tasks? Maybe you want to test all three aspects of the application.

> The first step in devising a testing plan is deciding what needs to be tested.

Along with their consultant, software programmer, and network designer, Mark and Marian made a long list of the items they felt needed to be tested. The following represents part of their list:

- *Daily Start-Up:* Beginning-of-day system totals should be the same as the preceding day's end-of-day totals (also called *run-to-run controls*).
- *Data Entry Screens:* All information required for a special order should be requested by the system.
- *Data Entry Screens:* The order in which information is requested should be in accordance with the written system specification.
- *Price Calculation:* Prices for custom items should be calculated accurately.
- *Customer's Order:* Orders should contain all entered information, calculated prices, shipping times, sales taxes, and estimated delivery times. Customer ID number, with customer name/phone/address

information, should be printed. Order number should be printed, should be assigned automatically, and should be one greater than the preceding order number.

- ❑ *End-of-Day Reports:* Daily reports should be accurate and complete.
- ❑ *End-of-Week Reports:* Weekly reports should be accurate and complete. Special reports sorted by vendor for the actual placing of a single blanket order of all items should be generated and be complete and accurate.
- ❑ *Other Reports:* All other reports, including aging of open orders, partially filled orders, and orders received but not picked up, should be checked.
- ❑ *Printed Notices:* Check printing of post cards to notify customers of arrival of goods.
- ❑ *File Maintenance:* Add, delete, and modify customer files, vendor files, stock number files, pricing information files, shipping charge files, etc.
- ❑ *Receipts:* A receipt for all items picked up should be printed. (This will be signed by the customer and kept on file.)
- ❑ *Payments:* Check customer payments to make sure they are accurately logged.
- ❑ *Activity Reports:* Reports listing activity by sales associate and commission calculation should be accurate and complete.
- ❑ *Returns:* Procedures for returning damaged merchandise including customer refunds, return to vendor, whether or not to re-order should be checked.

Get the idea? This list (only partially reproduced here) doesn't suggest how to perform the test; the list defines only items that Mark and Marian decided actually require testing. That list is the first step in the testing procedure.

Next, the team devised a testing plan. This plan is simply a schedule of events. You don't go to the theater and watch Act III of a play before you see Act I, and testing is no different. If Mark and Marian ran the activity by sales associate report before any transactions had been entered, the reports should show no activity. But if someone thought that transactions had already been entered, he or she would conclude that the sales associates were not selling anything. So a plan simply lists all the testing events in the order in which they are to take place. And because an exhaustive test can take several days or even weeks, each day must be identified.

You probably think the first testing day is day #1. That makes perfect sense, but imagine the analogy of a rocket lifting off from its launch pad. The clock begins counting up (elapsed time) at the time of liftoff. Before liftoff occurs, the clock actually counts backward in a countdown. (Remember "T minus 1 minute and counting"?) Mark and Marian certainly weren't counting minutes and seconds, but they were counting days, and their plan called for the first day of transaction entry to be labeled day #1. Their schedule looked like the following:

Day # −2: Daily start-up
- Data entry of vendor file
- Data entry of item file
- Print vendor file reports
- Print item file reports
- Daily file backup
- Daily shut-down

Day # −1: Daily start-up
- Data entry of pricing file
- Data entry of shipping charges file
- Data entry of adds, deletes, changes to vendor file

Data entry of adds, deletes, changes to item file
Print pricing file reports
Print shipping charges file reports
Print vendor file reports
Print item file reports
Daily file backup
Daily shut-down

Day # 0: Daily start-up
Simulated loss of data
Restore all data from Day −1 daily backup
Run all reports (should yield same results as day # −1)
Daily backup
Daily shut-down

Day # 1: Daily start-up
Data entry of customer name and address information
Entry of custom orders
Print end-of-day reports
Daily file backup
Daily shut-down

Day # 2: Daily start-up
Entry of custom orders
Entry of custom-order changes
Print end-of-day reports
Daily file backup
Daily shut-down

Day # 3: Daily start-up
Entry of custom orders
Print end-of-day reports
Print end-of-week reports
Daily file backup
Daily shut-down

What's happening here is clear. A tightly controlled schedule of events is being laid out. Remember that several workstations (which are configured like cash registers) were installed, so some of these activities take place concurrently.

Keep in mind that all these activities have nothing to do with the real custom orders still being placed by live customers. You can't let your business suffer while you work with a system that in reality isn't doing anything for you yet.

Another factor to remember is that the testing process may go more slowly than you anticipate. You need not complete each day's testing procedures in a single calendar day. In fact, some activities, like data entry of customer information, may take more than one day. And if difficulties arise that require going back to a previous activity or previous day, the delay may cost you a few aspirin, but that is what testing is all about.

> Each "day" of your testing schedule can span several calendar days if necessary.

At the conclusion of each calendar day on which testing is performed, the entire testing team should get together to discuss the day's events. Carefully consider the objective of each testing step and whether that goal was attained. If the team agrees that the objective was successfully met, you can proceed to the next phase of the test schedule.

At any point where testing produces results that are unexpected, undesired, or erroneous, suspend the testing procedure until the cause of the problem is determined and corrected. After the correction is made, be sure to go back and rerun those steps to ensure that the modifications correct the problem without introducing any new problems.

> Proceed to the next step of your testing only after the preceding step has been concluded successfully.

Creating Test Data and Test Scripts

Your test script identifies the activities that require testing and the order in which the testing should occur. But what do you want to happen during each step? For example, when you undertake the data entry of vendor, item, and pricing information, what will you enter? You could certainly enter random information as the test proceeds, but it would be impossible to tell whether the processing of that data or the reports generated by the system are accurate. You must create test data and test transactions so that the results you obtain can be reconciled with the original test data. After all, you wouldn't try to reconcile your checkbook without knowing what checks you wrote during the month.

First, you need to create a complete set of test data. Mark and Marian started by creating a set of test vendors, the companies from which they order their inventory. The following is a vendor test record:

Vendor Name: Ace Curtain Company, Inc.

Vendor Address 1: 83 Gingham Road

Vendor Address 2: P.O. Box 9442

City: Needham Heights

State: MA

ZIP: 02194

Area Code: 617

Telephone: 444-9999

Contact Name: Jane Gingham

Vendor Short Name: Ace

Vendor ID Number: (assigned by system)

Terms: Net 30

Discount Allowed: 2% 10 days

Print Form 1099: Yes

Day of Month Due: 15

Comment: Ships via UPS unless told otherwise

Testing notes: Add this vendor on day # −2, and delete on day # 5 after custom orders for this vendor have been placed.

Mark and Marian created a total of 25 vendor records. Why so many? Remember that during the course of the testing, one system feature that requires testing is the deletion of vendors from the system. So you need to start with enough records to still have enough in the system after deleting a few. That process will be a crucial test: what should the system do if you try to delete a vendor while there are pending orders for that vendor? Obviously, the system should never allow such a deletion to occur nor should it allow you to cancel pending orders first.

In a manner similar to the vendor test record, Mark and Marian created test records for the item file (the products that can be custom ordered), the pricing file, the shipping charges file, and the transaction file.

The transaction file is what Mark and Marian's system is all about: the entry and processing of custom orders. Although all the other files are important, the system cannot function without the transaction files. The whole purpose of testing is to make sure that customer orders are entered and processed completely and accurately. For this reason, you will need to create a broad range of transactions to cover every conceivable situation.

What kinds of situations should be tested? Here is a partial list of test transaction types and the number of each that Mark and Marian created:

Type of Transaction	*Quantity of test transactions created*
Order of one item	75
Order of several items from one vendor	75
Order of several items from two vendors	75
Order of several items from three vendors	75
Addition of items to an existing order	25
Cancellation of an entire order	15
Cancellation of a partial order	15
Receipt of all items in an order	30
Receipt of partial order	40
Return of damaged merchandise from customer	15
Return of damaged merchandise to vendor	15

Each of these transactions is designed to test a different aspect of Mark and Marian's custom-order entry system.

As you can see from the chart, Mark and Marian created 75 of each of the 4 order-type transactions. Creating each test transaction takes time: you need to decide which items will be ordered; what colors, sizes, and shipping arrangements will be used; and how deposits will be handled. Design your test transactions so that they cover a wide range of situations, combinations of situations, and data. For your own reference purposes (not for data processing purposes), put each transaction on a separate sheet of paper in a loose-leaf notebook and assign an identification number to each transaction for easy reference by all parties participating in the test. And mix the transactions up. It's not wise to perform all the transactions of one type and then go on to the next. The idea is to simulate your actual business operation.

> To test your system completely, develop a comprehensive set of test transactions.

Performing the Test

You have developed a list of features you want to test, a schedule of events, a set of test data, and a set of test transactions. With these tasks completed, you are ready to begin the testing process. Remember that each "day" of the test can span several calendar days and that you can perform the testing after office or store hours so that your current business operations will not be interrupted.

Mark and Marian elected to start the testing process on a Monday morning at 8:00 a.m., giving them two full hours of testing before the store was scheduled to open at 10:00 a.m. They also decided to leave the equipment running all day so that they could continue the data entry process during slow periods. You can see that no schedule was established to run according to the clock. Given the fact that only a few people were involved in the actual performing of the test, the participants agreed that by-the-clock timetables weren't necessary. If your company is large enough to require more than a handful of people, consider establishing a timetable. That schedule will help ensure that time is not being wasted by people simply waiting for their piece of the test to start.

On Monday morning, Mark and Marian arrived at the store early—7:30 a.m. Why not 8:00 a.m.? The test is scheduled to *begin* at 8:00 a.m.; all preparation for testing should be done beforehand so that the actual testing process can begin on time. And because this is the first day of testing, Mark and Marian decided that the key team players, their consultant, their value-added reseller (the network expert), and the programmer of the custom software should also be present.

The next steps are purely mechanical. Turn on all the equipment, set dates and times if necessary, load the operating system if necessary, and make sure that everything is operating properly. Is the network operating system functioning properly? Are all the individual workstations recognized by the network? Have the workstations "attached" themselves to the network server? Are the printers turned on and loaded with paper?

After all these items, and any others required by your particular configuration, are verified, you can proceed to the next step: loading the application software.

Mark and Marian's custom-order entry system called for one software program to be loaded, or *invoked*, at the network server and a second program to be invoked at each workstation. Mark and Marian brought up the server program first, verified that it loaded successfully, and then went from workstation to workstation to load the individual copies of the program that would make each workstation function as a cash register.

Performing the Test Transactions

With all the hardware running and the software loaded and verified, it's finally time to begin the testing process. That begins at 8:00 a.m.

Like painting a house, the preparation work is the most difficult and time-consuming. In painting, you spend most of your time scraping, sanding, and washing walls. Testing a computer system is no different. You have spent a great deal of time planning your test, devising a schedule, and developing a catalog of test transactions. Now comes the easy part, the actual painting of the room—the keyboard entry of your test transactions.

Simply perform each transaction as if a customer were standing in front of you. As the system asks for information, enter it from your test transaction sheet.

When the transaction is complete, initial the page to indicate that you have completed the transaction and staple the cash register receipt and customer copies of any documents generated by the system to the page for future reference.

If you are satisfied that the results of the transaction match the information on the sheet as well as the results you expect to see for that transaction, proceed to the next transaction. Continue as long as you do not encounter difficulties.

When *any* unexpected event occurs, such as erroneous information being displayed, incorrect totals being calculated, receipts not being printed or printing incorrectly, or anything else that does not meet your expectations completely, stop the test immediately. Call your team together and examine the transaction and its results in an effort to determine the nature of the difficulty. If the problem arises from a simple data entry problem (you entered a quantity of 22 instead of 2, for example), you can just make a note of the error on your test transaction sheet and continue.

If the difficulty is more problematic, such as prices being calculated incorrectly, you must suspend the test and discover the cause of the difficulty. Most often, the error will stem from an error in the logic of a software program. Even hardware problems can be caused by flaws in programming. For example, if a cash drawer fails to open, the failure might be caused by a malfunction in the drawer's hardware, but the more likely cause is that the programmer neglected to send a command to open the cash drawer at the appropriate time. Similarly, the failure of the system to print a receipt may be caused by a faulty printer or simply because the program didn't ask for a receipt to be printed.

Write a short description of the difficulty, the transaction in which the difficulty was noticed (the reason you assigned each transaction an identification number), and the business problems the difficulty might create. For example, Mark and Marian reported the following problem:

Transaction:	#37
Type:	Partial cancellation of a pending order
Expected Result:	Print a customer receipt confirming the cancellation.
Actual Result:	System failed to print receipt
Business Impact:	If we try to bill the customer for the cancelled merchandise, the customer has no way to prove the items were previously cancelled.
Recommendation:	Modify software as necessary

With written copies of this *incident report* in hand, the programmer has all the information necessary to modify the transaction. At the time the error was noticed, testing was immediately stopped, and a discussion took place to determine whether the difficulty was serious enough to cause the test to stop until the error was corrected. The team decided to continue with testing because all computations were being performed correctly. The only omission was the part of the program that was to print a customer receipt for this specific transaction type.

Reconciling the Test Results

When all the transaction activity for the first day has been entered, even though you might have spread that single business day over several calendar days, perform the procedures for end-of-day shutdown—backing up files to disk, tape, or other media and generating all expected reports.

When all the reports are generated and every activity scheduled for day # 1 has been completed, it's time to reconcile the reports, a procedure much like reconciling your checkbook.

It's not enough to examine the reports and add up the columns of numbers to see whether they equal the totals printed at the end of the report. All that task would accomplish is to prove that the addition of the printed numbers is correct. But do you know for a fact that everything that is supposed to appear on the reports actually does? That's something impossible to tell from examining the report itself.

There is only one way to make sure that all entered transactions were processed as expected and included on all appropriate reports. That way is to calculate, *by hand*, the expected results of the transactions processed during the testing day. Not sure whether you will do that manual calculation accurately? Then have several people do the manual calculations and compare the results. You should check these results against your printed reports. Are all transactions printed that should be? Do the printed totals accurately reflect all the transactions actually performed?

Go back through your test transactions and check to see that each one appears on the printed reports where appropriate. If everything checks—and that means 100 percent, then you go on to the next step. But if anything does not reconcile, you must go back, find the cause of the error, modify programming as necessary, and retest.

Getting the Team Together

With the results of the first day's test complete and audited, it's time for a meeting of your principal players—those who are in charge of the test and those who are responsible for the system (your consultant and programmer, for example).

What do you discuss at this meeting? The subjects that Mark and Marian placed on the agenda are as follows:

What worked

What didn't work

Why not

What needs to be done

Things that should be in the system but aren't

Clearly, the second item of this agenda deserves the most attention. Every unexpected or erroneous result, no matter how small or insignificant, must be discussed in detail. Occasionally, what appears on the surface as a small error may be the tip of the iceberg representing a larger error in logic that has been built into the software. And those errors, big or small, must be corrected.

> Changes made in the software to correct errors of any scope must be fully retested.

Changing the code in a program to correct an error does not guarantee that the change was correctly applied. To be sure that new errors have not been introduced inadvertently, those transactions must be tried again. And to make sure that other errors have not been introduced, be sure to run other transactions as well.

The third part of the daily agenda is usually broken into two groups: features that must be added and features that "we would like to see." These changes, because they are not part of the original system specification, will cost extra.

Is the team satisfied with the results? Yes? Then it's on to day # 2. If the team is not satisfied, the team must decide whether to go back and perform the first day's test again or push forward. Most programmers and consultants recommend retesting for two reasons.

- ❑ It's unlikely that they will guarantee an error-free system unless retesting is performed.
- ❑ Owing to human nature, retesting requires more billable hours by these independent business people.

Running Parallel Systems

You have completed an exhaustive and minutely detailed testing process. If your test was structured correctly and included the correct assortment of test transactions, you should have tested every aspect of your system. This test has been a scavenger hunt, a game in which the person who finds the most system errors deserves a prize.

> The testing period is the best time to find errors. After a system has been placed into production is the worst time to find errors.

After the entire team have audited reports from the last day and have agreed that the test has concluded successfully, it's time to go on to the next step in the testing process: running parallel systems.

You thought that testing was completed? You're not done yet because you have been using hypothetical data until now. Parallel testing means running your system during business hours, parallel to the manual system you are currently using. For Mark and Marian, parallel testing meant entering customer transactions in the computer system while still writing orders by hand.

The parallel test is run to make sure that the system runs as expected and produces complete and accurate results in the actual environment in which it will be used with real data.

Before beginning the parallel test, be sure to re-initialize all of your system's data files in order to remove all the data you entered during the initial testing process.

Running the parallel test is a simple matter. You use the system exactly as you would if the system were actually in production. In a sense, it is in production, but because you are still using your manual systems, you are not yet actually running your business using computer-generated data.

At the end of each day, be sure to reconcile the manual data with the reports generated by the computer system. Apply all the rules that you used in the initial testing process. Check to make sure that all the transactions entered appear on the reports. And compare the computer-generated reports to your hand-produced reports. Mark and Marian did this step and discovered that the manual and automatic reports didn't agree, something which did not surprise them, given the history of inaccuracy they had in manually producing these reports. After carefully auditing both the manual and computer-generated reports, they discovered, to no one's surprise, that the computer-generated reports were correct.

Of course, if your computer is generating reports that have no equivalent in your old manual system, a line-by-line comparison will not be possible. Be sure, however, to examine all reports possible, and check your computer-generated reports against each other. For example, Mark and Marian's new system prints daily reports for special orders placed by customers. The reports are generated by customer, by vendor, and by sales associate. Obviously, the totals printed by these three reports must reconcile to each other.

> Reports that look at the same data in different ways must always reconcile to each other.

Run the parallel system for at least eight days. That length of time allows you to test the week-ending procedure. You can, of course, run in parallel as long as you feel a need to. It's nice to have the safety net of your old system under you, at least for a while. Eventually, you will conclude that the time for the big event has arrived: leaving your manual system behind for good.

Cutting the Cord

When you and your entire team of players are totally convinced that all aspects of your system work perfectly, it's finally time to cut the cord between your computerized and manual systems. Making sure that everything is working perfectly includes checking every aspect of your system:

- ❏ Data entry
- ❏ Report generation
- ❏ File maintenance
- ❏ Daily procedures

Checking the daily start-up, shut-down and file backup procedures is especially important.

And what's involved in cutting the cord? As it turns out, very little. All you need do is stop using the manual system.

Consider, however, the timing of switching over to your computerized system. While you can certainly do it at any time, it makes the most sense to continue with the manual system through the end of an appropriate fiscal period. That means continuing with the manual system through month-end, or, if reasonable, year-end. That way you will have all the reports you need in a consistent format for your accountant.

Chapter Summary

This is an important chapter, one that you should reread several times as you move carefully through the testing process.

Testing is a vital part of implementing any computer system. From the simplest scenario of getting your word processor and printer to work together to a complex scenario like Mark and Marian's custom-order entry system, testing is required to make sure that the system does exactly what you demand with complete accuracy.

In this chapter, you learned that deciding what to test is the foundation in building an overall testing plan. You saw that testing schedules are developed within that play. These schedules determine the sequence of events for testing particular aspects of your system. Next, you learned how to create files of test data and an assortment of test transactions. Armed with these tools, you moved on to the actual testing procedure.

You learned that running the test is the simulation of several day's business and that test transactions of a particular type should be spread out as they would be when you operate the system "for real." At the end of each day, it's important for the testing participants to get together and share their observations regarding the progress of testing. Based on that discussion and the reconciling of printed reports to the transactions performed, you decide whether to move forward with testing or to make and retest changes in software or hardware.

You learned that with initial testing completed, you should run your new and old systems in parallel, both running at the same time with identical real-world data, even though you are still running the business on the old system. This step ensures that your new system produces the expected results in the actual environment in which it will be used.

You learned that after you are completely satisfied with the operation and integrity of your new system, it's time to cut the cord—and take that giant step into your business's future by leaving your old system behind. What remains to be done is training, a process that begins during the testing phase and continues for the life of your system.

CHAPTER 10

Training

Did you take a driver's education course when you were learning to drive a car? Did you have instruction when you learned to play the clarinet?

These activities constituted training, an activity in which the operation of a device was explained to you, written materials were given to you for study, and hands-on practice was highly encouraged. Training in the use of your new computer system is similar and equally as important.

Training for the care and ongoing operation of a computer system may be provided in several different forms, by different people, and in different environments. And depending on the tasks your employees will be performing, each of them may require different levels of training.

Who Should Do the Training?

Nearly everyone seems to be in the personal computer training business. Storefront dealers almost always have classrooms equipped with a computer for each student. A value-added reseller may have a classroom, may use your site, or may rent classroom space and equipment from a third party. Now there are even companies whose sole business mission is to provide personal computer training. These companies maintain classrooms or come to your site.

Sometimes you may not have the luxury of a choice. Almost all training companies are willing to provide instruction for mass-market software like 1-2-3, but if you contracted for a custom one-of-a-kind software system, you have no alternative except to go to the developer of the software.

A few of the larger software companies offer their own training programs either at a site near their headquarters or in training seminars that move from city to city. Call the manufacturer of your software package to find out whether this form of training is available.

As a variation on the manufacturer's "traveling road show," several companies have sprung up that provide training seminars that move around the country. These seminars tend to be on the expensive side, but can be a good alternative if the timing and locale are right for you.

Authorized Trainers

One of the newer trends is for the major software development companies to authorize individuals or training centers to provide training for their products. The authorization process usually requires a prospective trainer to submit an application that must be accompanied by a fee, a resume, a list of references (presumably students), and a sampling of teaching materials. After receipt and approval by the software manufacturer, a written test may be required. WordPerfect Corporation, for example, issues a written examination that can take a bona fide expert nearly 100 hours to complete! WordPerfect also requires a videotape of the instructor in an actual teaching session and annual retesting. Most other companies are not so rigorous.

When you call a software company that has such a program, you will be referred to authorized trainers in your area. The lead referral service is the primary benefit to the trainer who has taken the time to go through the process.

Remember that an authorized trainer is someone who took the time to go through the authorization procedure mostly for the privilege of advertising themselves as "authorized" and for the referrals that come their way from the manufacturer. An authorized trainer is not necessarily a better trainer than one without authorization. People not officially authorized may be equally qualified and may have chosen not to apply for authorization because they have enough business and don't need the referrals.

How Much Should You Pay for Training?

Given all the variables in the training industry, it's not surprising to see fees that vary wildly. A few examples follow.

- ❑ An independent trainer that travels to your site might charge $100 per hour (or sometimes $1,000 for the day) plus $25 to $35 per student to cover the cost of training materials. Rates for an "authorized" trainer tend to be slightly higher.

- A third-party training seminar that is visiting your city as part of a country-wide swing will charge from $400 to $600 per day per student with volume discounts of 10 percent sometimes available. This fee includes all materials and normally includes lunch.

- Training in the classroom of a company that specializes in training can run from $100 to $300 per day per student depending on the difficulty of the software package. The wide fee range exists because teachers of more difficult programs are more experienced and demand higher fees than their counterparts who may be teaching a personal computing primer course. The price should include the cost of materials. Lunch usually is not provided, but arrangements can sometimes be made to have lunch brought in—at your expense.

- Training at the software company's headquarters usually is somewhat less expensive, in the range of $100 per day per student for a three-day seminar. Although the cost of the course may seem low, you must figure air fare, hotels, and dinner into the overall cost. The total cost may actually be highest in these circumstances. Because training is provided by the software manufacturer's own staff, however, you may get the best training available anywhere.

My Place or Yours?

Training can take place either in a formal classroom setting provided by your dealer, consultant, or programmer, or at the site of a third-party company that specializes in training. You may want to have training take place on your system on your premises, however, because no classroom situation, no matter how well-equipped, can duplicate your environment exactly.

Classroom Training

Classroom training is usually provided at a specialized training site away from your business. Training sites are best for courses that introduce the concepts of personal computing and techniques for using many general-purpose software packages, such as word processors, spreadsheets, or desktop publishing programs.

When seeking classroom training, look for "hands-on" teaching techniques. You cannot learn to drive a car by reading a book about driving, and you will never master a program unless you have the opportunity to use it, learn its capabilities and pitfalls, and become familiar with its idiosyncrasies.

Expect personalized attention from your instructor. A ratio of one instructor to ten students should not be exceeded because each student needs a great deal of individual attention. That instructor should be certified by the manufacturer of the software to provide instruction or should have a long, successful track record with the software to be taught.

Be sure that the training includes handouts the students can read and exercises they can practice when class is not in session. The handouts should include a telephone number where the instructor can be reached when questions arise.

Site Training

Classroom training is a good environment for introductory lessons in computing, but a trainer's environment cannot duplicate your individual business computing environment. Chances are you will have different equipment, different software, and perhaps even one-of-a-kind custom software. The only place to obtain training *for* your system is *on* your system.

Suppose that you have in your business ten people who will be performing the same type of work with your new computer system. In a legal office this group might consist of ten legal secretaries preparing legal documents; in a telemarketing operation the ten might be the telemarketing representatives tracking sales leads; and in a retail operation like Mark and Marian's bed and bath store, the group might be sales associates who are taking customer orders.

With a group of your employees needing to learn the same set of skills, classroom instruction is a good solution. Training in a group provides a sense of security for the trainees—they will see that others have the same questions. Group training also breeds a sense of camaraderie—it's not at all unusual to find trainees lending each other a helping hand.

Learn One Program at a Time

Did you ever hear the expression, "Jack of all trades, master of none"? That saying could have been written for computer users.

Just as the man who had seven home repair projects active at the same time and who finished none, so computer users need to focus on one program at a time. Learning to master the use of your computer requires concentration in one area at a time. Even with a word processing or spreadsheet program, you have hundreds of features and keystrokes to learn. Understanding these features and becoming so familiar with them that they become a reflex action rather than a conscious thought process is not something you can accomplish overnight.

Consider the word processing program WordPerfect, for example. It's not at all unusual to see introductory, intermediate, and advanced courses, each running a total of

15 to 20 hours. And for those who have the desire, you can find courses in writing macros, using the graphic features, and working with fonts. And all these courses are for a general purpose word processor! Can you imagine what would happen if you took these courses while also learning a spreadsheet like 1-2-3?

The best approach is for each of your employees to learn one aspect of the system at a time and become an expert in that aspect. In your legal practice, for example, you may be installing both word processing and time-billing software. Divide the training so that some receive training in the word processing software only, while the others learn the time-billing software only. Each group will have less to learn, will be less inundated with training materials, and will master their respective program more quickly. Only after each group is comfortable with the software they have learned should you consider another round of training so that each group can learn the other program.

Allotting Enough Time

There are two aspects to consider when allotting time. The first aspect focuses on how long the training for a particular software application will take. The second aspect focuses on how much time your users need to grow familiar with an application before learning another.

Allotting Time for Training

Different programs require different amounts of formal training. Because the tens of thousands of programs for IBM compatibles and Macintoshes vary so wildly in their breadth of features, user interface, and operating procedures, no simple guideline on allotting time exists.

Discuss the timetable with your trainer and consider the many factors that contribute to a training schedule. If the training is off-site, you need to allow for travel time and meals. Does the training consist of full eight-hour days or just partial days? Full-day training may teach more than your employees can absorb and the overflow is wasted. How many days per week does the training occur? Training five days a week may not afford the student adequate time to practice the materials covered each day.

Your trainer should plan a schedule that sets a reasonable pace and allows enough time for the subject matter to "sink in."

Here is an example. A small accounting firm installed a network of IBM-compatible personal computers. The only application software purchased initially was three modules of an accounting system: accounts payable, accounts receivable, and general ledger. The firm's owners hired a company whose sole business was training, and the training company was certified by the software's manufacturer. A total of ten people from the accounting firm needed to be trained: nine staff members and an office manager. The training company divided the nine staff members into three groups of three and taught each a different module. The training schedule was two full days a week for each group. This training lasted for three weeks and the days were rotated to make sure that someone was always in the office. Each employee thus received six days of training. Figuring a full day of training at six hours (allowing for lunch breaks and a mid-morning and afternoon brain-rest), each employee received thirty-six hours of training. That's just shy of a forty-hour work week.

The accounting company finished this first round of training with experts in each of the three accounting modules. The office manager floated during the training period to learn enough about each module to manage her staff of nine.

The accounting company could have stopped here. But the next phase of their plan was to cross-train one employee from each group in a second module to fill in when required.

Allotting Enough Time To Grow

Some software packages are like onions. With an onion you peel away layers only to discover more layers underneath. And with software you might choose a particular menu item only to discover another set of underlying menus that lead to even more capabilities and features. The process sometimes can seem to go on almost forever.

After your company's training period, you will notice eventually that your staff is settling into the routine of interacting with the computer and that the comfort factor has reached a sufficient level. Look for the following telltale positive signs:

- *Fewer questions are asked.* The absence of a constant stream of questions is a good indication that each operator has determined how to resolve questions on his or her own by working with the system or referring to the appropriate documentation.

- *Productivity increases begin to level off.* As your staff learns more about the system, productivity increases. When those increases lessen or level off, it's a good indication that your employees are approaching a level of expertise that guarantees consistent results. Look at productivity as a trend rather than as items for daily reports. Everyone has good and bad days, and your employees and customers are no exception.

- *Ambitious employees begin to get curious about other aspects of the system.* If your general ledger expert starts asking about the accounts payable module, that's a sure sign that he or she is ready to break new ground. Almost everyone likes a new challenge, and this employee is no different. In fact, the person who wants to learn every aspect of your system may turn out to be a good choice for system administrator.

When can you expect to see these signs? Again, no clear-cut answer exists. A clerk trained to do only data entry should be expected to build up expertise rapidly because the scope of his or her interaction with the computer is quite narrow. In this case, a couple of weeks may be all that's required. But the person in charge of the general ledger module of your accounting system will need much more time, perhaps several months, because the range of tasks involved, such as setting up charts of accounts, batching transactions, making journal entries, trial balancing, posting, closing each quarter and the year, and running reports, may run into the hundreds.

Cross-Training

Cross-training is teaching an operator a secondary application program or module (as in the accounting system). Think of cross-training as both insurance and enrichment.

The insurance is a direct benefit to you. If an employee is out on vacation or becomes ill for an extended period, it's imperative that you have someone else who can fill in. In the example used in this chapter, three people were trained in each accounting module. But what about a much smaller operation in which one person each is trained in payables, receivables, and general ledger? Losing one of those staff members for just a few days could cause your workflow to come to a halt.

The enrichment is an employee benefit. Most employees enjoy the challenge of learning something new, and your decision to broaden their range of expertise is almost always viewed as a vote of confidence in your staff. That message isn't lost either. It translates directly into loyalty to your company and lower employee turnover. It takes more than a decent salary to hold on to your valued employees, and the message sent by cross-training is a tool you should add to your arsenal.

As you saw in the last section of this chapter, it's important to allow sufficient time for each employee to become comfortable and reasonably expert with one function before adding another. Piling on too much too soon gives users a sense of suffocation. This feeling leads to frustration, high error rates, overall job dissatisfaction, and high employee turnover. That situation in turn requires more training for new employees and more out-of-pocket dollars on your part.

Chapter Summary

Training is a straightforward activity that is important for you and for your employees. In this chapter, you learned that training can be provided by a variety of sources—independent trainers, training centers, your software developer, or sometimes the software manufacturer—and that training can take place in a variety of locations—a classroom away from your business, at your business, or even across the country at the software manufacturer's headquarters. You also learned that it's critical not to overload your staff when providing training and that the pace of training is important. Finally, you learned that cross-training your employees is important so that voids left by vacations and illnesses do not cause your company to come screeching to a halt.

CHAPTER 11

Living with Your System

By now your system is in operation. The testing process has been completed successfully and your employees (as well as you) have gone through enough training at least to get you started.

A great deal of work has been done from the time, probably months ago, when you first looked at your business and decided there had to be a better way. You have weathered various sales pitches and made sound decisions based on your methodical analysis of your business as it was and as you wanted it to be.

Now that your system is up and running, it's time to learn how to coexist with it.

Day-to-Day Operations

Very few businesses are open 24 hours a day. This book assumes that you are operating a business with daily opening and closing times. Day-to-day operations are the tasks that you need to perform to keep your system operating at peak efficiency and to ensure the safety of the data without which your business could not run.

Daily Start-Up

Depending on your business requirements and the physical complexity of your system, daily start-up can vary from turning on a few switches to running start-of-day reports.

Clearly, the first task in a daily start-up is turning on your computing equipment. If you installed a local area network, the server should be turned on first because the individual workstations may be programmed to "look" for the server as they are switched on. Other than that, equipment need not be turned on in any special sequence. An individual computer, one not connected to a network, can be simply switched on.

Whoever is responsible for turning on the system in the morning should check to make sure that the data files scheduled to be backed up at the close of the preceding business day have actually been backed up. If they have not been backed up, now is the time to do it. (More on file backup later in this chapter.)

Some software programs may require the generation and printing of a start-of-day report. These reports are used for *run-to-run control*. Their totals should equal exactly the totals printed by the close-of-day reports generated during the preceding business day's shutdown routine. Clearly, Monday night's ending figures should be the same as Tuesday morning's opening figures. If the two reports don't reconcile exactly, proceed no further and call your first-line source of assistance. Depending on your installation and your contracts, that person may be a custom-software programmer, your consultant, your dealer, or the software manufacturer. The cause may be an error in the logic that generates the reports (something that should have been caught during the test phase), or it may indicate the corruption of one or more data files. Solve the problem before proceeding. (You see later in this chapter that a manual backup system is needed for situations like this.) Keep your start-of-day reports in a folder for easy reference.

If your run-to-run controls are in balance, your system should be ready to go. A quick check for sufficient paper in each printer should take care of the daily start-up routine.

Housekeeping and Administration

As with any system, automated or manual, certain administrative chores need to be done. The range of tasks required for your computer system varies depending on your hardware configuration and software requirements.

Disk Housekeeping for Nonnetworked Computers

For nonnetworked computers, housekeeping is primarily a matter of keeping floppy disks and hard disks organized. For example, if you elect to store your word processing files on individual floppy disks, you can have a separate disk for each customer, or for each person who sends correspondence. Locating a particular file becomes a far easier task if you use this method of organization. Carrying that thought to the next step, you may want a separate set of disks to store your spreadsheet files and still a third group for your database files.

If you store your files on a hard disk, and you should because hard disks are much faster than floppy disks, be sure to organize your hard disk in *subdirectories*, or volumes in which you can group your files. For IBM-compatible computers, see your DOS manual for a complete discussion of subdirectories.

From time to time, each hard disk requires housekeeping—the deletion of old, inactive files that waste space, and the reorganization, or *defragmenting*, of the hard disk so that files scattered across the entire disk are placed in a single contiguous area. Defragmenting a hard disk can greatly improve performance. Several utility programs for this purpose exist, the most popular being The Norton Utilities, Advanced Edition, from Peter Norton Computing, Inc.

Files that are inactive, but which you do not want to purge forever, can simply be copied to a disk and stored. After copying to the disk, be sure to delete the file from your hard disk.

Housekeeping and Administration of Networked Computers

In a networked environment, the *system administrator*, because he or she controls every user's access privileges and adds and deletes users from the network, wields a great deal of power and must be someone you can trust without question. You should be cross-trained in network administration in case the system administrator is absent at a crucial time or if it becomes necessary to deny network access to the administrator.

Adding and Deleting Users

People come and go in a company; that's just the nature of business. But as an employee leaves, that person should be deleted from the network to prevent any logging in after he or she is no longer employed by you.

In addition, you need to add new employees to the system. Adding an employee consists of assigning the employee a *user name*, sometimes composed of his or her initials, and a log-in *password*, which the user should never reveal to anyone. And depending on the application software, you may also need to create subdirectories on the network's hard disk where the user can, for example, store word processing documents.

Finally, you must determine a security level for the user, indicating what the user has access to.

Access Rights

The security features built into almost any local area network operating system require the maintenance of information that describes who can log in to the network and which application programs or system features each user can use. These *access rights* tables must be carefully controlled by the system administrator to ensure that individual users are granted access only to programs and data needed to perform their respective jobs.

In addition to overall access to the network, some application programs include their own security measures. For example, no one using the accounts payable module of an accounting system should have security clearance that would allow him or her to create new vendors. If access were allowed, a less-than-honest employee could create a "dummy" vendor and send checks to that vendor. And who do you think would cash those checks?

Maintenance

Modern computer equipment is remarkable for its reliability. It has become very unusual to see a piece of computing equipment put out of action for any reason. Obtaining outside service is covered elsewhere in this book, but there are several steps you can take to keep your equipment in tip-top physical condition.

- ❑ Vacuum air intakes and exhaust ports.

  Most personal computers (the older Macintoshes being a notable exception) have fans built in to draw air through the computer to help dissipate the heat built up by the electronic components inside the machine. Even in the cleanest environment, dust and dirt tends to build up at the air intake and exhaust ports. This buildup of dust restricts airflow, which causes heat to build up, resulting in the premature failure of sensitive, and sometimes expensive, electronic components. For an average office environment, vacuuming these ports two or three times a year can extend the life of your computer.

- ❑ Use a dust cover.

  If your equipment is located in a dusty location, frequent vacuuming and dust covers for your equipment will help. Several of the larger computer mail-order supply catalogs carry dust covers for just about any make of computer and printer. The investment of $20 to $40 now could save a great deal of money later.

- ❑ Control static electricity.

  In many offices as well as homes, carpeting may cause static electric shocks in the winter when, for example, you touch a metal doorknob. You may not realize it, but that small shock may actually be several thousand volts! That kind of a shock can wipe a disk clean of its data and render the components mounted on circuit boards utterly useless. If you experience static electricity problems, purchase a special static discharge mat to place under each computer. Touching the mat instead of the computer harmlessly discharges the electricity. Also consider installing a humidifier, but do not point it directly at your equipment. Your aim is to raise the relative humidity of the air, not to drench your equipment.

- ❑ Keep the screen clean.

  A computer display monitor seems to be a magnet for dust. A damp paper towel doesn't seem to help; it just spreads the dirt around and attracts more. Buy a box of specially treated, antistatic, premoistened wipes designed for monitors. Similar to the moist towelettes you can get in many restaurants, they remove the dirt from the screen without creating the static charge that attracts more.

- ❑ Clean the disk drive.

  Hard disk drives are sealed and never require cleaning. But heavily used floppy drives could use a good cleaning, perhaps twice a year. The best disk cleaning kits consist of a disk with a cleaning pad inside rather than the usual magnetic disk. You place a few drops of cleaning solution on the pad and insert it into your machine. Make this disk spin for a few seconds (try typing DIR and pressing Enter a few times), and you are finished.

  Don't overdo the disk cleaning routine. These disks are somewhat abrasive, and overuse shortens instead of lengthens the life of a disk drive.

- ❑ Clean your printers.

  Open your laser printer and vacuum out or use the special brush provided to remove any lint buildup. Be careful; some laser components are very hot, and other components, like the corona wire, are very fragile.

  Vacuum your daisywheel and dot-matrix printers for lint, too. Also check them for excess ink buildup around the printhead. A cotton swab dipped in alcohol should do the trick.

Backing Up Files

Whether your computers are networked or not, the one operation that must always be performed without exception is the backing up of data files. Without data, your business will come to a complete stop, and you may find it impossible to recreate the data. Can you imagine losing your accounts receivable files? You would have no way of knowing who owes you money!

You need back up only data files. All the files that constitute your programs do not require backing up because, presumably, you have stored those original program disks in a secure off-site location.

For nonnetworked computers equipped with a hard disk, install a utility program that backs up the hard disk's data to another device, such as disks, a small tape backup unit, or even a second hard disk. Such a utility program automates the procedure and helps speed up the operation. See Chapter 5 for a listing of hard disk backup software.

If you installed a network, most of your data is probably stored at the server. This centralized data storage makes backup a simple procedure because you need not remind individual operators. Backing up becomes the job of the network administrator.

The first rule in securing data is making backup copies of your data at least once a day and maintaining several sets of data—at least one week's worth. That's actually eight backup sets, not seven.

Why maintain a full week? Imagine that your custom programmer has just installed an updated version of your custom accounts receivable system. After using the system for three days, you discover a major flaw. The system properly posts payments within the thirty-day monthly billing cycle and correctly assesses finance charges for any payment received after thirty days. But what about payments received precisely on the thirtieth day of the billing cycle? If your programmer failed to consider this third possibility, your system might completely ignore payments received on the thirtieth day even though they were entered into the system by your computer operators. Going back to yesterday's backup data will not help because the problem has occurred for three days. You need to have the problem fixed by the programmer, turn the clock back four days by restoring the data on your backup from four days ago, and reenter all the payments received since that time. In fact, in large corporate systems, it's not unusual to keep 32 days' worth of backups—an entire month.

And why the extra day? Simple. Suppose it's Saturday night and you have just backed up the data for today's sales. After you do that, you discover that a new employee, who did not receive proper training, has been making data entry errors all week long. You call the software manufacturer, and they advise you to go back a full week instead of trying to correct an entire week's worth of mistakes. You need to turn the clock back to last Saturday (see fig. 11.1). With just seven backups you would have written over last Saturday's data, which you now need. The extra set always ensures that the last accounting period (week or month, for instance) is still intact.

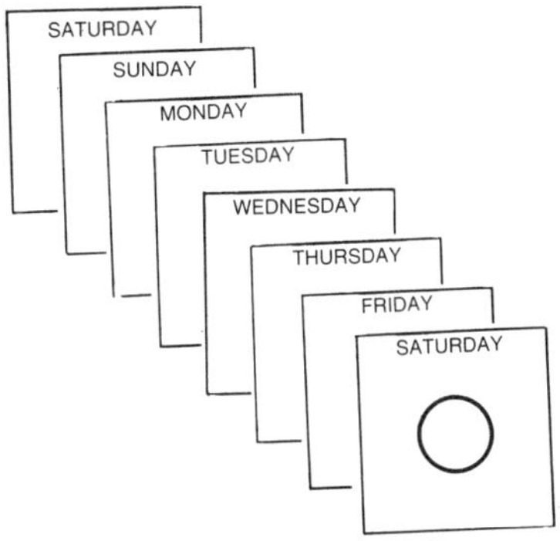

Fig. 11.1. *Keeping a week of data backups on floppy disks.*

Daily Shutdown

You should adopt planned shutdown procedures for the end of each business day, or carry out the daily shutdown steps that have been programmed into your software.

The most modest of shutdown procedures suggests that you back up critical files, store the backups in a safe place, and turn your system off. This applies whether your computers are networked or not.

Some software applications may contain programming logic that *requires* you to make file backups before leaving the program. Others may also generate a series of end-of-day reports. Most of the reports are simply printouts of the activity that occurred during the day, but your software may generate a special report of *control totals*. The control total report is special because it contains the figures that are compared to tomorrow's beginning-of-day reports, if your program generates them. The process of comparing end-of-day and beginning-of-day control totals, or run-to-run controls, always must be followed to ensure the integrity of your data.

Storing Data Off-Site

You already have learned about the importance of making daily backups of your data files. But what do you do with the stacks of disks that constitute your backups?

Here's an example of what not to do. Remember the small accounting firm, the one that services about 200 physicians and dentists? The personnel were trained to make backups of their data files every day. And they did. If backing up had been an Olympic event, they would have won the gold medal. Their mistake came after finishing the daily backup routine. *They left the box of disks containing the backup data right next to the computer containing the original data files.* It certainly was convenient, but one night a small electrical fire broke out, and there was a great deal of smoke and water damage.

You can imagine what happened next. All the equipment was ruined, but replaced within days thanks to the insurance coverage. The company, however, had to go to each client physician, borrow his or her personal records, and manually re-create all the lost data. That process took almost six months, and would have taken much longer except that a third of the clients took their business elsewhere.

Is there a moral here? You bet there is!

> Store backup data in a secure location away from your business premises.

That's too inconvenient? Did you know that most banks and large corporations make backups of their data files and store them in special climate-controlled warehouses, bank vaults, or underground vaults? And they pay a great deal of money to do so. If you're concerned about inconvenience, then make two backups. Keep one set in a convenient location *but away from your system*, and keep the second set in the secured, off-premises location. Remember, all the insurance in the world cannot replace lost data.

Controlling the Cost of Consumables

Did you ever read how computers would create the "paperless society?" As it turns out, that theory wasn't worth the paper it was printed on.

You will find that certain costs escalate as the direct result of your system. Your electrical bill certainly will be higher. And supply, or consumables, costs will probably rise. Plan on using a great deal of paper if you are doing word processing, generating reports, or producing desktop published pamphlets or newsletters. In the old days, you may have settled for a typewritten report that was close, but not perfect. But with a computer and a laser printer, it's easy to make minor changes and reprint the document several times. That desire to "get it just right" can cause paper to be used at alarming rates! Remind your employees to keep an eye on paper usage.

You also will find that disks seem to disappear into thin air. Each disk may cost only a dollar or two, but if you find yourself going through two dozen a week, that works out to an annual expense of $1,248 at a dollar each! Control your employees' appetites for disks by keeping them under lock and key. When you unlock that cabinet to hand out a disk or two, be sure that only one box of disks is stored there. Hide the rest of supply in a location that only you know. Why play these childish games? If your employees "see" only one box of disks in the cabinet, they are less likely to ask for one or two more.

The best solution to the disk disappearing act is to install a network with diskless workstations. If your employees have no disk drives, they have no need for disks!

Other consumables to watch are laser printer toner cartridges and printer ribbons. Laser cartridges cost close to $100 each, and although they are good for about 4,000 pages of average output, $100 is a great deal of money. Ribbons for dot-matrix or daisywheel printers and ink cartridges for inkjet printers cost considerably less, but as you know, their output can approach neither the speed nor the quality of laser output. This expenditure is directly tied to paper usage. As you control paper usage, so too will you control the appetite for toner cartridges, printer ribbons, and ink cartridges.

Keep an eye on your telephone bill for any calls to informational databases with which your company has accounts. Legal and other professional databases charge more than $70 per hour of connect time, and these charges can get out of hand without your realizing it. CompuServe charges $12.50 per hour at 1200 baud, but you may have to pay communications surcharges if you do not have a local telephone number for direct access to CompuServe. MCI Mail provides access to Dow Jones services for news retrieval and stock quotations. You can even get the latest sports scores. But you can easily run up monthly charges of several hundred dollars. Make it clear to your staff that such antics will not be permitted.

Standards

Some companies do nearly everything "by the book." Most companies, on the other hand, have no book. The book is a book of standards, the company-approved, prescribed manner in which procedures are to be carried out. You may hear the book of standards called different names—procedures manual, operations guide, or some other fancy name, but it remains a book of standards. As you enter the computer era, a book of operational procedures that is available to all employees can be a valuable tool.

What Standards Are Needed?

Your computerized business should be equipped with two types of standards guides: procedures and operational policies. Copies of each should be available to any employee at any time. And these volumes are *living documents*; they are always subject to revision and enhancement as your business grows and as you become more sophisticated in your use of computers.

Documented Procedures

Documented procedures are user guides and sometimes schedules. Each word processing package you buy comes with documentation that explains how to use the package, and it probably contains a reference section arranged alphabetically by feature. User documentation explains the proper way to achieve an intended result.

Software that was custom-developed for your business should also be accompanied by exhaustive documentation. If your programmer moves across the country without telling you, your documentation is all you have left. You also should have obtained a complete set of technical documentation that describes, in detail, the operation and processing logic of your custom software, and you should have a copy of the source code. These last two items belong in the vault and should not be made available to your employees.

Other procedure documentation may be developed by you or your own employees. Such procedure documentation may describe work flow, responsibilities for individual system chores, and the schedule for performing system housekeeping. For example, a section on data backups may include the text shown in figure 11.2.

This instructional text is *technical writing* at its finest. The process is broken down into small, easy-to-understand steps. Fancy words are not used in good technical writing when easy words make the same point. Each action performed by the operator is a numbered step. Tasks performed by the system in response are not numbered.

Operational Policies

The operational policies are the rules and regulations by which each employee is expected to live. These are your personnel policies, and they can cover areas as diverse as

At the end of each business day, the system administrator on duty is responsible for making backup copies of the company's most important data files. A backup copy is important because it allows the business to remain in operation even in the event of severe damage to our computing equipment.

The backup procedure can be performed only on the server. It cannot be done from individual workstations.

The steps that follow should be performed only by someone with security clearance to do so. If you do not have security clearance and attempt this procedure, a security violation will be logged by the system.

1. Insert the tape cassette labeled with the proper day of the week in the tape drive. (On Monday, use the cassette labeled Monday, and so on).

2. Log in on the network.

3. Type **backup** and then press the Enter key.

   The system will run the backup program and copy the appropriate files to the tape cassette.

4. If the files do not fit on one cassette, the system displays the message **cassette is full** and asks for a second cassette. Remove the first cassette, insert the cassette labeled '2' for the proper day of the week, and then press the Enter key. (On Monday you would use the cassette labeled Monday #2, and so forth.)

   When the backup process is complete, the system displays a message on-screen and prints a report.

5. Put the cassettes in the floor safe and then lock the safe.

6. Log off the system and turn off the server.

The daily backup procedure is complete.

Fig. 11.2. *A sample page from procedure documentation.*

dress codes, absenteeism, smoking on the premises, and so forth.

You should add computer-related rules and regulations to your operational policy manual. Be sure to word each policy in language that uses positive rather than negative phrasing. The following are some examples of the types of policies to include:

- Use of computers for nonbusiness-related work

  The company's computing equipment was purchased solely for the purpose of business-related work. Use of the equipment for nonbusiness purposes is not permitted.

- Eating, drinking, or smoking while using computing equipment

  Because food or beverages spilled on computing equipment can create a serious electrical shock hazard, eating or drinking are not permitted at any location where computing equipment is installed. Because smoke is known to harm computing equipment, employees should not smoke while working with the company's computing equipment. Eating, drinking, and smoking are permitted only in areas designated for those activities.

- Protecting your password

  Never give your password to anyone, and never write down your password. You are responsible for all activity attributed to your password, so guard it carefully. If you have any suspicion that the privacy of your password is being compromised, please advise the system administrator. He or she will be happy to assign a new password.

- Copying of files or willful destruction of files

  The copying or willful destruction of computer files is a serious offense and will not be tolerated. Either of these actions will result in your immediate dismissal.

- Security violations

  Attempts to run programs or use files to which access has not been granted results in that attempt being logged in a security violation report. Your supervisor will discuss each security violation with you. Fourth and fifth security violations result in a written warning that becomes a permanent part of your personnel file. A sixth security violation may be grounds for dismissal.

Clearly these rules reflect common sense and little else. But it is important that they are written and kept in your policy manual, and are available for all employees to see. In today's society, where disgruntled employees are so quick to file suit, it's crucial that everyone know the ground rules up front.

Why are Standards Necessary?

Writing standards and procedures isn't the most fun you will ever have, but it is as important a part of your computer system as the equipment and software itself.

Ensuring Operations Consistency

Imagine the simplest of scenarios. You have three employees who do nothing but word processing. Furthermore, the nature of your business requires you to send a great many form letters. Form letters require two files to generate, a *primary* file, which contains the text that is constant from letter to letter ("You may have won ten million dollars . . ."), and a *secondary* file, which contains the variable information—the personalized name and address information that is printed in the final form letter. Wouldn't it make sense for all three people to adopt the same naming conventions for their files?

In the IBM-compatible world, it wouldn't make much sense for the first operator to call the name and address file CONTEST.NAM, the second to call it PEOPLE.LST, and third to call it NEVER.WIN. If one operator is out sick, it might take another operator 10 to 15 minutes simply to locate the file containing the names and addresses. But if all three agreed that *any* name and address file contained the file extension SMF (for secondary merge file), then each operator could tell what files contain names and addresses without the need to actually examine the contents of each file. CONTEST.SMF, PEOPLE.SMF, and NEVER.SMF is consistent, and this consistency improves productivity.

The example illustrates the concept of *operational consistency*, ensuring that each employee performs the same task in the same way. Having one employee print the end-of-day reports an hour before your store closes even though all others wait until closing time yields erroneous reports. One day's figures will be low while the next day's are high.

Other factors that ensure operational consistency are training and the design of the system itself. It's one thing to develop a procedure that specifies that daily backups should be made *after* the store closes, but it is quite another to train your employees to do so. The design of the system may help. If your store is scheduled to close at 9:00 p.m., the system could check its internal clock when the backup procedure is requested. And, if it is not yet 9:00 p.m., the system might display the following message:

```
The system time is 9:28 a.m. Performing the daily
backup before 9:00 p.m. will be logged on the system
activity report with the message ''Backup Performed
Before Authorized to Do So.''
```

The system would then ask the operator

```
Continue with backup?
```

The operator would press Y or N in response to the question. Note that the system allows the early backup to take place. It's possible that a valid reason for the early backup exists, and the system should not prohibit the operator from starting the backup procedure.

Another way in which system design ensures consistent operation is the sequence in which data is entered. Because the system is programmed to ask for specific data elements (last name, first name, and so on) in a predetermined sequence, all operators have no choice but to perform in a consistent manner.

Early Problem Detection

Every Monday morning at 9:00 a.m. the president of a large corporation walks into his office. He is expecting to find on his desk the ideal executive decision-making tool: a one page report that summarizes last week's business and projects sales for this week. To make sure that the report is ready for 9:00 a.m., the director of the information systems department runs the program that produces the report at 6:30 a.m., 2 1/2 hours before the report is needed.

And the system always runs like a charm. The procedures call for the program to be run at 6:30 a.m., with the final report to be printed no later than 6:45 a.m.

But on *this* Monday morning there was no report by 6:45 a.m. and everyone knew it. Why? The standards dictated a specified result by a specified time. As soon as that standard was not met, the computer operator and the operations analyst on duty began an investigation. It turned out that the operator on duty the preceding night became ill and went home early. The remaining staff forgot to run the end-of-day routines that, in addition to printing reports, closed the files for the business day. Because the files had not been closed properly, the daily summary report would not run.

This situation worked out well for two reasons. First, the problem was detected early because the standards for operation were not met, and second, the 2 1/2-hour cushion before the 9:00 a.m. deadline allowed plenty of time to run last night's end-of-day routine, as well as the weekly business recap report.

Chapter Summary

In this chapter, you learned that the most difficult tasks of computerization are behind you. The daily routine consists of starting up the system (which may include running some start-of-day reports) and housekeeping (keeping hard disks purged of old unused files and defragmented for best performance). This chapter also covered the duties of a network system administrator. Finally, you learned about daily shutdown and data backup procedures, as well as about documented procedures and operational policies you need to have in effect.

CHAPTER 12

Expecting the Unexpected

With the months of planning, thousands of dollars invested, and exhaustive testing, it's difficult to imagine that anything unexpected would ever happen. That might be a wonderful world to live in, but that idyllic environment exists only in the movies. For the rest of us, that means things will surely go bump in the night. Accepting the unexpected as a given, this chapter examines how to prepare for that eventuality and deal with it when the time comes.

Allowing for Delays

One of the major tasks that you undertake when planning your computerization project is the project schedule. The idea of the schedule is to make every member of your project team (assuming that other people are involved) aware of certain milestones, such as selecting software; choosing hardware; and arranging delivery, installation, testing, and implementation dates.

No matter how carefully you plan when developing your project schedule, it's likely that a milestone date will be missed. Perhaps your custom software developer discovers that the programming aspect of the project is more complex than originally envisioned, or the electrician wiring your network finds concrete block behind the walls where nothing of the sort had been expected. These delays, though certainly undesired, are perfectly normal and should be planned for.

How can you prevent delays from pushing back the final implementation date of your system? The most logical adjustment is to build plenty of slack time into the original project plan. While opinion varies widely, adding at least 25 percent to time estimates provided by outside professionals is not at all unreasonable. Your dealer estimates 60 hours to unpack and install all of your equipment? Add 25 percent for a total of 75 hours, (round it up to 80, which is equivalent to two 40-hour work weeks), and use that figure in your project plan.

Custom programming, still considered something of a black art by many people, is more difficult to estimate. Here is how many programmers arrive at their estimates. After examining the final program specification, the programmer, based on experience, makes an educated guess at how long the project will take. And do you know what many programmers do next? They take that carefully arrived at figure and double it! That date is the date you are told.

If you contracted for custom programming, the programmer has already built in some slack of his or her own. After all, a missed delivery date may cause you to refrain from recommending that programmer to another potential customer, so pushing the date back is the programmer's safety margin.

Even knowing that your programmer already has built in a fudge factor, you should add your 25 percent to the estimate provided to you. The programmer is still bound by contract to deliver by the date spelled out in the contract, no matter what you write in your project plan.

Build slack into your plan all the way down the line. If certain aspects of the project take longer than initially expected, you already have allowed for that delay without causing later milestone dates to slip.

Review your project schedule on a regular basis and adjust the dates if necessary. If each task in the project is coming in ahead of schedule, you may be able to move up the remainder of the project dates. If dates are still slipping despite the slack you have built in, get together with your project team and readjust the remaining dates as necessary. By discussing the milestone dates on a regular basis (at least weekly), you should know early if remaining dates require adjustment.

Now, imagine a different scenario. Everything is on schedule. The electrical work has been completed, the custom software has been delivered, and all the hardware has been installed. But you get a call from the company printing your computer forms telling you that the printing press has broken down and that your order will be delayed three weeks. How do you react to this unplanned delay?

First, add your 25 percent fudge factor and round it off. Instead of a three-week delay, call it three and one-half weeks, or even four if you prefer. Gather your project team and adjust the project schedule as necessary. Be sure to get new copies of the schedule distributed to everyone involved in the project.

Next, make sure that your old system is still in place and that you can continue to use it to run your business even beyond the new planned changeover date. Make sure that you have adequate supplies of forms on hand for your old system. If not, now is the time to order more.

Nothing Is Perfect

After your system is up and running successfully, it's still possible, and in fact likely, that at some point events for which you didn't plan will happen. The two most likely occurrences are incorrect results and hardware failure.

Incorrect Results

No matter how careful and complete your testing procedure is, it is always possible that a rare combination of events or sequence of transactions that you never thought to test could combine to produce results that are incorrect.

For example, most fiscal years run for 52 weeks, just as you would expect. Occasionally, however, a company's fiscal year can run for 53 weeks. Can you imagine what would happen at year-end if your system calculated the total year's revenues based on the most recent 52-week period instead of the period since the last time the end-of-year procedure was performed?

Or what about the problem that happened to a colleague of Mark and Marian's? You know that in a number like 10.6 the 6 means six-tenths. But did you know that when measuring lengths of cloth (the colleague owned a drapery store), the number after the decimal point means *eighths* instead of tenths? In that case, 10.6 means 10 and six-eighths yards of material. Because the system was charging the customer for ten and six-tenths yards instead of ten and six-eighths, all orders with fractions of yards were being underbilled. Although all the reports seemed right, (the columns of numbers did add up), the store owner could not understand why the amounts invoiced by the vendor for nearly every order were more than he was expecting, while other orders (those without fractions) were exactly right.

It took considerable thought, but the store owner eventually determined what was wrong, and he angrily called the programmer who developed his custom system and demanded that the error be fixed and that the programmer pick up the tab for the billing differences. After checking the programming specifications, both parties discovered that the units of measurement were never discussed. The error was fixed, and because the store owner failed to discuss this requirement during the system design phase, he was forced to pay the programmer for the modification. And the programmer did not pay for the billing differences.

Fortunately, this error was not catastrophic enough to require suspending operation of the new system. Instead, the orders were manually adjusted while the fix was being developed and applied. It's possible, however, that errors crop up that are so significant that it makes no sense to continue operation of the system. If that happens, you need to *fall back* either to your old manual system, or go to a revised manual system designed for such an emergency. You will learn more about a fall-back system later in this chapter.

Hardware Failure

Do you remember the last time your car wouldn't start? Think about what you did. You probably tried to start it several times, and after giving up, decided to seek an alternative method of getting to work. Maybe you took a cab or a bus, or perhaps, after deciding you really needed the exercise, walked to work.

Your computer system is no different. A fact of life is that hardware occasionally fails. Although you cannot prevent hardware failures from occurring, you can do the next best thing: be prepared for hardware failures.

Depending on the size and complexity of your installation, a variety of alternatives are available to you, ranging from shifting the work to another computer or printer, to keeping spares on hand, to resorting to a manual backup system.

Automated Network Backup Systems

In each local area network scenario presented in this book, the configuration has consisted of several workstations but just one network server. Because the server contains all the software and data files used by each workstation, the server becomes the most critical component of the entire network. You should have protected the server with an uninterruptible power supply in case a power outage occurs, and you should be making daily backups of all the data files, but what happens when a component in the server fails, causing the server to become unavailable to the network?

With network operating system software becoming increasingly sophisticated, it is now possible to pursue two alternatives: backup disk storage, or a complete backup server.

Backup disk storage is a second hard disk that contains a *mirror-image* of the primary hard disk. When using a backup storage disk, a copy of every data file is maintained on each disk drive (on both the primary and backup drives). Every time a user adds, deletes, or edits data, the changes are written to both disks. If the primary disk fails, the network operating system software detects the failure. The first disk drive is placed out of service, and a message is sent to the network administrator advising him or her of the situation. With the backup disk now handling all network processing, the first disk can be removed from the network and repaired. When the first disk is reinstalled, it can resume its former position as the primary disk drive, or it can now take on the role of backup.

Of course, if another vital component of the server fails, no number of backup disk drives can keep the network in operation. To guarantee that a server failure will not cause the entire network to cease functioning calls for more drastic backup measures. More and more networks are installing a *second server* that is configured as a mirror-image of the first server. The second server provides no additional computing horsepower or file storage space, but acts as a silent, exact copy of the first, or primary server.

Mirrored servers add significantly to the expense of a network, but for mission-critical applications, where failure of the network could be dangerous, mirrored servers are a proper solution.

Are mirrored servers appropriate for you? Consider the facts before deciding. They are expensive. First, you have the cost of the server itself. That cost alone can be well over $10,000. Next, you must use a network operating system that supports mirrored servers. The increased complexity required to keep two servers running in perfect lock-step with each other does not come cheaply. And you may have to buy two copies of the network operating system—one for each server. Then consider the cost of application software. Most software is sold with a license to run the program on one server only. It may be necessary to purchase a second copy for your back-up server. If the software license says the software can be run on only one server *at a time*, purchasing a second copy may not be necessary. If in doubt, check with the software's manufacturer. Finally, don't forget the administrative cost of running two servers. Whoever you select to perform network administration will have more to do and will undoubtedly require more training.

Shifting the Workload

When one personal computer breaks down, the most common plan for getting the work done is to shift the workload to another computer. Depending on your business computing requirements, this can be done with varying degrees of success.

Each workstation in Mark and Marian's installation functions like a sophisticated cash register. Because Mark and Marian installed more than one workstation in the Custom Orders department, they could enter all transactions through just one of those workstations if necessary. During a busy time (mostly Saturdays), using only one workstation would reduce customer service levels, but Mark and Marian agreed that this was an acceptable risk.

Keeping Spares Ready

Here is a great idea that never works. The theory is that you keep a spare computer, workstation, printer, or modem tucked away in a closet, to be forgotten until you need it to fill in for a device in your system that has just failed. The problem here is obvious.

The urge to take the device and place it in everyday service is simply too great to resist. It doesn't make sense to tie up several thousand dollars worth of hardware to be prepared for a failure that might never occur. In a large corporation with several hundred personal computers, the department that supports personal computing (or end-user computing) usually can afford to squirrel away a couple of PCs. But in a small business, the cost usually cannot be justified.

Developing a Manual Backup System

The most important backup system of all is your manual system: a completely manual, nonautomated, paper-and-pencil-based system. A manual backup system is not necessarily the same manual system you used for all those years before computerizing. Your data requirements and procedures are probably very different from the good old days. You may remember from an earlier chapter that computerizing is your best opportunity to rethink your business operations and bring them up to date. If you followed that premise, the system you installed was not just a faster version of the old way of running the business. It was, rather, a new beginning.

Using the same reasoning, the manual backup to your computer system should follow your automated procedures as closely as possible. Mark and Marian's computer system requests data in a specific order. The manual system should follow the same order.

Having a manual backup system is not a luxury; it is a necessity. Imagine for a moment that Mark and Marian's custom-order entry system experiences a total failure. That failure could be caused by a hardware fault in their network server, a programming error in their custom software that produces an obscure incorrect result not caught during testing, or a pencil that accidentally falls into and jams their printer. They certainly cannot close their business until the problem is resolved. They must instead have a backup system in place, ready to go into operation on a moment's notice.

What are the requirements for a manual backup system? That depends on the types of application programs you are running, your hardware configuration, and the criticality of those applications.

Suppose that you are in a legal office, and your system consists of two computers. The first computer runs a word processing program, and the second runs word processing and time-billing programs. Now imagine that the second computer experiences a hard disk failure. How will you prepare the bills?

You should have current backup copies of your billing files from the last time you used the billing program. You certainly should have the original disks that came with your billing program. In this situation, you can install the billing program on the one computer still operating, load the current data from your backup disks, and get back into business. Keep in mind that you must erase the program from this computer when the other one is repaired because you are usually licensed to install the software on a single computer.

What if you don't have backup files? Shame on you, but that doesn't help now. You ought to have a set of printed reports generated by the billing program the last time you used it. With those reports you should be able to calculate manually and print new bills the old-fashioned way: using elbow grease, a calculator, and a typewriter (or word processor on another computer).

Mark and Marian understood that orders must continue to be taken even when their custom-order entry system is not available. Along with their consultant and programmer, they developed *and documented* a set of manual procedures to be used for taking orders, handling customer pickup of merchandise, inquiry, and placing orders with factories.

For taking custom orders, they developed a form that mimicked the data entry screens they see on the computer. The order of the fields on the manual form is exactly the same as the computer system in order to facilitate data entry when the system becomes available.

Because Mark and Marian have many regular customers, the automated system enables the employee to enter the customer's last name (McQuillan, for example) and the computer displays all McQuillans. The operator chooses the correct one; and the system automatically enters the name, address, telephone number, and payment method information for that customer. The manual system, of course, cannot do this, so complete entry of name and address information is required on the paper form.

The remainder of the form provides space for each item ordered, the vendor name, model number, dimensions, colors, materials, patterns, pricing, and special instructions.

Again, these fields for each item ordered appear in the same order as on the data entry screens.

These forms were printed in triplicate with a unique serial number. One copy goes to the customer, a second copy into a folder marked *Data Entry To Be Done*, and the third copy goes to a secure storage location off-site, because data protection is a must whether the data is on disk drives or paper forms.

Mark and Marian are back to the old way of doing things. They must manually compile a list of items to be ordered (by manufacturer) and call in the list. Without their computer system, however, they don't have the luxury of neatly printed reports sorted by manufacturer.

Chapter Summary

In this chapter you learned that comprehensive computer system design includes expecting the unexpected. As a safety cushion, you need to allow for delays in the initial project schedule, and you must keep everyone involved informed of revised schedules. You also were warned that you may be forced to do paperwork manually if software problems develop or hardware failure occurs. Always be prepared for such an occasion by having forms and documented procedures on hand.

APPENDIX A

Computer Publications

This appendix contains a representative sample of computer publications aimed at business audiences. Most (but not all) of the magazines you see on the shelves of your local bookstore or newsstand are not listed here because those magazines are aimed at the consumer market. That fact doesn't mean that you should ignore consumer publications; they serve a valuable purpose and are brimming with information you can use every day. This listing covers magazines you would not ordinarily know about. Most are available to the trade only, but you can almost always get a sample copy by calling the publisher.

Why would you want to check out these publications? Simple. If you read what your consultant, programmer, and dealer or reseller are reading, you not only can keep them on their toes, but you also can see the industry from their perspective. And the knowledge you soak up by reading trade publications will help you understand the recommendations presented to you.

Keep in mind that this list contains general computing publications only; I have made no attempt to list publications within particular lines of business. For example, publications specific to the floor-covering industry are not listed, but *Modern Floor Covering Business* magazine, published monthly by International Thompson Retail Press in New York City for people in the floor-covering business, lists articles on the use of computers in the editorial profile provided by its own publisher. Your membership in industry trade groups many times entitles you to their "house" publications, as well as to other types of counseling and assistance.

Finally, many software and hardware companies publish regular newsletters or magazines for *registered users* of their products. Sometimes these publications are free, sometimes they're not. Either way, it is to your advantage to know everything you can about your system, so remember to send in the product registration cards that come with virtually every product you buy.

Publication Name/Address	*Description*	*Frequency*
Amiga World IDG Communications, Inc. 80 Elm Street Peterborough, NH 03458 603/924-9471 603/924-9384 FAX	For owners of Amiga computers. Editorial content includes news, product reviews, trends, and how-to articles.	Monthly
Byte McGraw-Hill, Inc. One Phoenix Hill Lane Peterborough, NH 03458 603/924-9281	Provides information about performance, productivity, and efficiency of state-of-the-market microcomputer hardware and software products and computer industry developments. Includes features and product and technology news for experienced and knowledgeable users, advisors, buyers, and specifiers of microcomputers.	Monthly
Computer Buyer's Guide and Handbook Bedford Communications, Inc. 150 Fifth Avenue New York, NY 10011 212/807-8220	Product-intensive microcomputer magazine serving the business buyer. Comprehensive reviews appear regularly. Product specification charts compare products within categories. Each issue also contains feature articles on developments and trends pertinent to the purchase of computer systems, peripherals, and software. Special issues for the vertical product buyer, focusing on individual categories, such as printers or add-on devices, examine many products in a single edition.	Monthly

Publication Name/Address	*Description*	*Frequency*
Computer Currents Computer Currents Publishing, Inc. 5720 Hollis Street Emeryville, CA 94608 415/547-6800	Offers comprehensive product news and resource information for business and professional PC users. Articles include reviews, profiles, news stories, financial data, lists of new products and services, marketplace directories, questions and answers, and industry commentary. Also includes a calendar of local events, lists of user groups and associations, and a computer classified section.	Biweekly for San Francisco edition, monthly for other editions
Computer Graphics Today (Official publication of The National Computer Graphics Association) Media Horizons, Inc. 228 E. 45th Street New York, NY 10017 212/983-5888	Covers the complete computer graphics business scene with news of company developments, personalities, professional conferences, etc. Emphasis on computer graphics applications—the development, implementation, maintenance, and management of general-purpose and specialized graphics systems.	Monthly
Computer Graphics World PennWell Publishing Co. Advanced Technology Group P.O. Box 987 One Technology Park Drive Westford, MA 01886 508/692-0700	Covers technology and application areas for computer graphics worldwide. Editorial includes application stories, identification of new technologies, product announcements and round-ups, applications, interviews, and product evaluations.	Monthly
Computer Language Miller Freeman Publications, Inc. 500 Howard Street San Francisco, CA 94105 415/397-1881 415/995-2487 FAX	For the professional software developer and integrator who designs, writes, or customizes software. Editorial focuses on ways of improving productivity and aiding in the developers' efforts to design custom applications.	Monthly

Publication Name/Address	*Description*	*Frequency*
Computer Marketplace Magazine RK Productions, Inc. P.O. Box 18906 San Jose, CA 95158 408/978-7927	General-interest computer magazine, providing industry information, new product data, user group activities, and articles on a broad range of computer-related topics. For corporate purchasing agents, microcomputer-related resellers, value-added resellers, and computer buyers.	Bimonthly
Computer Reseller News CMP Publications, Inc. 600 Community Drive Manhasset, NY 11030 516/562-5000	For dealers, value-added resellers, distributors, and vendors of microcomputer products. Delivers timely news and provides comprehensive analysis of emerging market trends. Editorial coverage includes networking, hardware, software, the distribution channel, and company financials.	Weekly
Computer Shopper Coastal Associates Publishing L.P. 5211 S. Washington Avenue Titusville, FL 32780 407/269-1663 407/267-2950 FAX	Information about direct sellers of computer products for mail order buyers.	Monthly
Computer Systems News CMP Publications, Inc. 600 Community Drive Manhasset, NY 11030 516/562-5000	For management and decision-level technical executives in systems integration companies, value-added resellers, software development firms, and manufacturers of computer-related equipment. Editorial covers all aspects of the computer industry: news, trends, new products, people, business events, hardware and software developments, and product and technology updates.	Weekly

Publication Name/Address	*Description*	*Frequency*
Computer Technology Review West World Productions, Inc. 924 Westwood Blvd. Suite 650 Los Angeles, CA 90024 213/208-1335 213/208-1054 FAX	For corporate and engineering management of value-added resellers, original equipment manufacturers, systems integrators, and volume users. Provides an overview of new and emerging technologies and products, along with interviews and technology columns.	16 times a year
ComputerLand Magazine ComputerLand Corp. P.O. Box 9012 5964 W. Las Positas Blvd. Pleasanton, CA 94566-8575 415/734-4087	For preferred ComputerLand customers. Articles explore the role of high-technology information systems in contemporary life and focus on ways people are using computers in their work to accomplish a wide variety of tasks. Also featured are product reviews of new hardware, software, and peripherals.	Bimonthly
Computers in Accounting Warren, Gorham & Lamont One Penn Plaza 40th Floor New York, NY 10119 212/971-5000 212/971-5025 FAX	For the professional accountant who is a computer user or an advisor to clients who use or will use computers.	10 times a year
Computerworld CW Publishing, Inc. 375 Cochichuate Road Framingham, MA 01701 508/879-0700 800/343-6474 FAX	For the MIS/DP and other information systems professionals who are responsible for the planning, implementation, and management of computer-based information systems (including data and telecommunications) in business, government, vendor, and educational organizations. Includes news, features, spotlight sections, and in-depth articles on topics ranging from PCs to supercomputers.	Weekly

Publication Name/Address	*Description*	*Frequency*
Connect 3Com Corporation 3165 Kifer Road Santa Clara, CA 95052 408/562-6400	For resellers and users of local area and wide area networks that use the 3+Share or 3+Open network operating systems. Editorial includes user applications, news, product round-ups, and technical how-to articles.	Quarterly
Data Based Advisor Data Based Solutions, Inc. 4010 Morena Blvd. Suite 200 San Diego, CA 92117 619/483-6400	Specifically for database management system users. Features written by business and computer professionals provide practical techniques for improving DBMS productivity and efficiency. Articles include programming tips, software reviews, tutorials, and entire working computer programs. Specializes in dBASE language products like dBASE III Plus, dBASE IV, FoxBase, Clipper, and Quicksilver; also covers Revelation, R:base, Paradox, and SQL products.	Monthly
Data Sources Ziff-Davis Publishing Co. 1 Park Avenue New York, NY 10016 212/503-5178	Comprehensive 3-volume guide of available hardware, software, and data communications products for buyers of data processing and communications systems. Information is provided by vendors either through returned surveys or from provided technical manuals. Different sections cover product and vendor information. Product information includes technical data, manufacturer's make and model number, price, and installation data. Company listings include information on size of company, year established, phone numbers, and personnel.	Semiannually

Publication Name/Address	*Description*	*Frequency*
Data Training Weingarten Publications 38 Chauncy Street Boston, MA 02111 617/542-0146	For trainers and managers responsible for computer and information training. Covers new ideas and techniques and gives case studies of training and human resource management in the data processing, office automation, and computer technology fields. Topics include computer-based training, programmer and analyst training, end-user training, computer literacy, and implementation of new technology.	Monthly
Database Online, Inc. 11 Tannery Lane Weston, CT 06883 203/227-8466	Specifically for professional information specialists who search on-line databases. Contains in-depth, practical, how-to articles that provide comparative analyses and tips and techniques for on-line searching. Covers various types of databases: specific and technical, business, financial, social sciences, medical, and legal. An increasing amount of coverage is devoted to microcomputer applications for database creation, storage, and retrieval.	Bimonthly
Database Searcher Meckler Publishing Company 11 Ferry Lane Westport, CT 06880 203/226-6967	Assists both professional searchers and searching professionals in using on-line and microcomputer-based search aids and techniques for on-line systems.	Monthly

Publication Name/Address	*Description*	*Frequency*
Datamation Cahners Publishing 249 W. 17th Street New York, NY 10011 212/645-0067 212/463-6560 FAX	Focuses on significant challenges, which include implementing new technologies, protecting existing investments in hardware and software, connecting dissimilar systems, managing personnel inside and outside the MIS organization, and understanding where information technology fits their business.	Twice monthly
Information Center Weingarten Publications, Inc. 38 Chauncy Street Boston, MA 02111 617/542-0146	Serves readers who are responsible for the management of end-user computing in business organizations. Carries how-to articles, reports on trends, and "think pieces." Articles concern anything of interest to information center professionals, including topics such as software selection, information center staffing, and training of end-users. Also features regular departments for case studies, application stories, training techniques, and product news.	Monthly
InformationWEEK CMP Publications, Inc. 600 Community Drive Manhasset, NY 11030 516/562-5000	News magazine for information systems managers and senior staff in large and information-intensive organizations. Focuses on news but also provides news analysis, in-depth product coverage, and features that develop a picture of information management from systems and strategic viewpoints.	Weekly

Publication Name/Address	*Description*	*Frequency*
INFOWORLD INFOWORLD 1060 Marsh Road Suite C-200 Menlo Park, CA 94025 415/328-4602 415/328-1049 FAX	For personal computing professionals and business readers with volume-buying authority. Features news coverage, in-depth special reports, buyers' guides, and detailed product reviews.	Weekly
Journal of Accountancy 1211 Avenue of the Americas New York, NY 10036 212/575-6200	For certified public accountants and other accounting professionals. Editorial content focuses on the accounting business but includes coverage of technology as it applies to accounting.	Monthly
LAN: The Local Area Network Magazine Telecom Library, Inc. 12 W. 21st Street New York, NY 10010 212/691-8215	Devoted entirely to local area network products and peripherals. Primary readers are LAN users and managers. Distributors, dealers, and value-added resellers also make up a significant portion of the readership. Articles include using LANs to improve the bottom line. Every issue contains news; interviews; product round-ups; tests; tips; and tutorials to help readers sell, choose, install, use, maintain, or manage their networks.	Monthly
LAN Technology M & T Publishing, Inc. 501 Galveston Drive Redwood City, CA 94063 415/366-3600	Technical resource for network integrators, providing practical hands-on information. Readers are responsible for designing, installing, and maintaining LANs.	Monthly

Publication Name/Address	*Description*	*Frequency*
LAN Times McGraw-Hill 151 East 1700 South Suite 100 Provo, UT 84606 801/379-5850	Published for users and resellers of local area networks and developers of networking software applications, utility software, and hardware. Covers the industry, with a concentration on LANs running the Novell NetWare network operating system.	Monthly
Lotus Lotus Publishing P.O. Box 9123 Cambridge, MA 02139 617/494-1192	Computing magazine for managers and professionals who use personal computers and peripherals, Lotus spreadsheets, other software, and related materials and services. Editorial coverage includes information and perspectives on the computer industry and on general business trends; product reviews; tutorials on accomplishing tasks with Lotus software; and computing solutions for accounting, corporate and personal finance, real estate, manufacturing, education, and forecasting.	Monthly
M.D. Computing Springer-Verlag, Inc. 175 Fifth Avenue New York, NY 10010 212/460-1500	For physicians who use or are planning to use computers in their practice.	Monthly
MacGuide MacGuide Magazine, Inc. 550 S. Wadsworth Blvd. Suite 500 Lakewood, CO 80226 303/935-8100	Provides Apple Macintosh users with news, reviews, and feature articles on significant products. Editorial focus provides professional Macintosh users with in-depth knowledge of products and trends. Each issue contains product reviews and acts as a sourcebook for products in the Macintosh environment.	Monthly

Publication Name/Address	*Description*	*Frequency*
The Macintosh Buyer's Guide Redgate Communications Corp. 660 Beachland Blvd. Vero Beach, FL 32963-1794 407/231-6904	Provides an overview of products available to the business user of Macintosh computers. Each issue targets a specific area of interest, such as desktop publishing, desktop communications, and business productivity. Every issue contains product reviews, feature columns, and a product directory section.	Quarterly
Macintosh News CMP Publications, Inc. 600 Community Drive Manhasset, NY 11030 516/562-5000	For resellers, integrators, and developers of Macintosh computers and products. Provides news, marketing and distribution strategies, information on the corporate market for Macintosh products, and new product and technology coverage.	Weekly
MacUser Ziff-Davis Publishing Co. 950 Tower Lane 18th Floor Foster City, CA 94404 415/578-9770 415/378-5675 FAX	Source of product information for the serious business Macintosh user. Editorial focuses on analysis, tips, and insights, all aimed at increasing user productivity. In-depth coverage given to major products and trends, such as desktop publishing, desktop presentations, communications, networking, programming, and graphics.	Monthly
MacWEEK MacWEEK, Inc. 301 Howard Street 1st Floor San Francisco, CA 94105 415/243-3500 415/243-3650 FAX	For corporate and other volume users of Apple Macintosh computers and other graphics workstations. Includes product news, reviews, how-to articles, features, and opinion columns.	Weekly

Publication Name/Address	*Description*	*Frequency*
MacWorld PCW Communications, Inc. 501 Second Street San Francisco, CA 94107 415/243-0505 415/442-1891	Contains hands-on, in-depth product evaluations of Macintosh-compatible hardware and software. Includes product reviews, news, interviews, new product round-ups, how-to articles, and where-to-buy information.	Monthly
Modern Office Technology Penton Publications 1100 Superior Ave. Cleveland, OH 44114 216/696-7000 216/696-8765	Serves managers responsible for evaluating, buying, and managing business information-processing equipment and systems, office operations, and personnel. Editorial covers management information, equipment round-ups, procedures, software bestsellers, and new technology.	Monthly
Network World IDG Communications, Inc. P.O. Box 9171 375 Cochichuate Road Framingham, MA 01701-9171 508/820-2543 508/879-3167 FAX	For users of enterprise-wide local and wide area networks. Editorial mix includes news and features that provide strategic information on how to manage the enterprise network for corporate competitive edge.	Weekly
The Office Office Publications, Inc. 1600 Summer Street P.O. Box 1231 Stamford, CT 06904 203/327-9670	Contains practical articles on office automation management, software, word processing, telecommunications, office design and layout, and copying and reproduction. Editorial purpose is to assist administrative, MIS, information management, word processing, and data processing executives to develop more efficient and cost-saving business systems.	Monthly

Publication Name/Address	*Description*	*Frequency*
Online Online, Inc. 11 Tannery Lane Weston, CT 06883 203/227-8466	For professional users of on-line database services. Editorial includes feature articles, database searching tips, management of information centers, and equipment reviews.	Bimonthly
Online Today CompuServe, Inc. 5000 Arlington Center Blvd. Columbus, OH 43220 614/457-8600	For subscribers of the CompuServe Information Service. Editorial includes techniques for getting the most out of CompuServe's on-line databases; also covers special interest groups, electronic mail, interviews, product reviews, book reviews, and practical applications of communications to increase productivity.	Monthly
PC Computing Ziff-Davis Publishing Co. 4 Cambridge Center Ninth Floor Cambridge, MA 02142 617/492-7500	For active PC users. Provides information that helps readers seek new dimensions in their professional and personal PC applications.	Monthly
PC Magazine Ziff-Davis Publishing Co. One Park Avenue New York, NY 10016 212/503-5115	For buyers and users of IBM-compatible personal computers, software, peripherals, and accessories. Conducts extensive laboratory benchmark hardware and software product reviews, provides in-depth how-to articles, and includes several opinion columns that examine the industry from a variety of perspectives.	Biweekly (July and August are monthly)

Publication Name/Address	*Description*	*Frequency*
PC Publishing Hunter Publishing Limited Partnership 950 Lee Street Des Plaines, IL 60016 312/296-0770	Concentrates on desktop publishing and presentation graphics for IBM and compatible PC users. Feature articles deal with current hardware and software technology, including page design and layout, electronic production management, and publishing techniques.	Monthly
PC Today Peed Corporation 120 West Harvest Drive Lincoln, NE 68501 402/477-8900 402/477-9252	Contains articles for first-time buyers and users of PC systems and business applications using PC systems. Features lists of comparable equipment in the personal computer market.	Monthly
PC Week Ziff-Davis Publishing Co. 800 Boylston Street 11th Floor Boston, MA 02199 617/375-4000	Newspaper of corporate microcomputing targeted to provide volume users with news, buyers' guides, product reviews, and features on the strategies used by a variety of companies implementing PC-based business solutions.	Weekly
PC World PCW Communications, Inc. 501 Second Street San Francisco, CA 94107 415/243-0500 415/442-1891 FAX	Guide to IBM and IBM-compatible computers and products. Contains news, product reviews, how-to advice, and industry perspectives.	Monthly
Personal Computing VNU Business Publications, Inc. 10 Holland Drive Hasbrouck Heights, NJ 07604 201/393-6165	For experienced users of personal computers. Editorial content is designed to help readers enhance their productivity through the practical application of computing technology.	Monthly

Publication Name/Address	*Description*	*Frequency*
Personal Publishing Hitchcock Publishing Company 191 S. Gary Avenue Carol Stream, IL 60188 312/665-1000 312/462-2225 FAX	For individuals who use personal computers to create finished pages, documents, and publications.	Monthly
Physicians and Computers 2333 Waukegan Road Suite S-280 Bannockburn, IL 60015 312/940-8333	Addresses the interests of physicians in private practice, who have computerized their offices or are planning to do so. Articles cover many computer categories, such as medical and nonmedical software, product reviews, office management, patient education, hardware, peripherals, financial management, and telecommunications.	Monthly
Publish! PCW Communications, Inc. 501 Second Street San Francisco, CA 94107 415/243-0500 415/442-1891 FAX	Magazine of desktop and personal computer publishing. Source on how to use personal computers to integrate text and graphics into printed communication. Information ranges from laser printers and page-makeup software to commercial typesetting systems that interface with personal computers.	Monthly
Reseller Management Gordon Publications, Inc. 301 Gibraltar Drive Morris Plains, NJ 07950 201/292-5100 201/898-9281 FAX	For management and executives of value-added resellers, dealers, and distributors of personal computer hardware, software, accessories, and related products. Editorial content includes news, trends, success stories, and business issues affecting resellers.	Monthly

Publication Name/Address	*Description*	*Frequency*
Retail Info Systems News 21 Hilltop Circle Suite 150 Brookside, NJ 07926 201/543-4762 201/543-5753 FAX	Addresses systems solutions for corporate and financial operations, MIS, and merchandising management at retail. Also addresses various segments of retail as well as value-added resellers and manufacturers concerned with bar coding, point-of-sale, data capture, electronic data interchange, and other information advances.	9 times a year
Small Computers in Libraries Meckler Corp. 11 Ferry Lane West Westport, CT 06880 203/226-6967	Assists librarians in organizations using mini- and microcomputers. Provides information about computer reference services, software and courseware, user groups, product announcements, software reviews, and techniques for effective microcomputer operations.	Monthly
Software Magazine Sentry Publishing Company, Inc. Westborough Office Park 1900 W. Park Drive Westborough, MA 01581 508/366-2031 508/366-8104 FAX	Serves corporate software planners and purchasers in business markets who use, recommend, evaluate, select, or buy software for mainframe, minicomputer, and personal computer applications.	Monthly
Systems Integration Cahners Publishing Co. Cahners Building 275 Washington Street Newton Corner, MA 02158 617/964-3030 617/964-5490 FAX	For original equipment manufacturer (OEM) integrators, value-added resellers, and in-house systems integrators with the technology and product information needed to develop, configure, and integrate computer-based systems that solve specific application problems. Contains comprehensive and comparative details on products, including personal computers, workstations, input and output peripherals, systems and applications software, and communications hardware and software.	Monthly

Publication Name/Address	*Description*	*Frequency*
T.H.E. Journal (Technological Horizons in Education) Synergy, Inc. 2626 S. Pullman Suite 250 Santa Ana, CA 92705 714/261-0366	Forum in which administrators and managers in education and industry training share their experience in the use of technology-based educational aids.	10 times a year
TypeWorld TypeWorld Publications P.O. Box 170 35 Pelham Road Salem, NH 03079 603/898-2822 603/898-3393 FAX	For the electronic publishing industry. Contains news articles and tutorial information on the application and development of page-processing typographic devices, systems, and peripherals. Editorial content covers new equipment, installations, personnel, events, tutorials, and features.	24 times a year
Unix Review Miller Freeman Publications 5000 Howard Street San Francisco, CA 94105 415/397-1881 415/995-2487 FAX	Serves systems integrators, value-added resellers, professional developers, and end users building solutions using the UNIX or XENIX operating systems.	Monthly
UNIX Today! CMP Publication, Inc. 600 Community Drive Manhasset, NY 11030 516/562-5000	Provides news, news analysis, and feature stories for and about the UNIX user community. Contains features about UNIX-based business applications and the personalities creating those applications. Also covers industry trends, vendor strategies, and vendor financials.	Biweekly

Publication Name/Address	*Description*	*Frequency*
Unix World Tech Valley Publishing 444 Castro Street Mountain View, CA 94041 415/940-1500 415/967-1257 FAX	Covers systems integration and design topics for corporate and technical management of systems manufacturers, value-added resellers, independent software vendors, and large-volume end users.	Monthly
VAR Business CMP Publications, Inc. 600 Community Drive Manhasset, NY 11030 516/562-5000	For value-added resellers and dealers—companies that purchase computer products and services, add tangible value to them, and resell them to end users. Editorial focuses on management issues and trends designed to help VARs and dealers operate their businesses more effectively and profitably.	Monthly
Western Micro Market BAM Publications 5951 Canning Street Oakland, CA 94609 415/652-3810 415/652-4618	For resellers of personal computer hardware, software, accessories, supplies, and related products and services. Editorial content includes analysis of issues affecting resellers.	Monthly
WordPerfect Magazine WordPerfect Publishing Corp. 270 West Center Street Orem, UT 84057 801/226-5555 801/226-8804 FAX	For users of the WordPerfect family of software, including WordPerfect, DataPerfect, PlanPerfect, DrawPerfect, Library, Executive, and Repeat Performance. Editorial consists mostly of how-to articles to improve productivity. Also includes opinion pieces, product round-ups, news, and features.	Monthly

APPENDIX B

A Contract for Developing Custom Software

The contract shown in this appendix is similar to a formal contract you might see from a custom software development company.

Because no two attorneys develop identical contracts, even when the contracts are developed for the same type of transaction, what your developer presents to you may differ from this example.

Some software developers use contracts that are far less complicated than this sample. It is in your best interest to enter into an agreement that leaves little to the imagination. Getting everything down in black and white before the project begins is your best hope for resolving any disagreements that may arise.

A contract is a compromise—no one will sign a lopsided contract that favors only one party. For example, in this contract, the software developer (called the consultant) has the right to stop work if payments are not received on time, and the client has the right to reject the system if it does not perform as detailed in Exhibit A.

Contracts, like the price of a new car, are fully negotiable. The proposed contract presented to you probably is written in favor of the consultant. Read the contract carefully. If you see something that you don't like, cross it out. Maybe the consultant will agree to the deletion, and maybe he or she will not agree. You may get a counterproposal—one that both parties can agree to. Contract negotiation is a game of give and take.

One last bit of advice. Never, never sign a contract until the contract has been reviewed by your attorney, and you understand the ramifications of each section. After you sign, you are legally bound by the contract's terms and conditions. At that point, the only way to modify the contract is through an addendum.

Agreement for Custom Software Programming Services

This agreement (the *Agreement*) made as of March 19, 1990 (the *Effective Date*), is between Ace Consultants, Inc., 123 Main Street, Southborough, Massachusetts, 01772 (hereinafter called *Consultant*) and Mark and Marian, Inc., d/b/a Bed and Bath Accessories, Shopper's Universe Shopping Center, Framingham, Massachusetts 01701 (hereinafter called *Client*), for consulting services and development of computer software and related services in accordance with the terms and conditions set forth herein.

1. Definitions

As used in this Agreement, the term *system* refers collectively to computer magnetic media (disks), the software programs and other files recorded on said media, keyboard templates, and documentation, specifications, operations manuals, technical manuals, training materials, binders, and slipcases provided by Consultant.

2. Services

Consultant hereby agrees to design and create a computer system and provide services and documentation in accordance with the format guidelines and performance specifications set forth in Exhibit A attached to this Agreement and incorporated herein.

3. Additional work

This Agreement may be amended to add tasks that increase the scope of services set forth in Exhibit A. Any and all amendments to this Agreement shall be in writing and shall be agreed to and signed by both Client and Consultant. Start and completion dates as set forth in Exhibit C may be revised by said amendment. Payment for said additional services shall be made by the Client to the Consultant in accordance with the terms set forth in Exhibit D, unless otherwise superseded by terms specified in said amendment. In the event of multiple amendments, the services provided by the Consultant and payments made to the Consultant shall be defined as the aggregate of all services and payments set forth in Exhibits A and D and all amendments occurring in chronological order, unless otherwise specified.

4. Support services

The Client shall supply support services as set forth in Exhibit B.

5. Testing and acceptance

Client shall have a period of thirty (30) days to test the system at Client's business location. Consultant shall provide reasonable support to Client's employees during the test period. The thirty-day (30) test period shall commence on the day following delivery to Client of programs and other materials specified in Exhibit C.

5.1 Client shall notify Consultant in writing whether or not the system has been accepted. Client acknowledges that Client's failure to provide said written notice before the end of the thirty-day (30) period shall be deemed an acceptance of the system. If Client elects to reject the system, Client shall notify Consultant in writing, and Client shall return all copies of disks, programs, and documentation and all other materials to Consultant. Consultant shall, upon receipt of said disks, programs, documentation, and other materials, return, within thirty (30) days, all payments except the initial deposit and expense reimbursements that Consultant shall retain as sole compensation under this Agreement.

5.2 The sole permissible grounds for Client's rejection of the system is the failure to comply with the specifications set forth in Exhibit A.

6. Work delegation

All services performed shall be those of the Consultant unless permission to subcontract or otherwise delegate obligations is granted in writing by the Client.

7. Termination

This Agreement shall terminate fifteen (15) days after Consultant's receipt of written notification from Client. Furthermore, Consultant may terminate this agreement by providing Client with fifteen (15) days written notice.

8. Notices

All notices and other communications herein provided for shall be sent by overnight air courier, service fee prepaid, or certified or registered mail, postage prepaid, return receipt requested, to the parties at the addresses set forth at the beginning of this Agreement until such time as either party shall give the other notice of change of address.

9. Employment status

Consultant shall perform under this Agreement as an *independent contractor*, and not as an employee of the Client. Consultant shall be prohibited from participation in Client's employee benefit programs.

10. Fees

Client shall pay fees to Consultant in accordance with terms and conditions set forth in Exhibit D.

11. Expenses

Client shall reimburse Consultant for job-related expenses. Client also shall reimburse Consultant for reasonable incidental expenses. Said reimbursements shall be made within ten (10) business days after date of billing of said expenses.

12. Late payment

Consultant's invoices remaining unpaid by Client after thirty (30) days from date of billing shall be assessed a monthly late payment charge of 1.5 percent of the unpaid amount.

13. Suspension of work

Consultant shall suspend work and this Agreement shall terminate after sixty (60) days of nonpayment by Client of fees and expenses billed by Consultant.

14. Warranties

Consultant warrants that the system will perform in accordance with the specifications set forth in Exhibit A for a period of ninety (90) days from acceptance. Defects reported by Client to Consultant in writing during the warranty period shall be corrected by Consultant within fifteen (15) business days after receipt of such report. Consultant shall have no further obligations under this Agreement to provide maintenance after the conclusion of the ninety-day (90) warranty period.

14.1 Consultant shall replace defective disks at no charge—provided that the defective disk is returned to Consultant within twenty (20) days after acceptance by Client. After the twenty-day (20) period, Consultant shall replace defective disks for a charge of $20 each—provided that the defective disk first is returned to Consultant. All such disk replacements shall be returned to Client via First Class mail, or, if requested by Client, via overnight courier service at Client's expense.

14.2 In no event shall Consultant be liable to Client for any damages, including lost profits, lost savings, or other incidental or consequential damages arising from Client's use or inability to use the system even if Consultant has been advised of the possibility of such damages, or for any claim by any other party. Some states do not allow the limitation or exclusion of liability for incidental or consequential damages, in which case, this limitation may not apply to Client. Client further agrees that the system is not intended as *Consumer Goods* under state or federal warranty laws.

15. Confidentiality

Consultant and Client agree that neither party will disclose, duplicate, copy, or make use of any material or information that has or will come into possession of either party in connection with this Agreement for any purpose other than for the performance of this Agreement and shall treat as confidential and as proprietary to each other any information which relates to the other party's research, development, trade secrets, and business affairs, provided, however, that the obligation to treat such information as proprietary and confidential shall not apply to information which (i) is or becomes publicly available through no fault of the other party, (ii) is in the disclosing party's possession on the Effective Date provided that it shall not have been obtained from the other party, (iii) is developed by the disclosing party outside the scope of any agreement with the other party, (iv) is obtained lawfully and in good faith by the disclosing party, or (v) is required to be disclosed by a court or other governmental authority after reasonable notice is given to the other party. The parties hereby acknowledge that the burden of proving the exceptions set for in clauses (i) through (v) hereinabove resides with the disclosing party.

16. Legal process

In the event that a subpoena or other legal process concerning information disclosed by Client to Consultant or otherwise learned by Consultant is served upon Consultant at any time, Consultant shall notify Client immediately and cooperate, at Client's expense, in any lawful effort by Client to contest the legal validity of such a subpoena or other legal process. This provision shall in no way limit Consultant's ability to satisfy any governmentally required disclosure. The obligation in this paragraph survives termination of this Agreement.

17. Product ownership

Client shall own all materials and ideas embodied therein resulting from the services provided by the Consultant except that Consultant shall retain ownership of proposed plans and ideas rejected by Client.

18. Advertising

Neither party shall use the other party's name, directly or indirectly, in any advertisement, promotional literature, news release, or release to any publication without the written consent of such other party.

19. Remedies

Prior to formal acceptance of the system, Client and Consultant shall both have the right to terminate this Agreement in the event of a breach of any of its provisions by the other party. If the Agreement is so terminated, neither party shall have any rights under the Agreement. Consultant shall return to Client all payments made by Client under this Agreement, and exclusive rights to the system shall revert to Consultant.

20. Arbitration

Consultant and Client shall exercise good faith to resolve disputes that arise relative to the terms, performance, or interpretation of this Agreement. Disputes that cannot be resolved between Consultant and Client themselves shall be resolved through binding arbitration that shall be conducted in accordance with the rules of the American Arbitration Association. Arbitration shall constitute the sole option for resolving disputes. Neither party shall have the right to initiate litigation.

21. Scope of Agreement

This Agreement and the attachments set forth constitute the complete and exclusive statement of the terms and conditions between Consultant and Client covering the performance hereof and cannot be altered except in writing and executed by an authorized representative of each party.

22. Waiver of compliance

Any failure by any party hereto to enforce at any time any term or condition under this Agreement shall not be considered a waiver of that party's right thereafter to enforce each and every term and condition of this Agreement.

23. Partial invalidity

If any provision of this Agreement or the application thereof to any party or circumstances shall be declared void, illegal, or unenforceable, the remainder of this Agreement shall be valid and enforceable to the extent permitted by applicable law. In such event, the parties shall use their best efforts to replace the invalid or unenforceable provision by a provision that, to the extent permitted by the applicable law, achieves the purposes intended under the invalid or unenforceable provision. Any deviation by either party from the terms and provisions of the Agreement to comply with applicable laws, rules, or regulations shall not be considered a breach of this Agreement.

24. Applicable law

    This Agreement and its performance shall be governed and construed in accordance with the laws of the Commonwealth of Massachusetts.

25. Assignment

    This Agreement is not assignable by either party by operation of law or otherwise, except with the written permission of the other party.

26. Force majeure

    Neither party shall be responsible for delays resulting from acts beyond the control of such party, including but not limited to strikes, job actions, accidents, or acts of God, provided that the nonperforming party shall use reasonable commercial efforts to avoid or remove such causes of nonperformance, and shall continue performance hereunder with reasonable dispatch whenever such causes are removed.

27. Counterparts

    This Agreement may be executed in counterparts, each of which shall be deemed to be an original and all of which together shall be deemed to be one and the same instrument.

IN WITNESS WHEREOF, the parties hereto have caused this Agreement to be executed by their duly authorized representatives as of the Effective Date.

Ace Consultants, Inc.	Mark and Marian, Inc. d/b/a Bed and Bath Accessories
______________________	______________________
Signature	Signature
John Smith, President Typed name and title	Marian Jones, President Type name and title
______________________	______________________
Date	Date

Exhibit A

System Specifications

(You would attach the entire systems analysis, design requirements, report layouts, and functional specifications at this point in the Agreement. Exhibit A lays out in minute detail everything to be included in the system.)

Exhibit B

Client Responsibilities

The following shall be provided by Client for the duration of this agreement.

1. Access to Bed and Bath Accessories key employees for interviews and other necessary interaction during the course of analysis, development, installation, testing, and training.

2. Adequate space, working facilities, and support resources at Client's site to carry out tasks on a timely basis.

Exhibit C

Consultant's Deliverables and Schedule

Items to be provided by Consultant:

1. Weekly written status reports

2. Two copies of machine-readable executable code in magnetic disk form

3. One complete set of documentation

Computer Operating Environment: The system shall be designed to operate on IBM Personal Computers employing the PC DOS operating system Version 3.0 or later and other computers that are 100 percent compatible with this configuration. Applications designed for a networking environment shall be compatible with servers running any of the following network operating systems: NetWare 386 Version 3.1 or greater, manufactured by Novell, Inc., of Provo, Utah; VINES/386 Version 4.0 or later, manufactured by Banyan Systems, Inc., of Westborough, Massachusetts; or 3+Open Version 1.1 or later, manufactured by 3Com Corporation of Santa Clara, California.

Starting Date: Work by Consultant shall begin not later than April 1, 1990.

Ending Date: Work shall be completed on or before September 30, 1990.

Training Services: Consultant shall provide training services to Client's staff during the acceptance testing period. This training shall be sufficient to enable Client's staff to learn all aspects of operation.

Exhibit D

Payment Schedule

Client shall pay Consultant the sum of $25,000 for services provided under this agreement.

Consultant shall maintain a detailed log of time expended under this Agreement. If Consultant expends more than 250 hours on the project, Client shall make additional payments at the rate of $50 per hour for each additional hour of work up to a maximum additional amount of $2,500.

Payments shall be made as follows:

1. $8,000 at the signing of this agreement
2. $12,000 upon delivery to Client of items specified in the section of Exhibit A entitled "Items to be provided by Consultant"

3. $5,000 and all other additional payments, if any, upon Client's formal acceptance of the system under the terms set forth in this Agreement

APPENDIX C

Cost/Benefit Analysis

Unless you are independently wealthy or a philanthropist, you are in business to make money—to show a profit. The reason you elected to install a computer in the first place was not to prove that it could be done or to be the first on your block; the reason you began this long process was to improve the bottom line.

Before you reach the point of no return by committing to equipment and services, you must undertake a *cost/benefit analysis* to determine whether the money you invest in a computer system is worth it. After all, if you invest $60,000 in computerization for a return of 5 percent, you would be better off taking that same money and buying a certificate of deposit at your local bank. That way your return might be 9 percent or more!

> The cost of obtaining information must not exceed the value of that information.

Installing a $100,000 computer system to improve your sales by $10,000 a year is a case where the cost of obtaining the information ($100,000) is much greater than the value of the information, say $50,000 ($10,000 in increased sales per year over five years). Although this is a gross oversimplification, the intent of the cost/benefit exercise becomes clear.

The theory behind a cost/benefit analysis is simple. For a five-year period, calculate *all* the costs associated with your computerization project. Also calculate the costs of operating business *without* computers. Then through simple subtraction you can see the improvement (or loss) for each of the five years. You will use a little high school algebra to determine how long it will take to recover your costs and finally calculate the *return on investment*, an indication of the profitability of your initial investment.

A Simple Cost-Justification Model

Here's a very clearcut example. Suppose that you have one secretary who spends 75 percent (30 hours per week) of his or her time typing memos and correspondence. Examine the time spent and determine how much is allocated to the creation of new documents and how much is spent revising existing documents. For purposes of this model, you can assume that the time is divided half and half, or 15 hours creating and 15 hours revising.

What are the costs associated with this effort? For now forget the typewriter (you already own it) and supplies like paper and ribbons (you will continue to buy supplies with your new system). The only factor remaining is the cost of the secretary's labor and benefits. Assume that the secretary is paid $20,000 per year and that benefits add another 30 percent. The *fully loaded* cost of labor for the entire year is then $26,000 ($20,000 + 30%). But remember that only 75 percent of the secretary's time is spent on word processing, so you can count only 75 percent of the $26,000. So the final word processing labor cost today is $19,500 ($26,000 × 75%).

Next, break the $19,500 into its two component costs: creating new documents and revising existing documents. Because this example split that effort 50/50, the labor cost now looks like this:

Salary	$20,000	
Benefits	6,000	(30% of salary)
Fully loaded salary	$26,000	
% of time word processing	75	
Salary spent word proc.	$19,500	
50% creating	$ 9,750	
50% revising	$ 9,750	

Good! You now know, within reasonable accuracy, your current cost for word processing *for the current year*. If you have additional staff performing similar duties, you calculate the labor cost for each in a similar manner.

Next comes a little educated guesswork. You need to derive an estimate of the time saved by installing a word processing system. It should come as no surprise that far greater time savings can be achieved in the revision of existing documents than in the creation of new documents. That discrepancy is the reason you separate the tasks.

Suppose that the time to create new documents can be cut by 30 percent. Don't be surprised by the minimal gain. Fancy word processing programs that produce near typeset results will raise your expectations. And those raised expectations will take time to fulfill when formatting new documents. If you are currently spending $9,750 per year for document creation, a 30 percent cost reduction produces a new cost of $6,825 ($9,750 − 30%). But the real savings lies in revisions. The cost of revising documents can drop by 80 percent or more because these documents are retrieved from disk and easily modified. They need not be retyped in their entirety, and correction fluid becomes a thing of the past. Calculating an 80 percent savings here results in a cost of only $1,950 ($9,750 – 80%).

The labor costs with automation look like this:

Document creation	$6,825
Document revision	$1,950
Total word proc. cost	$8,775

That's quite a savings compared to $19,500! And this is for just one year. But this figure represents only the reduction in labor costs, or the *cost-avoidance.* You still need to figure in the equipment costs.

Suppose that you buy one personal computer, one laser printer, and a word processing software package for use by a single employee. Assume also that you send this employee to a three-day training seminar. (That constitutes initial, as opposed to on-going, training.)

The costs are

Computer	$5,000
Printer	$1,800
Software	$ 500
Training	$1,000
Total Initial Cost	$8,300

Finally, you will need to make a few more assumptions for this exercise. Assume that you give your secretary a 5 percent raise every year, plan on spending $100 per year for upgrading your word processing software to a new version, and remember to pay sales tax on your purchases. Finally, you send your secretary to a refresher course each year at an annual cost of $500. Now you have all the pieces needed to perform the simple cost/benefit analysis.

The chart in table C.1 conveniently pulls together all the calculations and assumptions you have made so far.

Table C.1
Sample Cost/Benefit Analysis

	Year					
Description	*1*	*2*	*3*	*4*	*5*	*Total*
Current salary expense	$19,500	$20,475	$21,499	$22,574	$23,703	$107,751
Projected salary expense	8,775	9,214	9,675	10,159	10,667	48,490
Improvement or (Loss)	10,725	11,261	11,824	12,415	13,036	59,261
Hardware cost	6,800	0	0	0	0	6,800
Software cost	500	100	100	100	100	900
Sales tax (5% Mass.)	365	5	5	5	5	385
Training	1,000	500	500	500	500	3,000
Total new system cost	$ 9,030	$ 610	$ 610	$ 610	$ 610	$ 11,470

This cost/benefit analysis paints a somewhat rosy picture in the first year. It's not likely that the improvements talked about earlier will be realized in the first year. Installation, training, the learning curve, and migration from the old system all take time.

In fact, the projected salary expense for the first year could actually *exceed* the current salary expense! Why? Suppose that the only training course is at night; you may be expected to pay overtime and travel expenses. And the migration from the old to the new system means that many documents will have to be "typed" all over again so that they can be saved on the computer's hard disk. That double duty may lead to a great deal of overtime.

> Modest benefits and higher than expected costs have a way of becoming reality. Refrain from making your cost/benefit analyses too optimistic.

The next step is to perform some math.

Calculating the *average annual benefit* is important. This figure represents the average number of salary dollars saved per year. Divide the total improvement figure ($59,261) by the number of years (5) to obtain an annual average benefit of $11,852.20.

Calculating the Payback Period

Now you can calculate how long you will need to recover your costs. For this example, ignore the minimal on-going cost of $610 per year and concentrate on the initial investment of $9,030. That figure represents a good chunk of money, and you can reasonably ask how long it will take for you to recover that outlay.

You can look at the cost recovery in two ways: average and actual. The average method is based on the average annual benefit you just calculated and is most useful when the improvement or loss (salary in the example) remains steady for each year. The actual method adds each year's actual improvement or loss until the total exceeds the initial expenditure. Using the average method, calculate the payback period with the formula

$$\text{Payback} = \frac{c}{b} \times 12$$

where c = the cost, b = the average annual benefit, and 12 causes the result to be expressed as a number of months. Plugging the numbers in yields the following:

$$\frac{9{,}030}{11{,}852.2} \times 12 = 9.14 \text{ months}$$

Using this method, you see that you can recover your initial investment in just over nine months! You can see why word processing is such a cost saver. A larger, more complex system like Mark and Marian's custom-order entry system could take two to three years to pay back its initial investment.

> Any system that takes longer than three years to pay back the initial investment may not be worth undertaking.

In the actual cost method, you simply add the actual annual improvement or loss figures until you reach your initial investment. In this example, the first year's savings of $10,725 is greater than the initial investment of $9,030 so you already know that the break-even point will be reached in the first year. Dividing the cost of $9,030 by $10,725 yields a result of 0.84 years, or a little more than 10 months.

With large projects the actual payback can occur a year or more after the theoretical average break-even point.

Calculating the Return on Investment

The last item to calculate is the *return on investment*. This abstract number provides a method for comparing several projects that you may be considering. As with any investment, the better the rate of return, the more attractive a particular project becomes.

Suppose that you are considering two projects and that one is far more expensive than the other. Which one is the better investment? You can find out by using the return on investment formula:

$$R = \frac{b - \frac{c}{t}}{c}$$

where

R = the return on investment expressed as a percentage
b = the annual average benefit
t = the number of years over which the money is being invested
c = the cost of developing the system.

Which of these two proposed systems will provide the best return on investment?

System 1: A $75,000 system expected to return $30,000 annually for 7 years

System 2: A $20,000 system expected to return $8,000 per year for 4 years

System 1 calculations are as follows:

$$R = \frac{30{,}000 - \frac{75{,}000}{7}}{75{,}000} = .26 = 26\%$$

System 2 calculations are as follows:

$$R = \frac{8{,}000 - \frac{20{,}000}{4}}{20{,}000} = .15 = 15\%$$

You can see that even though System 1 calls for a much larger initial investment, the projected return will be greater than that of System 2. Again, certain factors have not been brought into the calculation; inflation has not been accounted for, nor has the cost of money been included.

When Operating Costs Go Up

The secretarial example noted that the salary could go up in the first year due to overtime and training. If that trend quickly reverses itself, benefits can begin to accrue. Still, it is possible for expenses to remain higher with an automated system.

Instead of analyzing secretarial salaries, imagine that you are now looking at the entire spectrum of operating costs. Those costs include not only salaries and benefits, but on-going training costs, computer repair, custom continuous forms, telephone expenses, electrical expenses, increased air conditioning expenses, and so on. Clearly your computerized business may cost much more to run than the methods of the good old days.

Although increased operating expenses might suggest trouble, that is usually not the case. Depending on the size of your computer system and its complexity, you should *expect* operating costs to rise.

In Mark and Marian's case, their higher operating costs were more than offset by increased sales. First, they reduced the errors in custom orders. That meant fewer canceled orders, the cost of which Mark and Marian had to absorb. In addition, as customers became more satisfied with the store's customer service levels, word-of-mouth advertising brought in new business. Although the new business couldn't be quantified at the beginning of the project, the net improvement in sales not only covered the increased cost of operation but also directly affected the business's bottom line.

Summary

Undertaking a cost/benefit analysis can be a real pain. But the consequences of not doing one can be far worse. True, calculating costs of operation and proposed sales volumes can be a time-consuming, tedious task, but the results are as important as any other aspect of your computerization project.

A cost/benefit analysis tells you whether to proceed with your project. If the numbers add up in a way that you and your accountant like, that result is a signal to proceed to the next phase of your project.

If the numbers simply aren't there, you have come to a crossroads. An unfavorable analysis could mean that your project is not worth doing, but it also could indicate that you haven't included all the factors. The most important thing you can do after seeing an unfavorable cost/benefit analysis is to go back and reconsider your objectives. Are you trying to undertake too large a project, or does your proposed system treat the symptom rather than the disease?

The cost/benefit analysis and return on investment projection are two of the many tools that come together when you are automating processes of any kind. These two tools act as guideposts along the route to automation.

APPENDIX D

An Overview of DOS

This appendix acquaints you with an important link between the hardware, the software, and you. This link is the *disk operating system*, or *DOS*.

Anyone intending to use a personal computer will benefit from some knowledge of DOS. Consider the fact that you cannot use your computer at all unless you start it with DOS. You can rely on someone to do DOS-related work for you, but you will be less proficient at computing. Learn about DOS, and the results will greatly exceed your efforts.

After reading this appendix, you should

- ❑ Understand the fundamentals of disk operating systems (DOS)
- ❑ Be able to describe the structure of DOS

- ❑ Comprehend the purpose of DOS and be able to explain its principal functions
- ❑ Be familiar with the versions of DOS

Key Terms Used in This Appendix

You need to understand certain terms before you progress through this appendix.

Term	*Definition*
Disk operating system	A set of programs that lets a user and other programs use the hardware of a computer system
.Command interpreter	A command file (COMMAND.COM in DOS) that translates your keyboard instructions into actions by the computer
BIOS	Basic Input/Output System; the software that performs basic communications between the computer and the peripherals
Utility program	A program that performs a housekeeping task
Interface	A connection between parts of the computer, especially between hardware devices; also the interaction between a user and an application program

The DOS Shell	A graphical interface available with DOS 4.0 that provides an easy-to-use alternative for selecting commands
Redirection	A change in the source or destination normally used for input and output
Application program	A set of instructions that tells the computer to perform a specific task, such as word processing
Formatting	Preparing a disk so that it can be used by the computer
Batch file	A series of DOS commands placed in a disk file. DOS executes batch-file commands one at a time.
Extension	One to three characters that follow the dot (.) in a file name. The extension often indicates the file's function. For example, a COM extension is used for a command file.

What Is a Disk Operating System?

A disk *operating system* is a collection of computer programs that provides recurring services to other programs or to the user of a computer. If the computer's operating system did not provide these services, the user would have to deal directly with the details of the hardware. Without a disk operating system, for example, every computer program would have to contain instructions telling the hardware each step it should take to do its job. But because an operating system already contains instructions, any program can call on it. Disk operating systems get their name from the attention they give to the disks in the computer system.

Companies that develop commercial programs rely on this standard method for gaining access to the computer's resources. Personal computer operators rely on this standard to be able to operate computers as word processors, database managers, electronic spreadsheets, and even diversionary game opponents. Because the core of DOS remains constant in its many versions, manufacturers of personal computer products as well as end users of personal computers have a stable operating basis for their work.

From your point of view, DOS is likely to be a set of commands typed on your keyboard. This is the practical, user's point of view. Learning these DOS commands takes you from seeing a personal computer as a mysterious box of complicated equipment to using a personal computer as a system for independence and productivity.

IBM-compatible personal computers use versions of DOS called MS-DOS, the world's most popular disk operating system, developed by Microsoft Corporation. Manufacturers of personal computers, such as Zenith, IBM, and COMPAQ, tailor MS-DOS for use on their computers. The manufacturers may put their own names on the disks and package a different manual for the supplied version of DOS. But all these versions of DOS are similar when they operate on a PC. When you read about DOS in this book, you can assume that the material is relevant for your manufacturer's version of DOS.

The Three Parts of DOS

DOS has three main components. They are the following:

- COMMAND.COM, the command interpreter
- The Input/Output System
- The Utility Files

These components are contained in files that come with your DOS package. The following sections introduce you to the components and their functions.

The Command Interpreter

The *command interpreter* is DOS's "friendly host." It interacts with you through the keyboard and screen when you operate your computer. The command interpreter is also known as the command processor and often is referred to simply as COMMAND.COM ("command dot com"). All your communications with DOS are actually instructions to COMMAND.COM.

Because you instruct COMMAND.COM rather than the hardware, you never need to know the details of how the hardware operates. COMMAND.COM prints DOS requests on your display. When you enter a command, COMMAND.COM interprets what you have typed and processes your input so that DOS can take appropriate action. COMMAND.COM handles the technical details of such common tasks as displaying a list of the contents of a disk; copying files; and, of course, starting your programs.

The *DOS Shell* is a user-friendly program *interface* between your need for DOS services and the details of DOS commands. The Shell, available with version 4.0, is an additional layer that insulates you from having to know how to control details of the computer's hardware electronically.

The Input/Output System

System files, known simply as the *input/output system*, are another part of the operating system. These files are two or three special "hidden" files (the number depends on your computer) that define the hardware to the software. When you start a computer, these DOS system files are loaded into RAM. Combined, the files provide a unified set of routines for controlling the computer's operations.

The hidden files interact with special ROM on the motherboard. The special ROM is called the ROM Basic Input/Output System, or *BIOS* (pronounced BYE-oss). Responding to a program's request for service, the system files translate the request and pass it on to the ROM BIOS. The BIOS provides a further translation of the request that links the request to the hardware.

The DOS input/output system, through the special BIOS, largely determines the degree to which a non-IBM PC is "IBM compatible."

The Utility Files

DOS has certain *utility programs* that carry out useful housekeeping tasks, such as preparing disks, comparing files, finding free space on a disk, and background printing. Some of the utilities provide statistics on disk size and available memory. The utility programs are files that reside on disk and are loaded into memory by COMMAND.COM when you type their command names. Because the programs are not built into DOS, they are often called *external commands.*

Disk operating systems eliminate the need for you and your programs to know exactly how to make the hardware work. For example, to list the contents of a disk in a disk drive, you don't need to know the capacity or recording format of the disk or how to get the computer to direct the output to the screen. Another example: An application program that needs to store data on the disk does not have to reserve space on the disk, keep track of where on the disk the data is stored, or know how the data was encoded. DOS takes care of all these tasks.

DOS provides a uniform service to the hardware by getting assistance from the permanent ROM BIOS in the computer. ROM BIOS can vary among computer makers, but the computers will be highly compatible if the design of the ROM BIOS is integrated with DOS.

DOS Files and Extensions

Disk operating systems are collections of programs that carry out specific tasks. The kinds of files that hold these programs can be identified by the last three letters of the file name. These letters are called the *file extension*. Table D.1 lists the names of the DOS files and the meaning of their extensions.

Table D.1
File Names and Extensions

File Name		*File Extension Meaning*
ASSIGN	COM	The COM file extension identifies a *com*mand file. Command files are derived from the earliest operating system for personal computers, CP/M. As you learn DOS, you will recognize that these file names are the names of external DOS commands.
BACKUP	COM	
BASIC	COM	
BASICA	COM	
CHKDSK	COM	
COMMAND	COM	

Table D.1—*continued*

File Name		*File Extension Meaning*
COMP	COM	
DEBUG	COM	
DISKCOMP	COM	
DISKCOPY	COM	
EDLIN	COM	
FDISK	COM	
FORMAT	COM	
GRAFTABL	COM	
GRAPHICS	COM	
KEYB	COM	
LABEL	COM	
MODE	COM	
MORE	COM	
PRINT	COM	
RECOVER	COM	
RESTORE	COM	
SELECT	COM	
SHELLB	COM	
SYS	COM	
TREE	COM	
5202	CPI	Files with CPI extensions operate the display screen.
4208	CPI	
4201	CPI	
EGA	CPI	
LCD	CPI	
SELECT	DAT	A file with the extension DAT is a data file.
012345	678	The 678 files are used by a program that teaches aspects of DOS version 4.0.
012345	678	
MORTGAGE	BAS	BAS indicates a program file written in the BASIC language.

AUTOEXEC	BAT	BAT is a batch file. In this case, it is a special batch file that runs automatically when you start the computer.
SHELL	CLR	The CLR is a color configuration file that indicates to DOS version 4.0 how to display the Shell program.
ATTRIB	EXE	EXE files are *exe*cutable program files. Except for technical details of their internal structure, EXE files are much like COM files.
FASTOPEN	EXE	
FILESYS	EXE	
APPEND	EXE	
FIND	EXE	
IFSFUNC	EXE	
JOIN	EXE	
MEM	EXE	
NLSFUNC	EXE	
REPLACE	EXE	
SELECT	EXE	
SHARE	EXE	
SHELLC	EXE	
SORT	EXE	
SUBST	EXE	
XCOPY	EXE	
SELECT	HLP	HLP files display on-screen assistance.
SHELL	HLP	
DOSUTIL	MEU	MEU extensions indicate that the files handle on-screen menus from which you make selections.
SHELL	MEU	
PCIBMDRV	MOS	These MOS file extensions identify files that operate the mouse.
PCMSDRV	MOS	
PCMSPDRV	MOS	

Table D.1—*continued*

File Name		*File Extension Meaning*
GRAPHICS	PRO	The GRAPHICS.PRO file contains profiles of graphics-mode printers supported by DOS version 4.0.
ANSI	SYS	SYS files are *sys*tem files. They are also called *device drivers.*
CONFIG	SYS	
COUNTRY	SYS	
DISPLAY	SYS	
DRIVER	SYS	
KEYBOARD	SYS	
PRINTER	SYS	
VDISK	SYS	
XMA2EMS	SYS	
XMAEM	SYS	

The Functions of DOS

DOS provides standard routines or functions that you and your programs can use to access the services of your PC's components. Although DOS has some miscellaneous functions, like setting the computer's calendar and clock, the most important DOS functions include managing disks and files, redirecting input and output, and running batch files and application programs.

Managing Files

One of the primary functions of DOS is to help you organize the files that you store on your disks. Organized files are a sign of good computer housekeeping. Good housekeeping becomes crucial once you begin to take advantage of the storage capacity available on today's disks.

Think, for example, about the fact that the smallest-capacity disk can hold the equivalent of 100 letter-sized pages of information. Now, imagine that each sheet of information makes up one file: you have 100 files to keep track of. If you use disks (such as a hard disk) that can hold more information than a standard disk, file organization becomes even more crucial.

Fortunately, DOS gives you the tools to be a good computer housekeeper. DOS lists files for you, tells you their names and sizes, and gives you the dates when they were created. And you can use this information for many organizational purposes. In addition to organizing files, DOS can duplicate files, discard files no longer useful, and replace files with matching file names.

Managing Disks

Certain DOS functions are essential to all computer users. For example, all disks must be prepared before they can be used in your computer. This preparation is called *formatting* and includes checking disks for available space. Here is a list of other DOS disk-management functions:

- ❏ Labeling disks electronically
- ❏ Making restorable backup copies of files for security purposes
- ❏ Restoring damaged files on a disk
- ❏ Copying disks
- ❏ Viewing the contents of files on a disk

Redirecting Input and Output

DOS "expects" its input to come from a standard place, such as the keyboard. DOS sends its output to a standard place, such as the display screen. Designers of DOS recognized that it would sometimes be convenient to send output to another device, such as a printer. These designers provided DOS with the ability to redirect, or send in another direction, the output that normally goes to the standard output. Through *redirection*, a list of files that usually appears on the screen can be sent to the printer.

Running Application Programs

Computers require complex and exact instructions, or programs, to provide useful output. Computing would be altogether impractical if you had to write a program each time you had a job to do. Happily, that is not the case. Programmers spend months doing the specialized work that allows a computer to function as many different things, such as a spreadsheet, a word processor, or a database manipulator. Through a program, the computer's capabilities are applied to a task—thus, the term *application programs*. The programs covered in Appendixes E, F, and G—1-2-3, WordPerfect, and dBASE—are some of the most popular application programs.

Application programs are distributed on floppy disks. DOS is the go-between that gives you access to these programs through the computer. By simply inserting a disk into a computer's drive and pressing a few keys on the keyboard, you can instantly have an astonishingly wide variety of easy-to-use applications at your disposal.

Applications constantly need to read data from disk files, to see what you have typed, and to send information to the screen or printer. These input and output tasks are common, repetitive computer tasks. DOS provides applications with an easy-to-use connection, or program interface, that sees to the details of these repetitive activities. As the user of the computer, you want easy-to-understand information about disk files, memory size, and computer configuration. DOS provides this information.

Running Batch Files

Most of your interaction with DOS takes place through the keyboard. You type commands for COMMAND.COM to carry out. However, commands also can be placed in a disk file called a *batch file* and "played back" to COMMAND.COM. COMMAND.COM responds to these batches of commands from the file just as it would respond to commands typed from the keyboard. Batch files can automate often-used command sequences, making keyboard operation simpler. Difficult-to-remember command sequences are ideal candidates for batch-file treatment.

The Versions of DOS

The first version of MS-DOS appeared in 1981. Each new version or version upgrade (signified by the version number and a decimal) contained changes to accommodate developments in computer hardware. Table D.2 lists the new features of the various versions and upgrades.

Table D.2
Quick Reference to Versions of DOS

Version	*Significant Change(s)*
1.0	Original version of DOS
1.25	Accommodates double-sided disks
2.0	Includes multiple directories needed to organize hard disks
3.0	Uses high-capacity disks, the RAM disk, volume names, and the ATTRIB command. The ATTRIB command allows you to mark and unmark files, making them *read-only*. This means that they cannot be accidentally changed or erased while being used.
3.1	Includes networking
3.2	Accommodates 3 1/2-inch drives
3.3	Accommodates high-capacity 3 1/2-inch drives; includes new commands
4.0	Introduces the DOS Shell and the MEM command; accommodates larger files and disk capacities

Hardware Requirements

The type of personal computer most likely to use MS-DOS is one that is compatible to a great extent with the IBM PC. COMPAQ, Zenith Data Systems, Tandy, AT&T, AST, EPSON, WANG, NEC, Toshiba, Sharp, Leading Edge, Hewlett-Packard, and many other companies manufacture or market MS-DOS-based personal computers.

The computer should have at least 256K of system RAM, at least one floppy disk drive, a monitor (screen), and a keyboard. These suggestions are minimal; most MS-DOS PCs sold today exceed these requirements. For convenience and processing power, you may want to include a second floppy disk drive, a hard disk with at least 10M of storage capacity, a printer, and a color graphics display.

Summary

This appendix introduced the fundamentals of disk operating systems, which enable users to access computer hardware and run specific application programs, such as spreadsheets, word processors, and databases. MS-DOS, the world's most popular disk operating system, was first released in 1981 and has continued to evolve since then.

MS-DOS consists of a command processor, an input/output system, and utility files. Perhaps the most important component is the command processor, which interacts with you through the keyboard and screen when you operate the computer. The input/output system consists of several hidden files that interact with the computer's ROM and control the computer's use of hardware components in the system. The utility files are external commands that COMMAND.COM loads to carry out housekeeping tasks like formatting disks; determining disk size; listing, copying, comparing, backing up, and deleting files; and checking available memory.

Knowing how to use MS-DOS is important because it performs tasks essential for computing. It manages disks and preserves their information. DOS redirects output to different devices. Batch files can automate some of these tasks by replacing instructions normally typed on the keyboard.

APPENDIX E

An Overview of 1-2-3

1-2-3 is designed as an electronic replacement for the traditional tools of accounting. The columnar pad, pencil, and calculator have been replaced with a screen, cursor, and coprocessor that together give users more power, speed, and accuracy for all their financial calculations. When you start 1-2-3, your computer screen displays an area of columns and rows into which you can enter text, numbers, or formulas, just as an accountant makes entries on one sheet of a columnar pad (and, with the help of a calculator, makes calculations).

Although there are several popular spreadsheet programs on the market, 1-2-3 has been the dominant spreadsheet software product used in businesses worldwide since 1983. 1-2-3 has been popular because it provides users with three fundamental applications integrated into one program. Without having to learn three separate kinds of software, you can perform financial analysis with the 1-2-3 worksheet, create database applications, and create graphs.

But before you put your fingers to a keyboard and start using 1-2-3, you need to know what a spreadsheet is and how it is used. This appendix begins with contrasting examples of "manual" and "electronic" spreadsheets, shows you the wide range of capabilities offered by 1-2-3, and helps you understand how 1-2-3 is useful for many business applications.

After reading this appendix, you should be able to describe the following:

- ❑ 1-2-3's integrated spreadsheet
- ❑ 1-2-3's commands and functions
- ❑ 1-2-3's graphics capabilities
- ❑ 1-2-3's data manager
- ❑ 1-2-3's macros and the Command Language
- ❑ 1-2-3 Release 2.01's hardware requirements
- ❑ The major enhancements with 1-2-3 Release 2.2 and 3

Key Terms Used in This Appendix

You need to know the meanings of certain key terms before you read through this appendix.

Term	*Definition*
Electronic spreadsheet	An electronic replacement for the accountant's pad

Window	The portion of the spreadsheet that is on the screen
Cell	The intersection of a row and a column in the 1-2-3 spreadsheet. Cells are identified by their column and row coordinates (such as A2, B4, and F10).
Cell pointer	The highlighted bar that indicates where you can enter data into the spreadsheet
Formula	A mathematical relationship between cells or ranges of cells
Function	A "shorthand" method of expressing formulas. For example, instead of typing the formula +A1+B1+C1+D1+E1+F1, you could use the @SUM function—@SUM(A1..F1).
Command	A statement or menu instruction for carrying out an operation on the spreadsheet

What Is a Spreadsheet?

Sometimes known as a "ledger sheet" or accountant's pad, a *spreadsheet* is a specialized piece of paper on which information is recorded in columns and rows. Spreadsheets usually contain a mix of descriptive text with accompanying numbers and calculations. Typical business applications include balance sheets, income statements, inventory sheets, and sales reports.

Although you may be unfamiliar with business applications for spreadsheets, if you keep a checkbook, you're already using a rudimentary spreadsheet. Similar to an accountant's pad, a checkbook register is a paper grid divided by lines into rows and columns. Within this grid, you record the number of the check, the date, a description of the transaction, the amount of the check, a record of any deposits, and a running balance, as shown in figure E.1.

NUMBER	DATE	DESCRIPTION OF TRANSACTION	PAYMENT/DEBT (−)		FEE (IF ANY) (−)	DEPOSIT/CREDIT (+)	BALANCE
							$1000 00
1001	9/3/89	Department Store Credit	51 08				948 97
1002	9/13/89	Electric	95 12				853 85
1003	9/14/89	Grocery	74 25				779 60
1004	9/15/89	Class Supplies	354 57				425 03
	9/16/89	Deposit				250 00	675 03
1005	9/21/89	Telephone	49 43				625 60

Fig. E.1. A manual checkbook register.

What happens when you make an invalid entry in your checkbook register, or have to void an entry? Such procedures can be quite messy because you have to erase or cross out entries, rewrite them, and perform all your calculations once again. The limitations of manual spreadsheets are apparent even with the simple example of a checkbook register.

For complex business applications, the dynamic quality of an "electronic" spreadsheet like 1-2-3 is indispensable. You can change one number and recalculate the entire spreadsheet in an instant. Entering new values is nearly effortless. Calculating a column or row of numbers is done by formulas—the same type of formula that you use on a calculator.

Compare the manual checkbook register to the one shown in figure E.2. Notice that the electronic checkbook register is set up with columns and rows. Columns are marked by letters; rows are numbered. Each transaction is recorded on a row just as you record transactions in a manual checkbook register.

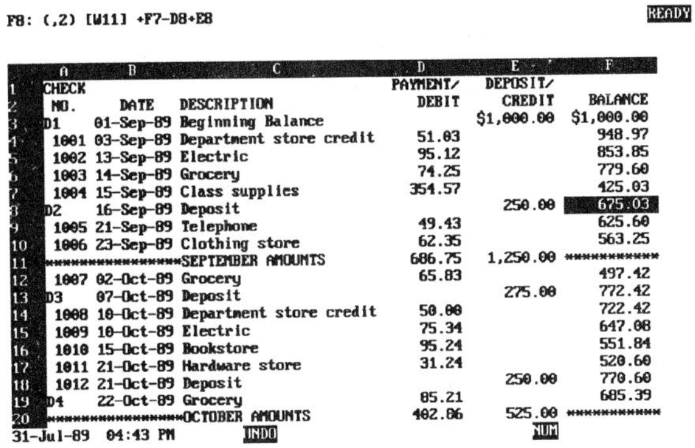
F8: (,2) [W11] +F7-D8+E8 READY

	A	B	C	D	E	F
1	CHECK			PAYMENT/	DEPOSIT/	
2	NO.	DATE	DESCRIPTION	DEBIT	CREDIT	BALANCE
3	D1	01-Sep-89	Beginning Balance		$1,000.00	$1,000.00
4	1001	03-Sep-89	Department store credit	51.03		948.97
5	1002	13-Sep-89	Electric	95.12		853.85
6	1003	14-Sep-89	Grocery	74.25		779.60
7	1004	15-Sep-89	Class supplies	354.57		425.03
8	D2	16-Sep-89	Deposit		250.00	675.03
9	1005	21-Sep-89	Telephone	49.43		625.60
10	1006	23-Sep-89	Clothing store	62.35		563.25
11	******************		SEPTEMBER AMOUNTS	686.75	1,250.00	***********
12	1007	02-Oct-89	Grocery	65.83		497.42
13	D3	07-Oct-89	Deposit		275.00	772.42
14	1008	10-Oct-89	Department store credit	50.00		722.42
15	1009	10-Oct-89	Electric	75.34		647.08
16	1010	15-Oct-89	Bookstore	95.24		551.84
17	1011	21-Oct-89	Hardware store	31.24		520.60
18	1012	21-Oct-89	Deposit		250.00	770.60
19	D4	22-Oct-89	Grocery	85.21		685.39
20	******************		OCTOBER AMOUNTS	402.86	525.00	***********

31-Jul-89 04:43 PM UNDO NUM

Fig. E.2. *An electronic checkbook register.*

Assigning column letters and row numbers lends itself well to creating formulas. Note the following formula in the upper left corner of the electronic checkbook:

+F7 − D8 + E8

These instructions to 1-2-3 translate as

Previous BALANCE minus PAYMENT/DEBIT plus DEPOSIT/CREDIT

As you can see from this simple example, formulas let you establish mathematical relationships among values stored in certain places on your spreadsheet. The principal calculation involved in your checkbook is to keep an accurate running balance. Formulas make it easy to make changes to a spreadsheet and see the results quickly. In the electronic checkbook, if you delete an entire transaction (row), the spreadsheet automatically recalculates itself. Or you may change an amount and not have to worry about recalculating your balance. The electronic spreadsheet takes care of updating all balances.

If you find that you forgot to record a check or deposit, 1-2-3 enables you to insert a new row at the point where the transaction was omitted and enter the transaction information. Subsequent entries are moved down one row. Inserting new columns is just as easy. You indicate where you want the new column to go, and 1-2-3 inserts a blank column at that point, moving information to the right over one column.

What if you want to calculate how much you have spent at the local department store since the beginning of the year? With a manual checkbook, you have to look for each check written to the department store and then total the amounts. Not only does this search take considerable time, but you may overlook one of the checks. An electronic checkbook lets you sort your checks by description so that all like transactions are together. You can create a formula that totals all the checks written to the department store, for example.

This simple example of a checkbook suggests the tremendous value of an electronic spreadsheet for maintaining financial data. Although you may not want to use 1-2-3 to balance your checkbook, an electronic spreadsheet is an indispensable tool in today's modern office.

The 1-2-3 Integrated Spreadsheet

1-2-3 has a number of capabilities, but the electronic spreadsheet is the foundation of the 1-2-3 program. The framework of this spreadsheet contains the graphics and data management elements of the program. You produce graphics through the use of spreadsheet commands. Data management occurs in the standard row-column spreadsheet layout.

The importance of the spreadsheet as the basis for the whole product cannot be overemphasized. All the commands for the related features are initiated from the same main command menu as the spreadsheet commands and have the same style. All of 1-2-3's special features originate from the spreadsheet. All the commands for displaying graphs refer to entries in the spreadsheet and use these entries to draw graphs on the screen (see fig. E.3). In data management, the database is composed of records that are cell entries in a spreadsheet (see fig. E.4).

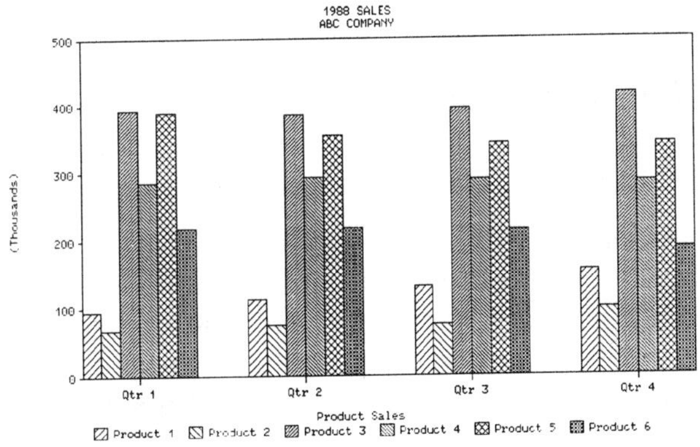

Fig. E.3. A 1-2-3 graph.

```
A1: [W25] 'Physical Inventory:  Hand tool stores #3                      READY

                  A                B     C     D        E        F
1   Physical Inventory:  Hand tool stores #3
2
3
                              ON HAND  UNIT OF UNIT  INVENTORY P.O.
4   DESCRIPTION               QUANTITY ISSUE   COST  VALUE     DATE
5   Hammer, claw                     2 EA      6.75     13.50 02-Aug-87
6   Screwdriver, flat tip set       17 EA      9.95    169.15
7   Tack hammer, 3/8' drive         24 EA      4.30    103.20
8   Air hammer, magnetized           1 KT     67.32     67.32 24-Aug-87
9   Phillips screwdriver set         8 EA      8.73     69.84
10  Hack saw                         3 EA     11.89     35.67 08-Sep-87
11  Counter sink set, 10pc           3 KT     13.44     40.32 15-Sep-87
12  Drop light, 100 foot             4 EA     17.99     71.96
13  Square                           0 EA     37.50      0.00 15-Sep-87
14  Hex wrench set                   2 KT     14.50     29.00
15  Wrench, box/open                 0 ST     46.70      0.00 31-Aug-87
16  Pipe wrench, 14 inch             4 EA     56.70    226.80
17
18
19
20
09-Aug-88  03:02 PM                                          NUM
```

Fig. E.4. A 1-2-3 database.

Understanding the Size of 1-2-3's Spreadsheet

With 256 columns and 8,192 rows, the 1-2-3 worksheet contains more than 2,000,000 cells. Each column is assigned a letter value ranging from A for the first column to IV for the last. A good way to visualize the worksheet is to picture it as one giant sheet of grid paper about 21 feet wide and 171 feet high.

Although the 1-2-3 spreadsheet contains that many columns and rows, there are some limitations to using the entire sheet. If you imagine storing just one character in each of the 2,097,152 available cells, you end up with a worksheet that is far larger than the 640K maximum RAM of an IBM PC.

Understanding the Worksheet Window

Because the 1-2-3 grid is large, you cannot view the entire spreadsheet on the screen at one time. The screen thus serves as a *window* to the worksheet. To view other parts of the sheet, you use the arrow keys to scroll the cell pointer across and down (or up) the worksheet. When the cell pointer reaches the edge of the current window, the window begins to shift to follow the cell pointer across and down (or up) the spreadsheet.

To illustrate the window concept, imagine cutting a one-inch square in a piece of cardboard. If you placed the cardboard on this page, you would be able to see only a one-inch square piece of text. Naturally, the rest of the text is still on the page; it is simply hidden from view. When you move the cardboard around the page (in much the same way that the window moves when the cursor-movement keys are used), different parts of the page become visible.

The default 1-2-3 window displays 8 columns (each 9 characters wide) and 20 rows (see fig. E.5). The width of the columns is adjustable; therefore, the number of displayed columns is variable. If you reduce the width of one or more columns, the window displays more columns; if you the expand the width of one or more columns, the screen displays fewer columns.

Fig. E.5. *The default 1-2-3 window displaying 8 columns (each 9 characters wide) and 20 rows.*

Understanding Cells

Each row in 1-2-3 is assigned a number, and each column is assigned a letter. The intersections of the rows and columns are called *cells*. Cells are identified by their row-column coordinates. For example, the cell located at the intersection of column A and row 1 is called A1. Cells can be filled with three kinds of information: numbers; mathematical formulas, including special spreadsheet functions; and text (or labels).

A *cell pointer* enables you to write information into the cells much as a pencil enables you to write on a piece of paper. In 1-2-3, as in most spreadsheets, the cell pointer looks like a bright rectangle on the computer's screen. The cell pointer typically is one column wide and one row high (see fig. E.6).

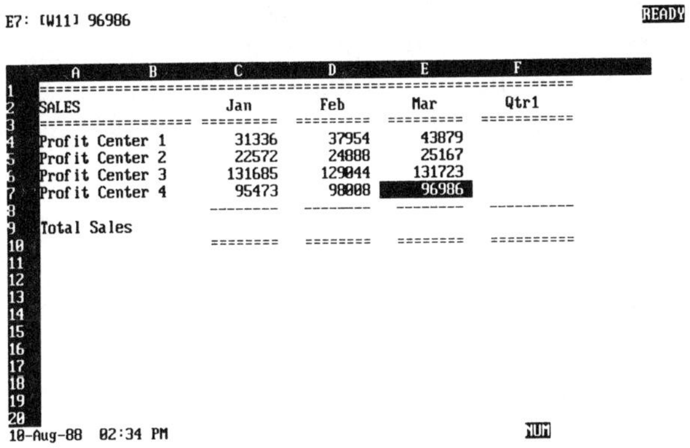

Fig. E.6. Cell pointer highlighting a numeric value in cell E7.

Electronic spreadsheets allow mathematical relationships to be created between cells. For example, suppose that the cell named C1 contains the formula

+A1+B1

C1 displays the sum of the contents of cells A1 and B1. (The + sign before A1 tells 1-2-3 that what you have entered into this cell is a formula, not text.) The cell references serve as variables in the equation. No matter what numbers you enter into cells A1 and B1, cell C1 always returns their sum.

Playing "What If"

Because 1-2-3 remembers the relationships between cells and does not simply calculate values, you can change a value in a cell and see what happens when your formulas recalculate automatically. This "what if" capability makes 1-2-3 an incredibly powerful tool for many types of analysis. You can, for example, analyze the effect of an expected increase in the cost of goods and determine what kind of price increase may be needed to maintain your current profit margins.

Understanding 1-2-3's Functions

As you know, you can create simple formulas involving only a few cells if you refer to the cell addresses and use the appropriate operators (+, −, /, *). These formulas are stored in memory, and you see the values of the formulas in the cells.

If you want to create complex formulas, you can use 1-2-3 functions. Spreadsheet functions are shortcuts that help the user perform common mathematical computations with a minimum of typing. Functions are like abbreviations for otherwise long and cumbersome formulas. You use an @ symbol to signal 1-2-3 that an expression is a function. For instance, the @SUM function in 1-2-3 is written as @SUM(A1..C1).

Without the capabilities to calculate complex mathematical, statistical, logical, financial, and other types of formulas, creating applications in 1-2-3 would be difficult. 1-2-3 comes with many functions that enable you to create complex formulas for a wide range of applications, including business, scientific, and engineering applications.

Understanding 1-2-3's Commands

You use spreadsheet commands at every phase of creating and using an application. You activate commands by pressing the slash (/) key. This action displays a menu of commands from which you can choose the command you want.

1-2-3 has many commands that enable you to perform a number of tasks in the spreadsheet. Commands are available to format the worksheet, name ranges, erase and copy data, perform calculations, store files, protect worksheet cells, protect files with passwords, and print your spreadsheets.

Understanding 1-2-3 Graphics

The spreadsheet alone makes 1-2-3 a powerful program with all the capabilities needed by many users. Another feature further enhances 1-2-3's usefulness: graphics. 1-2-3 has five basic graph types: bar, stacked bar, line, scatter, and pie. You can represent up to six ranges of data on a single graph (except for pie graphs and scatter diagrams). This capability means, for example, that you can create a line graph with six different lines. Figure. E.7 shows a 1-2-3 line graph.

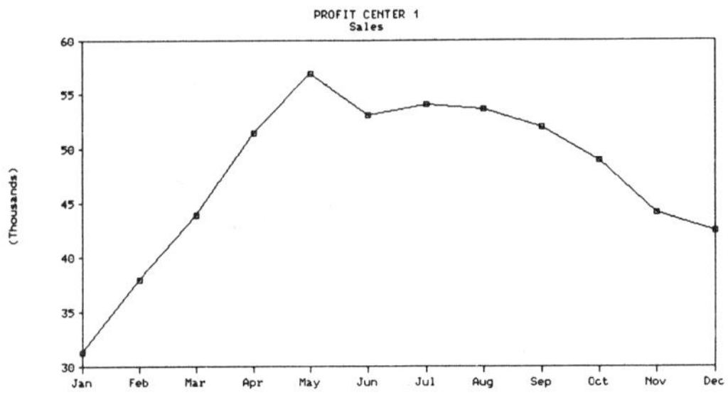

Fig. E.7. *A 1-2-3 line graph.*

A bar graph often compares two or more data items and typically shows the trend of numeric data across time (see fig. E.8).

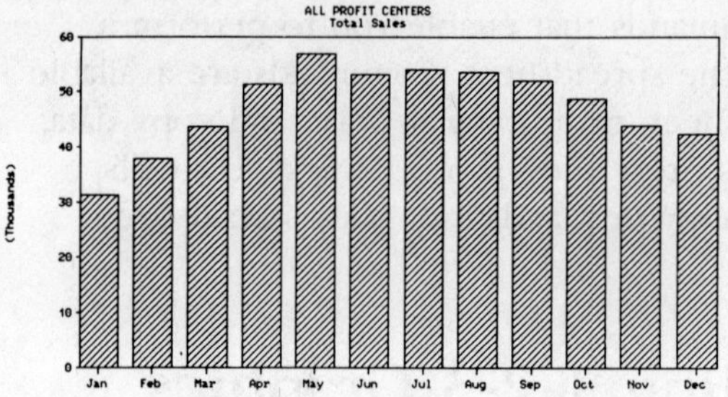

Fig. E.8. *A 1-2-3 bar graph.*

An XY graph compares two numeric data series across time and shows how one set of values appears to depend on the other, as in figure E.9.

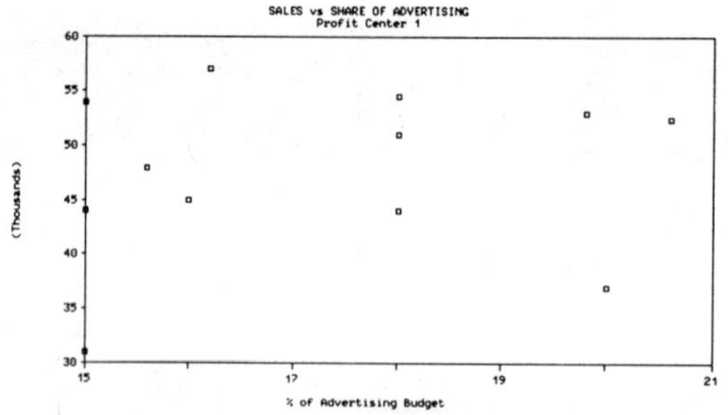

Fig. E.9. *A 1-2-3 XY graph.*

A stacked-bar graph compares two or more data series that total 100 percent of a specific category (see fig. E.10).

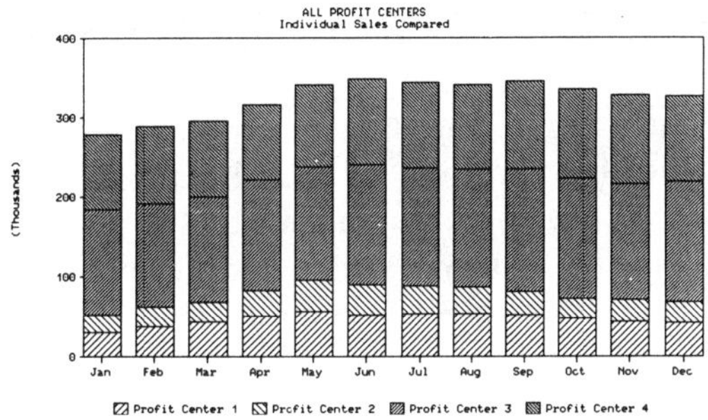

Fig. E.10. *A stacked-bar graph created in 1-2-3.*

A pie graph illustrates only one data series, the components of which total 100 percent of a specific numeric category (see fig. E.11).

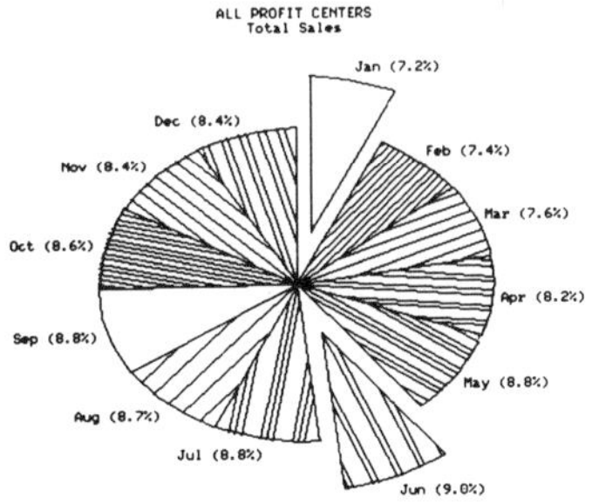

Fig. E.11. *A pie graph created in 1-2-3.*

Understanding the 1-2-3 Database

The column-row structure for storing data in a spreadsheet program is similar to the structure of a relational database. 1-2-3 provides database management commands and functions so that you can sort, query, extract, and perform statistical analyses on data in up to 8,192 records.

A row in 1-2-3 is equal to a record in a conventional database. In that record, you might store a client's name, address, and phone number. With 1-2-3's sort and search operations, you can organize the database based on any number of items and by a number of criteria, and you can locate a particular record with a few simple keystrokes. Figure E.12 shows a deductible expenses database created in 1-2-3.

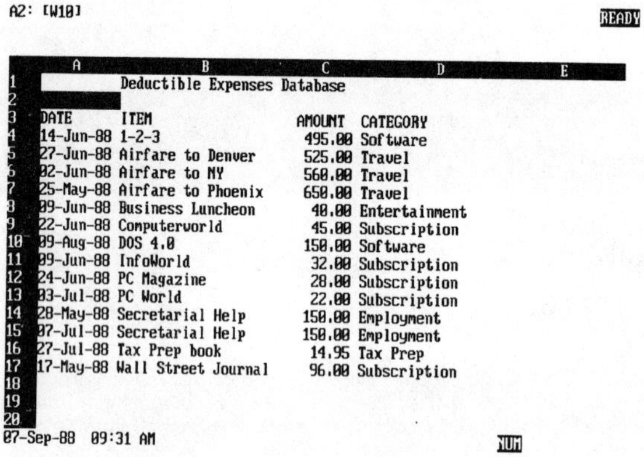
A2: [W10] READY

	A	B	C	D
1		Deductible Expenses Database		
2				
3	DATE	ITEM	AMOUNT	CATEGORY
4	14-Jun-88	1-2-3	495.00	Software
5	27-Jun-88	Airfare to Denver	525.00	Travel
6	02-Jun-88	Airfare to NY	560.00	Travel
7	25-May-88	Airfare to Phoenix	650.00	Travel
8	09-Jun-88	Business Luncheon	40.00	Entertainment
9	22-Jun-88	Computerworld	45.00	Subscription
10	09-Aug-88	DOS 4.0	150.00	Software
11	09-Jun-88	InfoWorld	32.00	Subscription
12	24-Jun-88	PC Magazine	28.00	Subscription
13	03-Jul-88	PC World	22.00	Subscription
14	28-May-88	Secretarial Help	150.00	Employment
15	07-Jul-88	Secretarial Help	150.00	Employment
16	27-Jul-88	Tax Prep book	14.95	Tax Prep
17	17-May-88	Wall Street Journal	96.00	Subscription
18				
19				
20				

07-Sep-88 09:31 AM NUM

Fig. E.12. *A database created in 1-2-3.*

Macros and the Command Language

In addition to all the capabilities available from the commands in 1-2-3's main menu, two other features make 1-2-3 extremely versatile. Using 1-2-3's macros and Command Language, you can automate and customize 1-2-3 for your particular applications.

With 1-2-3 macros, you can reduce multiple keystrokes to a two-keystroke operation. Simply press two keys, and 1-2-3 does the rest, whether you're formatting a range, creating a graph, or printing a spreadsheet.

You can create a macro, for example, to move the cell pointer to a specific part of the worksheet. Suppose that you have positioned a database section in the range R23..Z100. Because 1-2-3 is first displayed with the cell pointer at A1, you will have to use quite a few keystrokes to get to cell R23 when you want to work with the database. You can create a macro that will, in effect, "record" your actions as you specify the keystrokes necessary to get to cell R23. Then, after you assign a name and save the macro, you can access that part of the worksheet by simply typing the macro name.

You can best think of macros as the building blocks for Command Language programs. When you begin to add commands from the Command Language to simple keystroke macros, you can control and automate many of the actions required to create, modify, and update 1-2-3 models. At its most sophisticated level, 1-2-3's Command Language can be used as a full-fledged programming language for developing custom business applications.

Hardware Requirements

You can run 1-2-3 Release 2.01 on an IBM personal computer or compatible with 256K of RAM and at least one double-sided disk drive. For convenience and processing power, you may want to include a second floppy disk drive and a hard disk with at least 10M of storage capacity. If you want to view 1-2-3's color graphics, you need a color monitor.

1-2-3 Releases 2.2 and 3

You should know that Lotus introduced Releases 3 and 2.2, in that order, within two months of each other in 1989. Release 3 represents a total rewrite of the software, but Release 2.2 maintains much of the "look and feel" of Release 2.01 and previous releases.

The major enhancements to Release 2.2 over all previous releases include the capability to "link" the cells of one worksheet to another worksheet, improved report and graph printing, the capability to undo a worksheet change or command operation, a minimal recalculation capability that lets 1-2-3 Release 2.2 recalculate only those cells affected by a change in the worksheet, and new macro commands and capabilities.

Release 3 represents a dramatic change in the software. Unlike Releases 2.2 and 2.01, you cannot run Release 3 on an 8088- or 8086-based personal computer—you must have at least an AT-type 80286-based system. Among the major enhancements to Release 3 are the capability to have up to 256 worksheets in one file and multiple files in memory at one time, the capability to create graphs automatically, higher quality printed reports and on-screen and printed graphs, and the capability to access external databases.

Summary

In this appendix, you saw how one of the simplest examples of a spreadsheet—a checkbook register—could become easier to use in electronic form.

You were introduced to the features of 1-2-3's spreadsheet, such as its size, window, and cells. You learned how spreadsheets are designated and can be recalculated for "what if" analyses. And you had your first look at 1-2-3's powerful commands and functions, with which you can build formulas for a wide variety of applications.

This appendix gave you a glimpse at 1-2-3's flexible graphics capabilities and the types available. You had a quick view of 1-2-3's database and its power for managing and reporting on stored data. The appendix touched on macros and the Command Language, with which you can automate and customize your use of 1-2-3 and its integrated graphics and database. Finally, you got a quick glimpse of the enhancements provided by Releases 2.2 and 3 of 1-2-3.

APPENDIX F

An Overview of WordPerfect

WordPerfect is one of the most popular word processing software programs because it has all the "basic" features you would expect in a word processing package, plus a full complement of advanced features. The program is suited to your needs, whether they entail short memos or complex documents.

This appendix begins with the basics of WordPerfect: starting the program, looking at the editing screen, learning the keyboard, and using the Help feature. You learn some fundamental skills for using a word processor, including how to move around the editing screen, save a document, and exit WordPerfect. After you master these skills, you can begin to explore the program's many features.

After reading this appendix, you should have a basic understanding of the following:

- ❑ WordPerfect's basic and specialized features
- ❑ Starting WordPerfect on a hard disk system and on a dual floppy system
- ❑ The parts of the editing screen
- ❑ The use of the keyboard in WordPerfect
- ❑ Accessing the help feature and tutorial
- ❑ WordPerfect's built-in settings
- ❑ Typing text
- ❑ Moving the cursor
- ❑ Making a menu selection
- ❑ Saving, exiting, and clearing

Key Terms Used in This Appendix

You need to understand certain terms before you progress through this appendix.

Term	*Definition*
Defaults	Standard WordPerfect settings that are automatically put into effect each time you start the program
Status line	The bottom line on the WordPerfect editing screen. The status line indicates the disk drive, file name, and the position of the cursor.
Cursor	An on-screen marker that indicates where a character will appear when typed

Word wrap — A WordPerfect feature that eliminates the need to press the Enter (Return) key each time you reach the right margin. With word wrap, you need to press Enter only when you come to the end of a paragraph, a short line, or a command.

An Overview of WordPerfect Features

WordPerfect offers a range of basic features for making your word processing tasks convenient and efficient. The program also offers specialized features that enable you to create documents more quickly and to generate valuable reference materials.

Basic Features

One of the first characteristics you notice when you start WordPerfect is the uncluttered editing screen. Although many word processors display a number of indicators and codes on-screen while you edit, WordPerfect keeps these down to a minimum—freeing most of the screen for text. In addition, the screen display looks much like your document will appear when printed (see fig. F.1).

WordPerfect's two document windows (areas on-screen in which you work) give you the flexibility to work on different parts of the same document at once, or on two different documents. You can shift between a full-screen view of each window, or you can split the screen to display both windows.

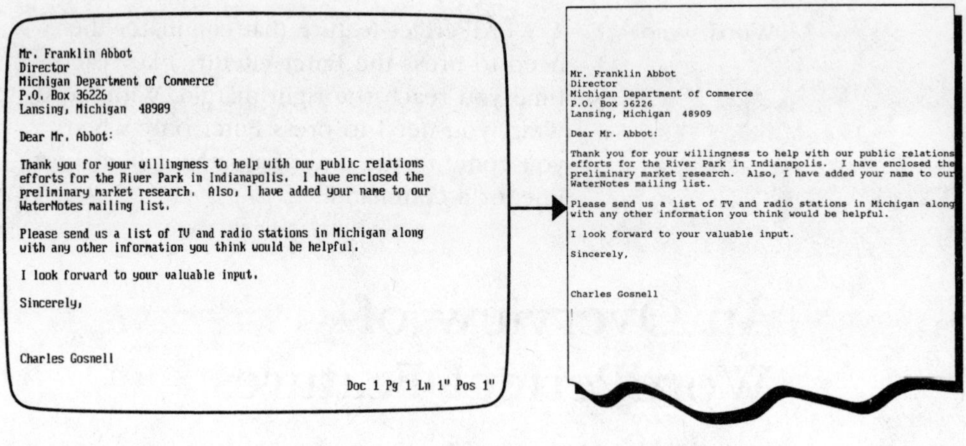

Fig. F.1. *The WordPerfect screen and printed document.*

The Block features in WordPerfect enable you to designate a specific portion of the document on which you want certain commands to have an effect. For example, you can use this feature to move and copy blocks of text, to display a certain portion of text in boldface, or to delete particular passages.

You can enhance the appearance of your text in WordPerfect with a multitude of formatting features. You can adjust margins, use boldface and italic typefaces, center text, justify text, change the line spacing and line height, instruct the printer to shift (left, right, up, or down) before printing, design headers and footers, choose page numbering positions, and control where pages break.

Some other features are useful in particular situations. The Redline and Strikeout features are excellent tools for marking suggested editing changes in a manuscript. The Compose and Overstrike features enable you to create special characters you might need for foreign languages or equations. The subscripts, superscripts, and half-line spacing options also are useful for typing equations.

WordPerfect's Styles feature is a powerful tool that lets you control the format of one document or a group of documents. You specify the formats you want in a particular style, and then you can apply that style to any future documents. You even can create a library of styles for use in a variety of document formats.

The built-in spell checker and thesaurus give you access to a 115,000-word dictionary and lists of alternative synonyms and antonyms you can access from the editing screen. Among the special printing features is View Document, with which you can preview your document on-screen before you print.

File management is handled efficiently through the List Files screen. From that screen, you can manipulate files and directories from within WordPerfect to a much greater degree than most word processors allow. And with WordPerfect's Document Summary feature, you can easily keep track of your files' contents.

Specialized Features

A feature that can help you perform repetitive tasks more efficiently is WordPerfect's Macro feature. The keystrokes and commands you want to include in a macro are recorded and then "played back" when you need them. You can keep macros for different tasks on-hand and call on them with as few as two keystrokes.

WordPerfect's Merge feature lets you merge text files and thereby increase office productivity. For example, you can merge data from an address list into a form letter, or piece together complicated reports. Other tools for handling data are WordPerfect's Sort and Select features. These features enable you to sort phone lists, for example, or extract certain ZIP codes from a mailing list.

Two kinds of columns are available in WordPerfect: text columns and math columns. With text columns, you can prepare text in newspaper-style format (for magazine articles or newsletters) or in parallel-column format (for inventory lists or duty schedules). WordPerfect's Math-columns feature, although limited in its utility, performs simple calculations.

WordPerfect's referencing features are quite broad in scope. You can supplement your documents with footnotes and endnotes, date and time codes, outlines, line numbers, document comments, indexes, tables of authorities, lists, and automatic cross-references. You also can piece together a large project by creating a master document to keep track of all the subdocument files that make up the project. You can use WordPerfect's Document Comparison feature to compare a new version of a document with a previous one.

By using WordPerfect's graphics capabilities, you can import graphic images; create text boxes; and enhance your document with borders, rules, shading, and many other features. These options are ideal for creating newsletters, brochures, and fliers.

Although WordPerfect comes with built-in settings for formatting, screen display, and file locations, you can customize the program with the Setup menu. After you become familiar with WordPerfect's standard settings, you may change a number of these options for all your future documents.

Hardware Requirements

You can run WordPerfect 5 on an IBM PC or compatible computer with a hard disk drive or dual floppy disk drives. WordPerfect requires DOS 2.0 or later and at least 384K of memory. At least 512K RAM is recommended.

Because WordPerfect comes on approximately twelve 5 1/4-inch floppy disks or seven 3 1/2-inch microfloppy disks, you frequently must swap disks in and out of your drives if you have a dual floppy system. To run WordPerfect with fewer interruptions, you probably should invest in a hard disk. Although WordPerfect is already a speedy program, it runs faster and performs better on a hard disk system.

WordPerfect runs on a wide variety of printers, from dot-matrix to laser. To take full advantage of WordPerfect's graphics capabilities, you need a graphics card, such as a Hercules Graphics Card or an InColor card.

Starting WordPerfect

This section tells you how to start WordPerfect on a hard disk system and on a dual floppy disk system. Before you start the program, you must install it.

Starting WordPerfect on a Hard Disk System

To start WordPerfect on a hard disk system, first check to be sure that the floppy drive(s) is empty. Then turn on your computer. If necessary, respond to the prompts for date and time. When the C> prompt appears, type

```
cd \wp50
```

and press Enter. Type

```
wp
```

and press Enter. You should see the opening screen for just a moment, and then the editing screen is displayed.

Starting WordPerfect on a Dual Floppy System

To start WordPerfect on a dual floppy disk system, first insert the working copy of your WordPerfect 1 disk into drive A and insert a formatted data disk into drive B. Then turn on your computer. If necessary, respond to the prompts for date and time. When the A› prompt appears, type

b:

and press Enter. Drive B is now the default drive, which means that any data you save to disk is saved to the disk in drive B. Type

a:wp

and press Enter. WordPerfect's opening screen appears. This screen contains WordPerfect copyright information, the version number of your copy, and an indication of the default directory that the system will use. Remove the WordPerfect 1 disk from drive A and insert the WordPerfect 2 disk into drive A. Press any key.

Learning WordPerfect Basics

Before you begin to use WordPerfect, you should take a few minutes to become familiar with WordPerfect's screen display and keyboard. You also should know that WordPerfect has an on-line Help feature you can access while working on WordPerfect documents, as well as a tutorial that can help you get started learning the program. Among other basics you need as you start using WordPerfect is knowledge about

WordPerfect's built-in settings that help you begin to create documents easily. You also need to learn how to enter text, move around the screen, save your work, and exit the program.

Understanding the Editing Screen

WordPerfect displays your document almost exactly as it will appear when it is printed. What you see on-screen is approximately one-half of a standard typed page. The main portion of the screen displays the document (see fig. F.2).

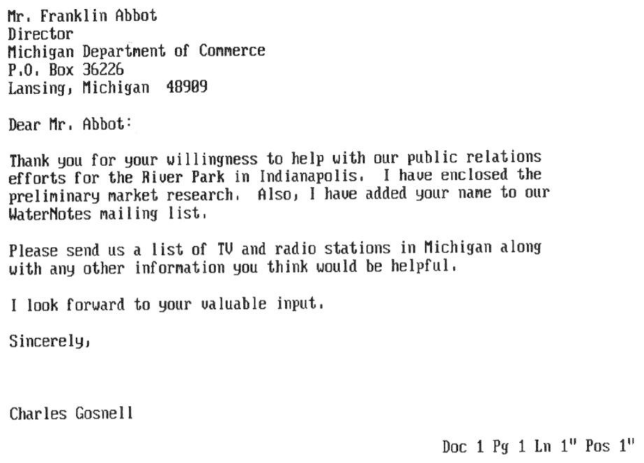

Mr. Franklin Abbot
Director
Michigan Department of Commerce
P.O. Box 36226
Lansing, Michigan 48909

Dear Mr. Abbot:

Thank you for your willingness to help with our public relations efforts for the River Park in Indianapolis. I have enclosed the preliminary market research. Also, I have added your name to our WaterNotes mailing list.

Please send us a list of TV and radio stations in Michigan along with any other information you think would be helpful.

I look forward to your valuable input.

Sincerely,

Charles Gosnell

Doc 1 Pg 1 Ln 1" Pos 1"

Fig. F.2. *The WordPerfect editing screen.*

The line of information that appears at the bottom of the screen is called the *status line*, because that information describes the cursor's status. The left side of the status line shows the current document's name. From time to time, the document name is replaced temporarily by system messages and prompts.

The next item in the status line (`Doc 1` or `Doc 2`) indicates which of two available documents is currently displayed on-screen. WordPerfect is capable of holding two documents in memory simultaneously.

`Pg` identifies the number of the page on which the cursor currently rests.

`Ln` indicates the cursor's vertical position, in inches, centimeters, points, or lines on your document page.

`Pos` is called the *position indicator*. This part of the status line tells you the cursor's horizontal position on the document page.

Note: Through the Setup menu, you can customize many aspects of WordPerfect's screen display. For example, you can change the appearance and color of normal text (if you have a color monitor), specify whether the current file name is displayed on the status line, and change the way menu letter options are displayed on-screen.

Learning the Keyboard

WordPerfect uses the following three main areas of the keyboard:

- The function keys, labeled F1 to F12 at the top of the IBM Enhanced Keyboard (or F1 to F10 at the left of the PC keyboard)

- The alphanumeric or "typing" keys, located in the center of the keyboard. (These keys are most familiar to you from your experience with typewriter keyboards.)

❑ The numeric and cursor keys, found at the right end of the keyboard

Function Keys

As the WordPerfect function key template illustrates, each function key can carry out four tasks when used by itself or in combination with another key (see fig. F.3). You routinely use the function keys to give your computer instructions called *commands*. To issue a WordPerfect command, you press a function key alone or in combination with the Ctrl, Shift, or Alt key.

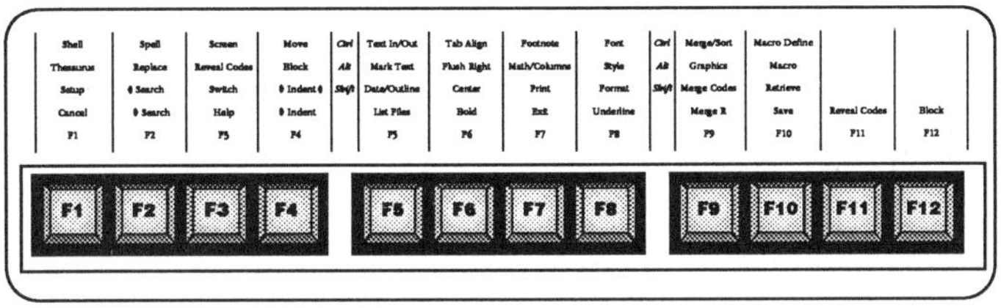

Fig. F.3. *The WordPerfect function key template.*

To issue the Spell command, for example, you press and hold the Ctrl key while you press the F2 key. Or to issue the Forward Search command, you press the F2 key alone.

The commands assigned to the functions keys when you first start WordPerfect are the default definitions for those keys. WordPerfect also gives you the option of switching to other keyboard definitions so that the keys on your keyboard—the function keys and other special keys—perform other commands or functions. The program also enables you to customize your keyboard by assigning alternative definitions to specified keys. To access WordPerfect's feature for alternative keyboard definitions, you use the Keyboard Layout option on the Setup menu.

Alphanumeric Keys

The alphanumeric keys work similarly to those on a typewriter. Keep in mind one critical but easily overlooked difference between composing with a typewriter and composing with WordPerfect: When you type normal text in WordPerfect, you do not need to end lines at the right margin by pressing the Enter key. When you type text in WordPerfect and reach the end of a line, the text "wraps" automatically to the next line.

The Enter key can be used as a carriage return. You also press Enter to insert blank lines in your text, such as the lines that separate paragraphs.

The Shift, Alt, and Ctrl keys are part of the alphanumeric keyboard. The Shift key creates uppercase letters and other special characters, just as it does on a typewriter keyboard. Shift is used also with the function keys to carry out certain operations in WordPerfect. The Alt and Ctrl keys are used in combination with other keys to provide WordPerfect capabilities that a single key cannot provide. The Alt and Ctrl keys don't do anything by themselves, but work with the function keys, number keys, or letter keys to operate various commands in WordPerfect.

Cursor-Movement Keys

The cursor is the blinking underline character that marks the location on the screen where the next character you type will appear. The cursor also marks the location in your text where codes (such as those used to create new margin settings) will be entered.

You use the keys marked with arrows at the far right of the keyboard to control cursor movement. When you press an arrow key, the cursor moves in the direction indicated by the arrow on that key. You will learn more about cursor movement later in this appendix.

When the Num Lock key is activated, the cursor-movement keys become the numeric keys used to perform math functions.

Note: WordPerfect offers an option for changing the rate of speed at which the cursor moves. The Cursor Speed option is available through the Setup menu.

Accessing the WordPerfect Help Feature and Tutorial

WordPerfect provides two tools for helping you learn the program: the Help feature and the tutorial. The screens in the Help system, which you can access while you are working in a document, can help you learn more about WordPerfect commands and keys. The Help system also provides an alphabetical listing of all WordPerfect features and an on-screen function key template. From within a document, press the F3 (Help) function key to access the Help system. Then press the key about which you want to know more.

WordPerfect's self-paced tutorial, WordPerfect Tutor, includes a series of lessons in which you gain experience with the program's features. Most of the lessons range from 12 to 20 minutes, for a total of about 2 1/2 hours.

Typing Text

With a word processor, you can get words on-screen as fast as you can type them. In a short time, you will realize that putting words on-screen can be far easier than putting them on paper. WordPerfect doesn't think or plan for you, of course, but it certainly simplifies self-expression.

At any stage of the writing process, you can easily revise your words on-screen. With a word processor, you can freely alter what you write; you can easily insert new words, delete ones you don't want, or move up and down through a document to see what you have written. Because altering text can be accomplished so effortlessly, you can focus on first getting words on-screen. Then you can wait until later to edit, revise, and spell-check the text. If you're a poor typist, you can leave spelling errors for WordPerfect's speller to catch.

WordPerfect's Built-In Settings

Before you even put fingers to keys and begin typing, WordPerfect has been at work for you. You will recall from your experience with a typewriter that you must set margins, line spacing, and tabs, for example, before you begin composing. With WordPerfect, you don't need to make any formatting decisions before you begin unless the preset values do not suit you.

WordPerfect comes with a number of default settings—for margins, page numbers, tab settings, base font (basic character style), line spacing, and other features (see fig. F.4).

You should be familiar with the basic default settings before you begin writing. Subsequent chapters, especially those devoted to formatting and printing, explore the many ways you can alter the look of a document.

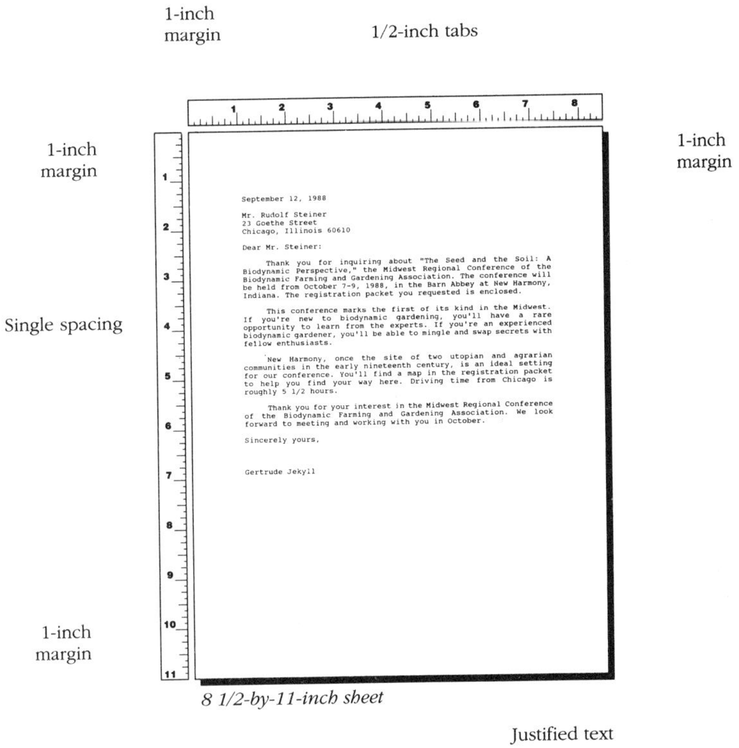

Fig. F.4. *WordPerfect's default settings.*

Note: Through the Initial Settings option on the Setup menu, you can change a number of WordPerfect's built-in settings. For example, you can change the formatting specifications for all future documents, change the date format, and turn off the feature that sounds a "beep" when you have made an error.

Entering Text

As you type in WordPerfect, characters appear at the position of the cursor, just as they do when you use a typewriter. After you type a few words, look at the Pos indicator on the status line. This value increases as you type and as the cursor moves horizontally across the line to the right. Unlike a typewriter, WordPerfect doesn't require you to press Enter to end a line. Word wrap inserts what is known as a soft return at the end of each line and wraps the text to the beginning of the next line.

Moving the Cursor

You move the cursor through text in WordPerfect with the cursor-movement keys: the up, down, left, and right arrow keys; the PgUp, PgDn, Screen Up, and Screen Down keys; the GoTo (Ctrl-Home) key combination; or the Repeat key (Esc). When you press an arrow key, the cursor moves in the direction indicated by the arrow on that key. Keep in mind that WordPerfect does not permit the cursor to move where nothing exists. The cursor moves only through text, spaces, or codes.

The following list describes the cursor-movement keys in WordPerfect.

Key	*Definition*
Arrow Keys	
↑	Moves the cursor up one line
↓	Moves the cursor down one line; this key also reformats existing text when you move the cursor through it with the down arrow.
←	Moves the cursor one position to the left

→	Moves the cursor one position to the right
Ctrl-→	Moves the cursor one word to the right
Ctrl-←	Moves the cursor one word to the left
Home-→ End	Moves the cursor to the right end of the line
Home-←	Moves the cursor to the left edge of the screen
PgUp	Moves the cursor to the top of the preceding page
PgDn	Moves the cursor to the top of the next page
−	Moves the cursor to the top of the screen or to the preceding screen (use the − key on the numeric keypad)
+	Moves the cursor to the bottom of the screen or to the next screen (use the + key on the numeric keypad)

To move to a specific page in your document, press Ctrl-Home, the page number, and Enter

To move to a specific character in your document, press Ctrl-Home and the character (nonnumeric).

To move to the top of the page, press Ctrl-Home-↑.

To move to the bottom of the page, press Ctrl-Home-↓.

To return to the cursor's original position, press Ctrl-Home.

To repeat an operation *n* number of times, press Esc, enter the number of repetitions (*n*), and press the key you want to repeat.

Making a Menu Selection

WordPerfect uses two types of menus. Many times when you press a function key combination, a one-line menu appears at the bottom of the screen (see fig. F.5). Other commands in WordPerfect display full-screen menus (see fig. F.6).

```
1 Math On; 2 Math Def; 3 Column On/Off; 4 Column Def: 0
```

Fig. F.5. *A WordPerfect one-line menu.*

Select an option from either type of menu in either of two ways:

- ❏ Press the number next to the menu selection.
- ❏ Press the highlighted letter in the name of the menu option.

When you press the Math/Columns key (Alt-F7), for instance, a one-line menu appears at the bottom of the screen. To turn on Math, press 1 or M for Math On.

```
Format

    1 - Line
            Hyphenation                      Line Spacing
            Justification                    Margins Left/Right
            Line Height                      Tab Set
            Line Numbering                   Widow/Orphan Protection

    2 - Page
            Center Page (top to bottom)      New Page Number
            Force Odd/Even Page              Page Numbering
            Headers and Footers              Paper Size/Type
            Margins Top/Bottom               Suppress

    3 - Document
            Display Pitch                    Redline Method
            Initial Codes/Font               Summary

    4 - Other
            Advance                          Overstrike
            Conditional End of Page          Printer Functions
            Decimal Characters               Underline Spaces/Tabs
            Language

Selection: 0
```

Fig. F.6. *A WordPerfect full-screen menu.*

When you press the Format key (Shift-F8), the Format menu appears on-screen. If you want to change the margins, for example, you press 1 or L for Line to choose that option. Another menu is then displayed, from which you can choose other options to adjust the margin settings.

Using the Cancel Key

The Cancel key (the F1 "oops" key) enables you to back out of a menu without making a selection, or to restore deleted text either to its original location or to another location.

When used to back out of a menu, F1 (Cancel) cancels the most recent command and returns you either to the preceding menu or to your document. When used to restore text, Cancel (F1) retrieves one of the last three items you have deleted. An *item* in this case means the characters (numbers, letters, or punctuation) deleted before moving the cursor. Cancel (F1) always acts as an "undelete" key when a menu is not visible.

Saving, Exiting, and Clearing

What you see on-screen is a *temporary* display; only the documents you transfer to disk storage are secured for future use. Usually you keep copies on disk of the documents you create. As a rule, you should save your work at least every 10 or 15 minutes. Use either of two methods to save a document to disk. Save the document with Save (F10) and remain in WordPerfect, or save the document with Exit (F7) and exit WordPerfect. Keep in mind that before you can work on a new document or before you can retrieve a document, you must clear the current document from the screen.

Note: WordPerfect offers two automatic backup features through the Setup menu: Timed Backup and Original Backup. With the Timed Backup option, at specified intervals, WordPerfect automatically saves to disk the document displayed on-screen. With the Original Backup option, WordPerfect saves both the original file and the edited version.

Saving a Document to Disk and Remaining in WordPerfect

The first time you save a document, WordPerfect prompts you for a file name. Suppose that you have created a document, and you now want to save the file. With your document on-screen, you press Save (F10). The prompt `Document to be saved:` appears on the status line. Next, you type a file name for the document and press Enter. When you name a file, you must observe your operating system's (MS-DOS or PC DOS) guidelines for naming files. After you name and save a file, the file name is displayed on the status line in the left corner of the screen. The document remains on-screen, and you can continue working.

WordPerfect responds a bit differently when you want to save a file you have saved before. When you press Save (F10), WordPerfect asks whether you want to replace the file on disk. You can press Y to replace the previous version of the file with the new version. Or, you can press N, rename the file, and save it under a different name.

Saving a Document to Disk and Exiting WordPerfect

The other method for saving a document to disk is to use Exit (F7). The prompt `Save document? (Y/N) Yes` is displayed. To begin the Save process, press Y. When WordPerfect prompts you to enter the name of the document to be saved, type the file name and press Enter.

If the document already exists, WordPerfect prompts `Replace (file name)? (Y/N) No`. Press Y to save the document with the old name; or press N, type the file name, and press Enter. Your document is stored to disk under the name you select. The message, `Exit WP? (Y/N) No` appears on-screen. Press Y to exit WordPerfect and return to DOS.

Clearing the Screen

You must clear the current document from the screen before you start work on a new document—or before you retrieve a document. You can use Exit (F7) to clear the screen without saving the document. If you do not clear the current document before starting a new document, or before retrieving a document from memory, the old and the new documents will merge with one another.

If you don't want to save the document you have created, or if you have saved the document previously but you want to clear your screen, press Exit (F7). In response to the `Save Document? (Y/N) Yes` prompt, press N.

The prompt `Exit WP? (Y/N) No` appears on-screen. In response to the prompt, press N or Enter to clear the screen and stay in WordPerfect. If you press Cancel (F1), you will return to the document displayed on-screen.

Summary

This appendix has introduced you to the range of word processing features available in WordPerfect. The program's basic features are convenient and efficient for creating, editing, formatting, and printing documents. WordPerfect's specialized features give you a full range of tools for further supplementing your documents with elements such as graphics, footnotes, and lists. You have learned about the hardware requirements for using WordPerfect. You also learned how to start the program on a hard disk and on a dual floppy system.

The appendix introduced the editing screen, from which you perform most of your work in WordPerfect, and explained how to use the keyboard, access the help feature and tutorial, type text, move the cursor, and make a menu selection. You also learned about WordPerfect's built-in settings that help you begin to create documents quickly. Finally, you learned to save your work, and exit the document and the program.

APPENDIX G

An Overview of dBASE

Businesses collect, hold, and process data in a variety of ways. They may, for example, generate follow-up letters to customers by using a word processor such as WordPerfect 5, or prepare budgets using the row-and-column format of a 1-2-3 spreadsheet. When data items are related, businesses often use a database management system (DBMS).

dBASE III Plus, published by Ashton-Tate, is one of the most popular and powerful database management system programs in use. (Although Ashton-Tate released an upgrade, dBASE IV, in early 1989, this text focuses primarily on dBASE III Plus.) Merchandising firms use a DBMS, such as dBASE III Plus, to maintain accurate data concerning the quantity of goods on hand and the lead times for reordering, as well as to schedule workers according to required skill levels.

Organizations providing services use a DBMS to monitor constraints on resources, such as the beds available in a hospital. And most firms receive payments from customers and generate payroll checks—tasks that can be handled with a DBMS.

Before you start using dBASE, you need to know what a database is and how it is used. This chapter begins with an explanation of a database management system and then contrasts "manual" and "electronic" databases. The text next shows you the wide range of capabilities offered by dBASE and helps you understand how dBASE is useful for many business applications.

After reading this appendix, you should have a general understanding of the following topics:

- ❑ The advantages of a computerized database over a manual one
- ❑ The characteristics of relational and multiple-interface databases
- ❑ The capabilities of dBASE

Key Terms Used in This Appendix

You need to understand certain terms before you progress through this appendix.

Term	*Definition*
Data	Basic elements of information, such as numbers, letters, words, or facts. For example, data includes phone numbers, dollar amounts, dates, descriptions, opinions, and assumptions.

Database	A collection of related data. An automobile dealership, for example, collects in a database the same data about each vehicle sold, such as customer name, vehicle identification number, price paid, and delivery date.
DBMS	Database management system; a systematic approach to storing, updating, reporting on, and deleting related data. For example, a DBMS can update the database for the current week's sales and print a list of vehicle sales for the month just ending, subtotaled by salesperson.
Field	A specific data item within a database record
Record	A collection of related fields in a database

What Is a Database Management System?

The systematic approach to storing, updating, reporting on, and deleting related data is called a database management system. A DBMS can be manual or automated. This section discusses the limitations of a manual database system and the advantages of an automated system.

Limitations of Manual Database Systems

You can store data in a manual database in your mind or on paper. If you store data only in your mind, you may not remember everything, and only you can access the data. The larger the database, the more important it is to store data in an organized manner and in a physical form accessible to others.

In a manual system of tracking vehicle sales data, the salesperson keeps records on paper about each sale, places the paper in a folder marked with the customer's name, and stores the folder in a file cabinet in alphabetical order by customer name. Periodically, clerical staff members remove folders to prepare required reports.

In database terminology, each data item in the folder—such as customer name, date of sale, and salesperson—is a *field*. The collection of related data items about one sale is a *record* (in this case, the folder). All the sales folders (records) in the file cabinet make up the sales *database*.

The manual process has several limitations. If you know the customer's name, you easily can find data in the file cabinet—the manual database. However, what if you want to know both the total sales for the month of January and the total sales made by a particular salesperson? Using this manual database, you must physically look at every record, remove the ones meeting your search conditions, manually calculate the required totals, and refile the records in their original order.

Report generation is often a time-consuming task; and during the activity, the removed folders are not readily available to other staff members. In addition, few firms make duplicate copies of their paper files and therefore place themselves at risk should fire or theft result in loss of data.

Advantages of Automated Database Systems

In an automated system of tracking vehicle sales data, the salesperson enters from the keyboard data about each sale and saves on disk the update to the vehicle sales database. With just a few keystrokes, a single clerical staff member can generate reports and labels, and create a backup of the database on disk.

In addition to the potential to reduce staff requirements, an automated DBMS has several other advantages over a manual one. Entering and editing data with a computer keyboard and monitor is faster and easier than manipulating data by hand. The computer performs the necessary calculations. Records can be organized on any field instead of being physically arranged by a single field such as last name.

Report generation is no longer a time-consuming task that prevents other staff members from accessing the database records. Using a computer database, you can copy data quickly to inexpensive disks or tapes and store these backup files in a separate, and safe, location.

How Do Automated Systems Vary?

Database management systems are classified according to two main criteria: the data storage method and the type of user interface. dBASE uses a relational storage method and a multiple-interface.

dBASE: A Relational DBMS

The file storage methods commonly used with IBM-compatible personal computer database management systems are *flat-file* and *relational*. Other types of file storage methods, which are more often associated with mainframes or with personal computers that are not IBM-compatible, are not included in this discussion.

A flat-file storage DBMS views each database as a unit independent of other database management systems. In other words, no two databases created under a flat-file DBMS can be connected or related to each other to produce a larger view of data.

For example, if you develop a database using 1-2-3 Release 2.01, you create a flat-file database. To access data in two 1-2-3 spreadsheets at the same time, you must use a /File Combine command sequence to copy one flat-file into another. In some cases, a flat-file storage feature may be adequate for your needs. For instance, if your database needs are fairly basic and relate to a simple list, such as names and addresses or records of investments, you can use a flat-file DBMS to define and maintain a database with ease.

Suppose, however, that you have certain fields that are repeated in different records. A car dealership, for example, maintains a vehicle sales database as well as a database for related warranty records, and both databases contain fields for a complete customer address. In this case, you may end up with redundant data in the databases. Although inefficient space utilization isn't a problem in small databases, it becomes a problem for a personal computer DBMS when databases grow to thousands of records.

Selecting a relational DBMS, such as dBASE, can significantly reduce this redundancy. The word *relational* indicates that the database management system provides a means to relate, or link, files by using a common field defined in more than one database. For example, customer name and address fields are included in the vehicle sales database but not the warranty records database. By linking the databases on the common field VIN (vehicle identification number), you can produce a warranty work report that contains name and address data.

With a relational DBMS, you easily can change database relationships as the need arises. Internal tables used in a relational DBMS define the relationships between fields in a record and link fields between databases. The internal tables, established when the database structure is entered into the DBMS, make a relational DBMS efficient to use and the process of relating databases relatively easy and dynamic.

dBASE: A Multiple-Interface DBMS

The link between the visual and keyboard work that people do in a DBMS environment is called the *user interface*. You can use four basic user interfaces to access DBMS services: a system of menus, commands issued on a command line, operation of a program that issues DBMS requests internally, or some combination of these. Using the menu approach, you select from menu options that are displayed on-screen. The command-line approach requires you to type the appropriate directions from the keyboard. If you use a program approach, you activate a series of instructions that are stored on disk.

A *menu-driven* DBMS, such as Paradox or R:BASE, guides you through the process of using a database by providing menus you must learn to navigate. One menu may lead to another and yet another. By knowing the menu structure and selecting individual menu items, you learn how to extract the needed information. Menu systems are easy to learn because they are tutorial by nature. Each possible action is available as a menu item.

A *command-driven* system performs basically the same tasks as a menu-driven system, but requires you to type commands instead of selecting menu items. Command-driven systems usually are more flexible than menu-driven systems but require that you learn many commands. Most DBMS users find that learning a command-driven DBMS is initially more difficult than using a menu-driven system. After learning the commands, however, users find that the command-driven approach is faster, more flexible, and more specific than a menu-driven system.

Program-driven user interfaces can be viewed at two levels. At one level, you simply operate a program (a series of instructions) that someone else has written. At the other level, you actually write programs to request DBMS services. The common feature of both levels is that a program must exist in order to use the DBMS resource.

If you operate a program that someone has written, you use the features provided by the program. Although using a prewritten program is convenient, it is by nature limiting. You cannot access information in a way other than the way provided by the program. On the other hand, DBMS programs that limit access to information are quite appropriate for activities involving routine data entry and report generation. For some users, the program is desirable because it makes using the DBMS less complicated. For users who want to create their own databases and update or query them in an *ad hoc* fashion, the preprogrammed DBMS is not an appropriate information tool.

An alternative to using prewritten programs with a program-driven DBMS is writing your own programs. This approach requires you to know a particular programming language, such as Oracle, in order to enter, retrieve, and otherwise manipulate data. Although by writing programs you can then perform sophisticated DBMS work, programming languages are beyond most people's expertise.

Most of the popular DBMS systems offer a *combination* of the three interfaces. dBASE offers a menu-driven interface, a command line, and a complete programming language. Paradox gives a choice of a menu-driven system or a programming language, but no command-driven feature. With the three user interfaces available in dBASE, a user can select the interface that best suits the activity at hand.

Why Is dBASE a Powerful System?

dBASE III Plus and dBASE IV are relational DBMS products. (Both versions of dBASE share common characteristics; for this overview discussion, you can think of the two collectively as dBASE.) dBASE includes all the features representative of the DBMS discipline of personal computer productivity. In addition, dBASE enjoys a larger user base than any other relational DBMS. The dBASE features enable you to complete common DBMS activities that include designing and creating a database; viewing, organizing, and updating data; searching the database; generating reports and labels; and writing programs.

Designing and Creating a Database

Before you start to implement a new DBMS, you should specify the database objectives, analyze the current system for flaws and potential enhancements, determine desired outputs, and then select appropriate inputs. These actions constitute *designing* the database.

To *create* a database, you must define its structure and enter records. The structure defines the characteristics of the fields you want your database to contain. A DBMS enables you to create, display, modify, and copy the database structure. After you establish the structure, you can add records.

Viewing, Organizing, and Updating Data

All database management systems, including dBASE, offer commands for viewing data after it has been entered. In this context, the word *view* means to look at data on-screen or produce printed output. dBASE enables you to view complete records or limit the output to only selected fields in a record. As an added dBASE feature, you can create new information to view by performing calculations on the contents of existing fields. dBASE also enables you to organize records in a database on the field(s) of your choice.

dBASE provides options for updating a database—to revise or delete existing records, as well as to add records. The program provides an Edit mode to revise one record on the screen and a Browse mode to edit multiple records. dBASE also enables you to replace contents of records and recall deleted records.

Searching the Database

Searching for records in your database may be the most important function you perform. Using the term *search* in a broad sense, you can use a search to tell a DBMS which records to access. dBASE enables you to limit the number of records you view by specifying a scope. You also can find only those records meeting simple or complex search conditions.

Generating Reports and Labels

Printing custom reports is a common feature of database management systems. A simple listing of selected database contents might suffice for some tasks, such as documenting the current day's sales. But a multiple-page listing of an entire month's sales activities warrants some enhanced features. You can, for example, add headings, page numbers, subtotals, and totals to create a custom report. The dBASE III Plus report generator creates columnar reports. Using dBASE IV, you can produce a wide variety of report formats. With both versions of the program, you also can create and print custom labels.

Writing Programs

dBASE offers a complete programming language that has become a standard for microcomputer use. If you know the language, you can write programming code to control a multitude of database activities. For example, a program to manage vehicle sales data might verify data entry (for example, reject inaccurate salespersons' initials) and offer the user a selection of custom reports.

Hardware Requirements

You can run dBASE on an IBM personal computer or compatible with DOS 2.0 or later and at least 256K of RAM for dBASE III Plus or 360K for dBASE IV. To run dBASE III Plus, the system should have either two 360K double-sided floppy disk drives or one 360K floppy drive and a hard disk drive. For larger databases and faster processing, a hard disk is highly recommended. To run dBASE IV, you must have a hard disk, as well as a 5 1/4-inch, 360K disk drive or a 3 1/2-inch, 720K disk drive. Other hardware requirements include a printer with a capacity of at least 80 columns, if you plan to print database reports.

Summary

Businesses process and store large amounts of data by developing database management systems. The systems can be manual or automated. Automated systems vary according to the type of file storage and user interface.

Three terms describe the components of a database: each data item is a *field*; the collection of related data items is a *record*; the records make up the *database*. The larger the database, the more important it is to store data in an organized manner, to make data accessible to a variety of users, and to provide backup copies of the data. You can achieve these results by using database management system software such as dBASE III Plus or dBASE IV.

In this appendix you learned that dBASE embodies the best features of a database management system: designing and creating a database; viewing, organizing, and updating data; searching the database; generating reports and labels; and writing programs. The power of dBASE is best realized in actually using the program.

Glossary

Adapter. A special-function, electronic component that fits in a slot within the computer itself. An adapter is also called a *board* or *card*. The adapter may have ports that allow you to plug in a monitor, printer cable, and so on.

Alignment. The positioning of lines of text on a page or in a column: aligned left (flush left, ragged right), centered, aligned right (flush right, ragged left), or justified (flush on both the left and right).

Application. A program that performs a specific function, such as word processing, database management, or accounting.

ASCII. America Standard Code for Information Interchange. ASCII format files can be saved and read by most database, spreadsheet, and word processing programs, making ASCII an ideal format for information exchange. ASCII files include all the characters of the text itself (including tabs and carriage returns), but not the non-ASCII codes used by some applications to indicate character and paragraph formats.

AUTOEXEC.BAT. A batch file that causes the computer to perform certain functions and procedures when the computer is first booted.

Background Operation. The execution of secondary tasks by a computer system during brief pauses in the execution of the system's primary ("foreground") task or tasks.

Backup. Duplicating files for storage and security. This practice safeguards important data from loss.

Backup Disk. A disk that holds previously backed-up files.

Bad Break. Term used to refer to line breaks that hyphenate words incorrectly or separate two words that need to stay together (such as *Mr. Smith*), and to page breaks and column breaks that result in widows or orphans.

Base Memory. The memory that is usable by DOS within the standard 640K memory area. This memory is directly addressable by DOS.

BASIC. Beginner's All-purpose Symbolic Instruction Code, a programming language often included with DOS.

Batch Command. A DOS command specifically used in a batch file.

Batch File. A text program that contains several DOS or batch commands. Batch files have an extension of BAT and are executed from the DOS prompt when you type the root name of the file.

Baud. The rate at which information is transferred between devices. The baud rate is the number of bits transmitted per second (bps). Also called the *communication speed.*

Binary File. A file that contains machine-language information, using the digits 1 and 0. Each binary digit (or bit) indicates the presence (1) or the absence (0) of voltage.

Bit. The smallest amount of information that a computer can process. Eight bits make a *byte*, and four bits a *nybble.*

Bit Map. A graphic image or text formed by a pattern of dots. The higher the number of dots, the greater the resolution and the sharper the image. Low-resolution images are sometimes called *paint* files, and they usually have a smaller number of dots per inch (dpi) than high-resolution images have.

Bleed. Term used to describe the part of a printed image that extends to the trimmed edge of the sheet or page.

Board. See **Adapter**.

Body Copy. The main part of the text of a publication, as distinguished from headings and captions.

Body Text. The body copy of a document. See also **Body Copy**.

Boot. Load and run the operating system.

Break. The flow of text from one paragraph to the next. Normally each paragraph continues directly below the previous paragraph or (if no more room is left on the column or page) continues at the top of the next column or page (line break).

Bus Mouse. A bus mouse is a mouse that is connected to a card inside the computer. See also **Mouse**.

Byte. A character. Each byte is composed of 8 bits. Approximately 2,000 bytes equals one page of text.

Card. An electronic circuit board about the size of an index card, which plugs into slots in a computer. See **Adapter.**

Carriage Return. A line break that you enter by pressing the carriage return (the Return or Enter key) at the end of a line or paragraph. Sometimes called a *hard carriage return* to distinguish it from the *soft carriage returns* that occur because of automatic word wrap at the right margin of a page or the right edge of a column.

Cell. A cell is the intersection of a column and a row on a spreadsheet.

Cell Address. The address of a cell is the cell's column and row number, such as C1 or R34.

CGA. Color Graphics Adapter: an electronic board that displays graphics and color on a monitor.

Character. A letter, number, or symbol (including the blank space produced by pressing the space bar).

Characters Per Inch (cpi). The number of characters a computer printer makes in one inch. Most printers are set to produce 10 characters per inch.

Chip. A computer circuit that integrates many electronic functions.

Click. To press and release a mouse button quickly.

Column. A vertical line down the screen. An "80-column" screen means you can put 80 letters on a line.

Command. An instruction, usually typed from the keyboard, given to the operating system for processing.

Communications Port. A port used to connect your computer to an external device, such as a serial printer, modem, or plotter. It is often referred to as an RS-232 or COM port.

Console. The main part of the computer, consisting of the cabinet, disk drives, motherboard, and power supply. The console often contains add-on boards that accept cables to the monitor and printer.

Control Key. A special key usually pressed in combination with another key to perform a computer operation (abbreviated *Ctrl*).

CPU. Central processing unit: the large chip within the computer that acts as the "brain." Also called the *microprocessor*. CPU types for IBM PC and PS/2 computers include the 8086, 8088, 80286, and 80386.

Ctrl. See **Control Key**.

Current Directory. The directory you are in or used last. Many DOS commands make the current directory the default directory.

Current Drive. The drive DOS uses to find files and other information unless another drive is specified in a command.

Cursor. The small flashing underline that marks the place where characters appear on-screen when you type.

Cursor Control Keypad. The keys on the right side of the computer keyboard that allow you to move the cursor. Sometimes this keypad is separate, and sometimes it functions as a toggle with the numeric keypad as well.

Daisywheel Printer. See **Letter-Quality Printer**.

Data. Information contained in files. The term data is often interchangeable with the word *information*.

Database. A file that holds groups of like information, such as a phone directory, mailing list, inventory records, and so on.

Database Management System (DBMS). A group of programs to manage similar groups of information, which are called databases.

Data Disk. A disk on which you save, and from which you recall, the files you make.

Data File. A set of information, other than a program file, saved on disk.

Debugging. The procedure of locating and correcting errors in a program.

Default. The program's initial setting of a value or option. Default settings usually can be changed by the operator.

Delete. A computer term meaning *erase* or *eliminate* characters or entire sections of files.

Delimited ASCII. A type of ASCII file in which data items are delimited by characters such as the comma or quotation marks.

Deselect. To cancel the current selection.

Desktop Publishing. The use of personal computers and software to produce camera-ready publications.

Device. A computer component or peripheral that can receive and/or send data; often termed an *I/O device*.

Dialog Box. A window or full-screen display that appears in response to a command.

Digitize. To convert an image to a system of dots that can be stored in the computer. See also **Scanned Image Files**.

Directory. A list of files, including subdirectories. A full directory begins with a heading that names the disk drive and path being displayed. The list itself includes file names and extensions, the date and time the file was created or modified, and the size of the file. Footer information includes a byte count that shows how much space is available on the disk.

Disk. A thin, circular piece of plastic coated with metal oxide and housed in a rigid or flexible plastic case. Disks are used to store data, usually from 180K to 1.44M. Disks are often referred to as floppy, micro-, or minifloppy disks.

Disk Drive. A computer peripheral that reads and writes data. Disk drives read and write both floppy and hard disks.

Disk Operating System. DOS: A system of commands that permit you to use disks with your computer; it interfaces computer hardware with software, thus controlling all I/O operations and computer functions. DOS itself is on a disk and is read from the disk (via the disk drive) when the computer is turned on or reset.

Display. The monitor screen that displays characters you type from your keyboard. A display is a specific type of device. See **Device**.

DOS. Disk operating system. See **Disk Operating System**.

Dot-Matrix Printer. A printer that creates text and graphics by pressing a matrix of pins through the printer ribbon onto the paper. These impact printers usually offer lower resolution (dots per inch) than non-impact laser printers.

Dots Per Inch (dpi). See **Resolution**.

Drag. Describes the operation of selecting something by clicking it, then holding the mouse button down while you move that object to a new location.

Drive. See **Disk Drive**.

Drive Name. The name given to a particular disk drive. A drive name consists of a letter and a colon, such as A:.

Drop-Down Menu. A list of commands that is displayed when you make a menu selection.

Edit. To change a text file.

EGA. Enhanced Graphics Adapter: a special video card that provides sharper video resolution than is available with CGA (Color Graphics Adapter).

EMS Memory. Expanded Memory Specification. Using EMS memory frees conventional memory and enables you to work on longer documents.

Enter Key. A key you press to break a line. See also **Carriage Return**.

Escape Key. A key often used to abort or cancel an operation. Use this key to cancel a DOS command line if you haven't yet pressed Enter.

Expanded Memory. Memory above the base 640K memory that DOS directly addresses. Expanded memory is accessible through special software and by some DOS commands, such as VDISK.

Expansion Slot. A slot on the computer that accepts add-on cards. Depending on the brand and model, computers can provide from 3 to 12 expansion slots.

Export. To send a file created in one program to a file in a different program.

Extended Memory. An accessory that increases the amount of information the computer can remember at once (RAM).

Extension. The three-letter suffix, preceded by a period (.), that follows a file name. For example, in the file name MYFILE.EXE, the extension is .EXE.

Field. One piece of information in a single record. For example, if a record contains a name and address, the name, street, city, state, and ZIP code are each contained in a field.

File. A grouping of related data from application programs, text material, or other data.

File Name. Identifier given to a file. The name can contain up to eight characters, followed by a three-character extension. FILENAME.EXE is an example of a file name.

File Server. A single computer whose disk drive contains, in a single, centralized location, all the database files to be used by an application running on a network.

Filter. A command that alters the input of a file before sending the input to an output device. FIND, MORE, and SORT are three DOS filters.

Fixed Disk. See **Hard Disk**.

Fixed-Length ASCII. A type of ASCII file in which the data items are stored in a columnar format.

Floppy Disk. See **Disk**.

Footer. One or more lines of text that appear at the bottom of every page of a document.

Format. An operation that prepares a disk for use by the computer system.

Function Keys. Programmable keys that provide special functions, depending on the software you are using. Function keys may be labeled F1 through F10 or F12, depending on your keyboard.

Graphic. An illustration placed in a document.

Gray Scale. Some scanners produce images that are shades of gray instead of a bit-mapped image that simulates gray.

Hard Carriage Return. See **Carriage Return**.

Hard Disk. A fixed or removable disk that can commonly store 10M or more of data. Hard disks can provide faster access to data than can floppy disks.

Hardware. The electronic components, boards, peripherals, and equipment that make up your computer system. The keyboard, system unit, disk drives, printer, and monitor are all hardware.

Header. One or more lines of text that appear at the top of every page of a document.

Hierarchical Directory. A file structure that allows you to store files on disk in compartments called *subdirectories*. This filing system can be compared to a manual filing system in which data is sorted by major groups in filing cabinets. Data is further sorted into minor groups within file drawers and re-sorted by topic in folders.

Highlight. To visually differentiate a selection on the screen. Usually, highlighting reverses the normal appearance of the selected text, graphics, or options (for example, black text on a white background will appear as white text on a black background).

Hyphenation. The method of dividing words over two lines to achieve better word spacing on each line.

Icon. A functional graphic representation of a tool, file, or command displayed on a screen.

Import. To bring text or graphics into one program file from other programs.

Initialize. To prepare a disk by dividing it into tracks and sectors for use by a computer. See **Format**.

Input. The data that a program reads, usually from a keyboard or disk drive.

Integrated Software. This term refers to the type of software that has several built-in applications that are capable of sharing data.

Interface. The interconnection and interrelationships between two devices or applications.

I/O. Input/output.

Justified Text. Text that is flush at both the left and right edges. See also **Alignment**.

K. Kilobyte: 1024 bytes of memory.

Kerning. The amount of space between letters, especially certain combinations of letters that must be moved close together in order to create visually consistent spacing between all letters. For example, the uppercase letters *AW* may appear to have a wider gap between them than the letters *MN* unless a special kerning formula is set up for the *AW* combination.

Keyboard. An input device that allows the user to communicate with the system.

Kilobyte. 1024 bytes of memory (abbreviated K).

LAN. Local area network: two or more computers connected in a linear or circular arrangement and sharing data.

Landscape Printing. The rotation of a page design to print text and graphics across the longer axis of the page or paper (usually 11 inches).

Laser Printing. Term used to describe printing with one of the toner-based laser printers that are available for PCs. These printers use laser technology to project an intense light beam with a narrow bandwidth (1/300th of an inch in 300-dots-per-inch printers) to create the electrical charge on the printer drum that picks up the toner and transfers it to the paper. Some typesetters also use laser technology in conjunction with their photochemical processing, but these devices are usually referred to as phototypesetters rather than laser printers.

Layout. The process of arranging text and graphics on a page. Also, a sketch or plan for the page or the final appearance of the page.

Leading. Historically, the insertion of thin strips of metal (made of a metal alloy that included some proportion of lead) between lines of cast type to add space between the lines and to make columns align vertically. In modern typography, leading is the vertical spacing between the baselines of two lines of text.

Letter-Quality Printer. A computer printer that produces fully formed characters, like a typewriter's, instead of producing characters made of dots.

Letter Spacing. The space between letters in a word. Also, the practice of adding space between letters.

Line Break. The end of a line of text that is created by automatic word wrap and hyphenation. See also **Carriage Return**.

Line Length. The horizontal measure of a column or a line of text.

Line Spacing. See **Leading**.

M. Megabyte: 1,048,576 bytes of memory (1K x 1K = 1024 x 1024 bytes).

Macro. A macro is a series of recorded keystrokes that you can activate by one key combination.

Mail Merge. You can mail merge form letters, labels, and envelopes by merging text in a document with data from a database.

Margin. Traditionally, the distance from the edge of the page to the edge of the layout area of the page.

Megabyte. 1,048,576 bytes of memory (abbreviated M).

Memory. The computer's temporary storage of information while you are working (also called *RAM*, for *random-access memory*). You copy the contents of memory onto disk by saving the document.

Menu. A set of options from which the user makes selections.

Menu-Driven. Term describing a program that is made to run via the selection of choices from a menu.

Microprocessor. See **CPU**.

Modem. An input/output device that permits communications through a serial port over telephone lines. The term *modem* is derived from the words *MO*dulation-*DEM*odulation.

Monitor. An output device that displays computer input and output.

Monochrome. A single-color display against a dark background.

Motherboard. A large computer circuit board that contains the CPU and expansion slots. The power supply, keyboard, add-on cards, and memory chips are attached to the motherboard.

Mouse. A small peripheral device used to point to and select menus, commands, options, tools, and graphic elements.

Mouse Driver. A program packaged with a mouse that communicates with the computer.

Multiuser. A system that accommodates more than one user. Multiuser software usually provides a file-locking capability to restrict access to another user's data. See **Network**.

Network. A hardware and software combination that allows users to share applications, data, and peripherals, such as printers.

Nonbreaking Space. A special character inserted between two words so that they cannot be separated by a line break.

Numeric Keypad. The numeric keypad is a separate set of keys used for entering numbers. On some computer keyboards, the numeric keypad also functions as a cursor control keypad.

Orientation. The page position: portrait or landscape. Portrait orientation means that the text runs horizontally across the narrower width of the page and the columns run down the longer length of the page. Landscape orientation means that the text runs horizontally across the wider measure of the page.

Output. The result of computer processing. Output can be displayed on an output device, such as a monitor.

Paper Size. Each size of paper a printer can print on. Standard sizes are letter (8.5 x 11 inches), legal (8.5 x 14 inches), double (11 x 17 inches), and European A4 (8.27 x 11.69 inches) and B5 (6.93 x 9.84 inches).

Paragraph. Any line or lines of text ended by pressing the Enter key.

Parallel Port. A port that sends information 8 bits at a time. The parallel port is primarily a printer port.

Password. A word you must enter to access files or projects that are password protected.

Path. The identifier that shows the subdirectory structure in which a file is located. For instance, in the full file name A:\DOS\MYFILE.EXE, the path is A:\DOS\.

Pica. A unit of measure equal to approximately 1/6 inch, or 12 points.

Pixel. The smallest unit on a computer screen display. Monitors can have different screen resolutions, or pixels per inch, as well as different overall sizes (total number of pixels).

Point. A standard unit of measure for type, measured roughly from the top of the ascenders to the bottom of the descenders in a line of type. A point is the smallest unit of measure in typographic measurement.

Pointer. The on-screen icon that moves when you move the mouse.

Pop-Up Menu. A submenu of choices that pops up after you make a menu selection.

Port. The connection point in the computer for peripherals such as a printer or mouse.

Portrait Printing. The normal printing orientation for a page: horizontally across the shorter axis of the page (usually, 8.5 inches).

PostScript. A page-description language, developed by Adobe Systems, Inc., that is used by the Apple LaserWriter and other high-resolution printers and typesetters. PostScript is used to describe how to print a page that consists of both text and pictures. This description is completely independent of the printing device. Therefore, the page can be printed on any printer or typesetter that uses PostScript, and the page will print at the full resolution that each printer or typesetter can produce.

Power Supply. A computer component that provides power to the system unit. Your computer's ON/OFF switch is connected to the power supply.

Print Area. The area of a piece of paper where a printer can reproduce text or graphics. The print area is usually smaller than the paper size.

Printer. A device that transfers computer output to paper.

Print Head. The mechanism in a printer that controls the placement of the pins on paper.

Program. A set of instructions for the computer to perform some specific function. Examples are BASIC, spreadsheet, database, and word processing programs.

Prompt. An on-screen computer request to provide additional information or to enter a command. PROMPT is also a DOS command that lets you change the appearance of the prompt.

Proportional Spacing. A style of printing by a computer printer in which narrow letters (such as *i*) take up less space than wide letters (such as *w*).

Protection. A procedure in many programs that keeps a file from being changed accidentally.

Ragged Right. Text in which lines end at different points near the right margin. Distinguished from flush right (justified) text. See also **Alignment**.

RAM. Random-access memory: the erasable memory in a computer where instructions and data are contained before and after being processed by the CPU. Once the computer is turned off, everything in RAM that has not been saved to disk is lost.

Read. The computer process of acquiring information from a device and placing it into memory.

Recalculation. The way in which the program computes the calculations on the worksheet.

Record. A single collection of related data items stored in a database file. A database file consists of many records, each record containing an identical set of fields that contain data items.

Redirect. To route input or output to a device other than the standard device.

Resetting the System. Making the computer start up again, as if you had turned it off and then on again.

Resolution. The number of dots per inch used to represent alphanumeric characters or graphic images. High-resolution images have more dots per inch and look smoother than low-resolution images. The resolution of images displayed on the screen is usually lower than the resolution of the laser printout. Laser printers print 300 dots per inch or more; typesetters print 1200 dots per inch or more. Resolution is a term used in reference to screen displays and printer output.

Return Key. See **Enter Key**.

Reverse. The opposite of a text's or graphic's normal appearance on the printed page. Normally, text and graphics are black on a white background; when reversed, they are white on a black background.

Right Justified. See **Alignment**.

ROM. Read-only memory: an area of computer memory containing instructions (programs), which are usually about start-up procedures. ROM is maintained even when the computer is turned off.

Root Directory. The main directory of a disk where files and other directories can be placed. The root directory is the highest directory in a hierarchical directory.

Rules. Black lines added to the page—for example, between columns—to enhance the design or readability of a publication. Rules can be horizontal or vertical, and of varying lengths and widths.

Scanned Image Files. Bit-map files created with hardware that digitizes images (converts a two- or three-dimensional image to a collection of dots stored in the computer's memory or on disk).

Scanner. A device that converts an image on paper into a computer image.

Scroll. To move through a file to information not on the current screen display.

Select. To click or drag the mouse to designate where the next action will take place.

Selected Text. Text that has been highlighted.

Serial Communications. A method by which the computer communicates, one bit at a time, with another device. The rate at which these bits are transferred is called the **baud rate**.

Serial Port. The connection where wires are attached to the system unit for serial communications. These wires are in turn attached to a modem, serial printer, or other device.

Soft Carriage Return. See **Carriage Return**.

Software. A series of instructions, usually on disk, used to control a computer. Software usually consists of several programs.

Source. The original location from which a command acquires information. During a copy operation, for example, the source disk is the location of the file to be copied. The files are copied from the source to the *target* disk.

Space Bar. The long key at the bottom of the keyboard that records a blank space.

Speed Keys. Key combinations that allow you to bypass certain menu selections.

Spell Check Program. A program that systematically checks the words in your word processor file against a built-in dictionary to see if the words are spelled correctly.

Spreadsheet. A program that enables you to manipulate and analyze numbers arranged in rows and columns.

Standard Input. A default device where data comes from unless otherwise specified. The standard input device is normally the keyboard.

Standard Output. The default device where data is sent unless otherwise specified. The standard output device is normally the monitor.

Subdirectory. A division of a directory. A subdirectory may contain files and other directories.

System Prompt. A symbol that DOS displays when it is ready to receive instructions or commands. The default system prompt is the drive letter followed by the greater-than sign, such as `A>`.

System Unit. The box containing the motherboard, power supply, memory chips, and disk drives.

Target. The target disk or drive is one that receives the effects of a command. For example, when you copy files, the target disk receives the newly copied files. See also **Source**.

Text. Alphanumeric characters that include upper- and lowercase letters, the numerals 1 to 9, and standard punctuation. Special characters below ASCII 32 and above ASCII 127, which include control characters, are not text.

Text Block. A highlighted section of text.

Text File. A file of alphanumeric characters.

Text-Only File. Text created with another application and then saved without any type specifications or other formatting. See also **ASCII**.

Toggle Switch. An on-off command. Used to describe cases in which the same command is invoked to turn a feature on and off.

Tractor Feeder. An accessory for your printer that holds continuous (fanfold) paper straight as it goes through the roller.

Typeface. A single "type family" of one type design in all sizes and styles. Times and Helvetica are two different typefaces, for instance. Each typeface has many fonts (that is, sizes and styles). Sometimes the terms *typeface* and *font* are used interchangeably.

Typeset. The act of producing a document on a typesetting machine.

User. The individual who actually uses the computer hardware and software (also called an "end user").

VGA. Video Graphics Array: a video card that provides sharper video resolution than is available with CGA and EGA.

Volume Label. The unique, identifying name assigned to a disk. The name must be no more than 11 characters.

What-If Analysis. Usually performed on a spreadsheet, what-if analysis allows you to show how the outcome of a specific change would affect different areas of the business.

White Space. Empty space on a page, not used for text or graphics.

Word Processor. A program that provides for general typing and editing of text and includes features such as spell checking.

Word Spacing. The space between words in a line or a paragraph. See also **Kerning** and **Letter Spacing**.

Word Wrap. The automatic adjustment of the number of words on a line of text in order to match the margin settings. The carriage returns that result from automatic word wrap are called *soft carriage returns* to distinguish them from the *hard carriage returns* that result when you press the Enter key.

Work Area. The area of the screen in which you perform word processing, spreadsheet, database, graphics, or communications tasks.

Workstation. A single-user computer or terminal connected in a local area network.

Write. To record information from the computer's RAM onto a device.

WYSIWYG. "What-You-See-Is-What-You-Get"—pronounced "wizzywig"—describes systems that display full pages on-screen with text and graphics. Some systems are more WYSIWYG than others in the accuracy of the display.

Index

E

F

K

L

M

N

O

P

Q

R

S

T

U

V

UPGRADING
AND
REPAIRING PCs
que

USING
WORDPERFECT 5
que

Special Edition
USING
1·2·3
RELEASE 2.2
que

USING
DOS
ERASE
MKDIR
COPY
que

Free Catalog!

Mail us this registration form today, and we'll send you a free catalog featuring Que's complete line of best-selling books.

Name of Book ________________________

Name ________________________

Title ________________________

Phone ( ) ________________________

Company ________________________

Address ________________________

City ________________________

State __________ ZIP __________

Please check the appropriate answers:

1. Where did you buy your Que book?
   - ☐ Bookstore (name: ________)
   - ☐ Computer store (name: ________)
   - ☐ Catalog (name: ________)
   - ☐ Direct from Que
   - ☐ Other: ________

2. How many computer books do you buy a year?
   - ☐ 1 or less
   - ☐ 2-5
   - ☐ 6-10
   - ☐ More than 10

3. How many Que books do you own?
   - ☐ 1
   - ☐ 2-5
   - ☐ 6-10
   - ☐ More than 10

4. How long have you been using this software?
   - ☐ Less than 6 months
   - ☐ 6 months to 1 year
   - ☐ 1-3 years
   - ☐ More than 3 years

5. What influenced your purchase of this Que book?
   - ☐ Personal recommendation
   - ☐ Advertisement
   - ☐ In-store display
   - ☐ Price
   - ☐ Que catalog
   - ☐ Que mailing
   - ☐ Que's reputation
   - ☐ Other: ________

6. How would you rate the overall content of the book?
   - ☐ Very good
   - ☐ Good
   - ☐ Satisfactory
   - ☐ Poor

7. What do you like *best* about this Que book?

____

____

8. What do you like *least* about this Que book?

____

____

9. Did you buy this book with your personal funds?
   - ☐ Yes ☐ No

10. Please feel free to list any other comments you may have about this Que book.

____

____

____

QUE

Order Your Que Books Today!

Name ________________________

Title ________________________

Company ________________________

City ________________________

State __________ ZIP __________

Phone No. ( ) ________________________

Method of Payment:

Check ☐ (Please enclose in envelope.)

Charge My: VISA ☐ MasterCard ☐

American Express ☐

Charge # ________________________

Expiration Date ________________________

Order No.	Title	Qty.	Price	Total

You can **FAX** your order to **1-317-573-2583.** Or call **1-800-428-5331, ext. ORDR** to order direct.
Please add $2.50 per title for shipping and handling.

Subtotal	
Shipping & Handling	
Total	

QUE

NO POSTAGE
NECESSARY
IF MAILED
IN THE
UNITED STATES

BUSINESS REPLY MAIL
First Class Permit No. 9918 Indianapolis, IN

Postage will be paid by addressee

que®

11711 N. College
Carmel, IN 46032

NO POSTAGE
NECESSARY
IF MAILED
IN THE
UNITED STATES

BUSINESS REPLY MAIL
First Class Permit No. 9918 Indianapolis, IN

Postage will be paid by addressee

que®

11711 N. College
Carmel, IN 46032